First World War
and Army of Occupation
War Diary
France, Belgium and Germany

74 (YEOMANRY) DIVISION
Headquarters, Branches and Services
General Staff
1 May 1918 - 30 November 1918

WO95/3148/1

The Naval & Military Press Ltd
www.nmarchive.com
Published in association with The National Archives

Published by

The Naval & Military Press Ltd

Unit 10 Ridgewood Industrial Park,

Uckfield, East Sussex,

TN22 5QE England

Tel: +44 (0) 1825 749494

www.naval-military-press.com

www.nmarchive.com

This diary has been reprinted in facsimile from the original. Any imperfections are inevitably reproduced and the quality may fall short of modern type and cartographic standards.

© **Crown Copyright**
Images reproduced by permission of The National Archives, London, England, 2015.

Contents

Document type	Place/Title	Date From	Date To
Heading	74th Division General Staff 1918 May-1918 Feb 1919		
Heading	War Diary of General Staff 74th (Yeo) Division 1st May To 31st May 1918		
War Diary	At Sea	01/05/1918	03/05/1918
War Diary	Marseilles	07/05/1918	07/05/1918
War Diary	Rue	09/05/1918	19/05/1918
War Diary	Roellecourt	21/05/1918	24/05/1918
War Diary	Le Cauroy	25/05/1918	31/05/1918
Operation(al) Order(s)	74th Division Order No.58	14/05/1918	14/05/1918
Operation(al) Order(s)	74th Division Order No.59	19/05/1918	19/05/1918
Operation(al) Order(s)	74th Division Order No.60	24/05/1916	24/05/1916
Miscellaneous	74th Division Warning Order	31/05/1918	31/05/1918
Miscellaneous	Cover For Branch Memoranda.		
Heading	General Staff 74th Division June 1918 Vol. 3		
War Diary	Le Cauroy	01/06/1918	25/06/1918
War Diary	Le Cauroy Norrent Fontes	26/06/1918	30/06/1918
Miscellaneous	Instructions for An Inter-Brigade and Tactical Exercise To Be Held on 1st June 1918	01/06/1918	01/06/1918
Miscellaneous	General Idea		
Miscellaneous	Special Idea "A"		
Miscellaneous	Open Warfare Brigade In The Attack	05/06/1918	05/06/1918
Operation(al) Order(s)	74th Division Order No.61	20/06/1918	20/06/1918
Operation(al) Order(s)	74th Division Order No.62	20/06/1918	20/06/1918
Miscellaneous	C Form Messages And Signals		
Miscellaneous	S.G.50	25/06/1918	25/06/1918
Operation(al) Order(s)	74th Division Order No.63	24/06/1918	24/06/1918
Miscellaneous	Move Table		
Map	Lestrem		
Operation(al) Order(s)	74th Division Order No.64	26/06/1918	26/06/1918
Map	Vieille Chapelle		
Map	Map		
Miscellaneous	Reference Sheet 44.b. 1/40,000	29/06/1918	29/06/1918
Miscellaneous	Headquarters 229th Infantry Brigade	28/06/1918	28/06/1918
Miscellaneous	Amendment To 74th Division Order No.65 Of 29/6/18	01/07/1918	01/07/1918
Operation(al) Order(s)	74th Division Order No.65	29/06/1918	29/06/1918
Heading	War Diary of General Staff, 74th (Yeo) Division From 1st July 1918 To 31st July 1918		
War Diary	Norrent Fontes	01/07/1918	13/07/1918
War Diary	Lilette Chateau H.Q. Right Div Sector XI Corps Front	14/07/1918	15/07/1918
War Diary	Lilette Chateau	20/07/1918	31/07/1918
Miscellaneous	Warning Order	08/07/1918	08/07/1918
Operation(al) Order(s)	74th Division Order No.66	08/07/1918	08/07/1918
Miscellaneous	Table To Accompany 74th Divisional Order No 66.		
Map	Map		
Map	France		
Miscellaneous	Table To Accompany 74th Divisional Order No 66.		
Map	Identification Trace For Use With Artillery Maps		
Miscellaneous	Amendment To 74th Division Order No.66	11/07/1918	11/07/1918
Miscellaneous	C Form Messages And Signals		
Operation(al) Order(s)	74th Division Order No.67	15/07/1918	15/07/1918

Type	Description	Date From	Date To
Miscellaneous	Minutes of Conference Held At Divisional Headquarters	15/07/1918	15/07/1918
Operation(al) Order(s)	74th Division Order No.68	15/07/1918	15/07/1918
Operation(al) Order(s)	74th Division Order No.69	20/07/1918	20/07/1918
Heading	General Staff With Appendices 74 (Yeomanry) Division August 1918		
War Diary	Lilette Chateau H.Q. Right Div. XIth Corps	01/08/1918	04/08/1918
War Diary	Lilette Chateau	05/08/1918	24/08/1918
War Diary	Busnes Chateau	24/08/1918	27/08/1918
War Diary	Norrent Fontes	28/08/1918	28/08/1918
War Diary	Beaucourt Chateau	29/08/1918	31/08/1918
Miscellaneous	Warning Order	04/08/1918	04/08/1918
Operation(al) Order(s)	74th Division Order No.70	31/07/1918	31/07/1918
Miscellaneous	A Form Messages And Signals		
Miscellaneous	Messages And Signals		
Miscellaneous	A Form Messages And Signals		
Miscellaneous	Reference XIth Corps Ss.24 (XIth Corps Policy)	04/08/1918	04/08/1918
Operation(al) Order(s)	74th Division Order No.71	04/08/1918	04/08/1918
Miscellaneous	A Form Messages And Signals		
Operation(al) Order(s)	74th Division Order No.72	09/08/1918	09/08/1918
Miscellaneous	A Form Messages And Signals		
Operation(al) Order(s)	74th Division Order No.73	09/08/1918	09/08/1918
Operation(al) Order(s)	74th Division Order No.74	11/08/1918	11/08/1918
Operation(al) Order(s)	74th Division Order No.75	14/08/1918	14/08/1918
Miscellaneous	A Form Messages And Signals		
Operation(al) Order(s)	74th Division Order No.76	17/08/1918	17/08/1918
Miscellaneous	A Form Messages And Signals		
Operation(al) Order(s)	74th Division Order No.77	20/08/1918	20/08/1918
Miscellaneous	Reference Divisional Order No 77	20/08/1918	20/08/1918
Miscellaneous	S.G.115	22/08/1918	22/08/1918
Miscellaneous	A Form Messages And Signals		
Miscellaneous	S.G.113	21/08/1918	21/08/1918
Operation(al) Order(s)	74th Division Order No.78	23/08/1918	23/08/1918
Operation(al) Order(s)	74th Division Order No.79	25/08/1918	25/08/1918
Miscellaneous	Relief Table		
Miscellaneous	Reference Divisional Order No 79 And Serial Nos Of Attached Relief Table As Under	25/08/1918	25/08/1918
Miscellaneous	A Form Messages And Signals		
Miscellaneous	C Form Messages And Signals		
Operation(al) Order(s)	74th Division Order No.80	28/08/1918	28/08/1918
Miscellaneous	A Form Messages And Signals		
Operation(al) Order(s)	74th Division Order No.81	31/08/1918	31/08/1918
Miscellaneous	Reference 74th Division Order No.81	31/08/1918	31/08/1918
Miscellaneous	Reference Map Sheet 620	31/08/1918	31/08/1918
Miscellaneous	Headquarters 229th Infantry Brigade	27/08/1918	27/08/1918
Map	Belgium		
Map	Tournai		
Miscellaneous	Headquarters 229th Infantry Brigade	24/08/1918	24/08/1918
Miscellaneous	Headquarters III Corps No. RA/2255	31/08/1918	31/08/1918
Heading	74th Division General Staff September 1918		
Miscellaneous	D.A.A.G	06/11/1918	06/11/1918
War Diary		01/09/1918	17/09/1918
War Diary	J.11.c.3.9	17/09/1918	28/09/1918
War Diary	Norrent Fontes	29/09/1918	30/09/1918
Miscellaneous	Narrative of Operations Carried Out By 74th (Yeomanry) Division	24/09/1918	24/09/1918
Operation(al) Order(s)	74th Division Order No.82	01/09/1918	01/09/1918

Miscellaneous	A Form Messages And Signals		
Operation(al) Order(s)	74th Division Order No.83	03/09/1918	03/09/1918
Operation(al) Order(s)	74th Division Order No.84	04/09/1918	04/09/1918
Miscellaneous	For Day of Month 5		
Miscellaneous	A Form Messages And Signals		
Miscellaneous	BM2/28	19/10/1918	19/10/1918
Operation(al) Order(s)	74th Division Order No 85	05/09/1918	05/09/1918
Miscellaneous	A Form Messages And Signals		
Operation(al) Order(s)	74th Division Order No.86	06/09/1918	06/09/1918
Miscellaneous	A Form Messages And Signals		
Miscellaneous	229 Bde.		
Miscellaneous	A Form Messages And Signals		
Miscellaneous	Urgent Operation Priority (Sd) A.C.T.		
Miscellaneous	Priority to 229 Bde And 231 Bde (Sgd) A.C.T.		
Operation(al) Order(s)	74th Division Order No 87	09/09/1918	09/09/1918
Operation(al) Order(s)	74th Division Order No 88	10/09/1918	10/09/1918
Miscellaneous	A Form Messages And Signals		
Miscellaneous	Defence Instructions No.1	12/09/1918	12/09/1918
Map	Sheet 62		
Map	Map		
Miscellaneous	A Form Messages And Signals		
Operation(al) Order(s)	74th Division Order No 89	14/09/1918	14/09/1918
Miscellaneous	A Form Messages And Signals		
Miscellaneous	Amendment To 74th Division Order No.90	17/09/1918	17/09/1918
Miscellaneous	Reference Divisional Order No 90 Para 1 Zero Hour	17/09/1918	17/09/1918
Miscellaneous	Reference Divisional Order No 90 Para 1	17/09/1918	17/09/1918
Miscellaneous	S.G65/7	16/09/1918	16/09/1918
Operation(al) Order(s)	74th Division Order No 90	15/09/1918	15/09/1918
Miscellaneous	A Form Messages And Signals		
Miscellaneous	Headquarters 229th Infantry Brigade	16/09/1918	16/09/1918
Map	Barrage Table		
Operation(al) Order(s)	74th Division Order No.91	20/09/1918	20/09/1918
Miscellaneous	A Form Messages And Signals		
Miscellaneous	Warning Order		
Operation(al) Order(s)	74th Division Order No.92	22/09/1918	22/09/1918
Operation(al) Order(s)	74th Division Order No.93	23/09/1918	23/09/1918
Miscellaneous	Addendum No 2 To 74th Division Order No 93	24/09/1918	24/09/1918
Miscellaneous	Addendum To 74th Division Order No 93	23/09/1918	23/09/1918
Operation(al) Order(s)	74th Division Order No.94	25/09/1918	25/09/1918
Miscellaneous			
Miscellaneous	Warning Order	27/09/1918	27/09/1918
Miscellaneous	Warning Order	28/09/1918	28/09/1918
Operation(al) Order(s)	74th Division Order No.95	28/09/1918	28/09/1918
Miscellaneous	Relief Table		
Operation(al) Order(s)	74th Division Order No. 96	29/09/1918	29/09/1918
Map	Bois Du		
Map	Biez		
Heading	War Diary of General Staff 74th (Yeo) Division From 1st Octr 1918 To 31st Octr 1918		
War Diary	Norrent Fontes	01/10/1918	18/10/1918
War Diary	Wattignies	18/10/1918	28/10/1918
War Diary	Pont A Tress In	27/10/1918	31/10/1918
Miscellaneous	C Form Messages And Signals		
Miscellaneous	A Form Messages And Signals		
Operation(al) Order(s)	74th Division Order No.98	08/10/1918	08/10/1918
Operation(al) Order(s)	74th Division Order No.97	07/10/1918	07/10/1918

Miscellaneous	A Form Messages And Signals		
Miscellaneous	Defence Instruction	09/10/1918	09/10/1918
Operation(al) Order(s)	74th Division Order No.99	10/10/1918	10/10/1918
Operation(al) Order(s)	74th Division Order No.100	12/10/1918	12/10/1918
Miscellaneous	A Form Messages And Signals		
Miscellaneous	C Form Messages And Signals		
Operation(al) Order(s)	74th Division Order No.101	17/10/1918	17/10/1918
Operation(al) Order(s)	74th Division Order No.102	18/10/1918	18/10/1918
Operation(al) Order(s)	74th Division Order No.103	19/10/1918	19/10/1918
Miscellaneous	A Form Messages And Signals		
Operation(al) Order(s)	74th Division Order No.104	20/10/1918	20/10/1918
Operation(al) Order(s)	74th Division Order No.105	21/10/1918	21/10/1918
Miscellaneous	Appendix 'A' Orders for the Military Occupation of Tournai		
Miscellaneous	Addendum No 1 To 74th Division Order No.105	22/10/1918	22/10/1918
Miscellaneous	Amendment No.2 To 74th Division Order No.105	25/10/1918	25/10/1918
Operation(al) Order(s)	74th Division Order No 106	22/10/1918	22/10/1918
Miscellaneous	To All Recipients Of O.O. 106	23/10/1918	23/10/1918
Miscellaneous	A Form Messages And Signals		
Operation(al) Order(s)	74th Division Order No.107	24/10/1918	24/10/1918
Miscellaneous	Reference Div. Order No.107	28/10/1918	28/10/1918
Operation(al) Order(s)	74th Division Order No.108	24/10/1918	24/10/1918
Operation(al) Order(s)	74th Division Order No.109	29/10/1918	29/10/1918
Miscellaneous	Appendix Orders for the Military Occupation of Tournai		
Miscellaneous	Amendment To Divisional Order 109	29/10/1918	29/10/1918
Operation(al) Order(s)	74th Division Order No 109	29/10/1918	29/10/1918
Miscellaneous	Orders For The Military Occupation of Tournai		
Operation(al) Order(s)	74th Division Order No 110	31/10/1918	31/10/1918
Miscellaneous	Proposed Bridging Arrangement For L'escaut River	29/10/1918	29/10/1918
Miscellaneous	B Form Messages And Signals		
Miscellaneous	S.G.24/7	11/10/1918	11/10/1918
Miscellaneous	Cover For Branch Memoranda. Unregistered.		
Heading	General Staff 74th Division November 1918		
War Diary	Field	01/11/1918	30/11/1918
Miscellaneous	Amendments To 74th (Yeomanry) Division Order No 109	05/11/1918	05/11/1918
Miscellaneous	A Form Messages And Signals		
Operation(al) Order(s)	74th Division Order No 111	08/11/1916	08/11/1916
Miscellaneous	A Form Messages And Signals		
Operation(al) Order(s)	74th Division Order No 113	09/11/1918	09/11/1918
Miscellaneous	A Form Messages And Signals		
Operation(al) Order(s)	74th Division Order No 114	14/11/1918	14/11/1918
Operation(al) Order(s)	74th Division Order No 115	15/11/1918	15/11/1918
Operation(al) Order(s)	74th Division Order No 116	16/11/1918	16/11/1918
Miscellaneous	A Form Messages And Signals		
Miscellaneous	Minutes of Conference At Divisional Sports Meeting 18th Inst		
Miscellaneous	Minutes of Conference Held By Divisional Recreation Committee on 23rd Inst		
Miscellaneous	74th (Yeomanry) Division Organisation Of Education	20/11/1918	20/11/1918
Operation(al) Order(s)	74th Division Order No.110	31/10/1918	31/10/1918
Miscellaneous	S.G.6	04/11/1918	04/11/1918
Operation(al) Order(s)	Royal Artillery Order No.66 By Brigadier General L.J. Hext C.M.G. Commanding Royal Artillery 74th (Yeo) Division	04/11/1918	04/11/1918
Map	Map		

Miscellaneous	Bombardment Table		
Map	Tournai		
Miscellaneous	Bombardment Table	04/11/1918	04/11/1918

74TH DIVISION

GENERAL STAFF
1918 MAY - ~~DEC 1918~~
~~JAN~~ - FEB 1919

74TH DIVISION

— CONFIDENTIAL — Vol 2

WAR DIARY

OF

GENERAL STAFF, 74TH (YEO) DIVISION

1st MAY TO 31st MAY 1918

Army Form C. 2118.

WAR DIARY
INTELLIGENCE SUMMARY
(Erase heading not required.)

74th (Yeomanry) Division
General Staff Branch.

Instructions regarding War Diaries and Intelligence Summaries are contained in F. S. Regs., Part II. and the Staff Manual respectively. Title Pages will be prepared in manuscript.

Place	Date	Hour	Summary of Events and Information	Remarks and references to Appendices
At Sea	May 1918 1st		The Division less artillery sailed from ALEXANDRIA and arrived without incident at MARSEILLES on the 7th. Divisional artillery embarked at ALEXANDRIA.	C.S.O's R.S.R's
	3rd			
MARSEILLES	7th		On arrival men were received to entrain for NOYELLES and the first trains left the same evening — Units who did not entrain on the 7th marched to rest camps.	C.S.O's R.S.R's C.S.O's
RUE	9th		Divisional Headquarters were established at RUE.	
	11th 14th 18th		Divisional artillery disembarked at MARSEILLES. Divisional area no 58 input. Concentration of the Division in the RUE area completed. During the time the Division was in the RUE area units were chiefly occupied in training in Gas defence. The chemical adviser VIII Corps and a staff of Gas N.C.O's were placed at the disposal of the Division to assist in carrying this out — lectures were given to all units in the Division and all Small Box Respirators were carefully examined. This was especially necessary	Appendix A R.S.R's

Army Form C. 2118.

74th (Yeomanry) Division
General Staff Branch.

WAR DIARY
INTELLIGENCE SUMMARY
(Erase heading not required.)

(2)

Instructions regarding War Diaries and Intelligence Summaries are contained in F.S. Regs., Part II. and the Staff Manual respectively. Title Pages will be prepared in manuscript.

Place	Date 1918 May	Hour	Summary of Events and Information	Remarks and references to Appendices
RUE	19th		As many of the S.B.R.'s issued in PALESTINE were faulty and as large number had to be exchanged. It was also necessary to exchange all the contaminated air trunks in possession of this Division had become obsolete. Demonstrations of the use of Gas projectors were also carried out in each Brigade Area. The Deputy Inspector of Physical and Bayonet Training gave lectures to Infantry Battalions on the 15th and 16th. He gave three lectures each day and two Battalions attended each lecture. Orders were received for the Division less artillery to move forward by rail into the First Army Area.	C.S.9a. Appendix B. C.S.9a / 9.9a Appendix C. C.S.9a C.S.9b
ROELLECOURT	21st	2 p.m.	Divisional Headquarters opened at ROELLECOURT.	
	24th		Division less artillery concentrated in First Army Area. Orders received for Division less artillery to move*	
LE CAUROY	25th		Division less artillery concentrated in new area by 2 p.m. Divisional Headquarters opened at LE CAUROY.	
	27th	1 p.m.	G.O.C. Inspected 229th Infantry Bde	

WAR DIARY

INTELLIGENCE SUMMARY
(Erase heading not required.)

74th (Yeomanry) Division
General Staff Branch

Army Form C. 2118.

Instructions regarding War Diaries and Intelligence Summaries are contained in F.S. Regs., Part II. and the Staff Manual respectively. Title Pages will be prepared in manuscript.

Place	Date 1918	Hour	Summary of Events and Information	Remarks and references to Appendices
LE CAUROY	May 28th		G.O.C. inspected 230th Infantry Bde.	Appx
	29th		G.O.C. inspected 231st Infantry Bde. Conference of Brigade Majors at Divl. Headquarters.	Appx Appx
	30th		74th Divisional Artillery arrived and were located in HOUVIN-HOUVIGNEUL area	Appendix D Appx
	31st		Division placed in G.H.Q. Reserve and held at 24 hours notice to move.	

(Signed) Slate-ded Major
General Staff 74th (Yeomanry) Division

1.6.18

Appendix A

SECRET.   Copy No...14....

74th DIVISION ORDER No.58.

14th May 1918.

1. The following temporary Brigade Groups will be formed; Brigade Commanders will assume responsibility for their administrative areas in accordance with F.S.R. Part I., Section 47.

229th BRIGADE GROUP.   Area.
   229th Infantry Brigade.   RUE - ST.FIRMIN -
   5th R.Anglesey R.E.   FAVIERES - BECQUERELLE
   448th Company, Div.Train.   - FOREST MONTIERS -
   229th Field Ambulance.   BERNAY.

230th BRIGADE GROUP.
   230th Infantry Brigade.   PONTHOILE - MORLAY -
   5th R. Monmouth R.E.   HAMEL - NOUVION -
   Machine Gun Battalion.   LAMOTTE BULEUX -
   449th Company, Div.Train.   FOREST L'ABBAYE -
   230th Field Ambulance.   SAILLY BRAY - LE TITRE.

231st BRIGADE GROUP.
   231st Infantry Brigade.   CANCHY - DOMVAST -
   439th Field Coy. R.E.   MARCHEVILLE -
   Pioneer Battalion.   HAUTVILLERS.
   450th Company, Div.Train.
   231st Field Ambulance.

ARTILLERY GROUP.
   44th Brigade R.F.A.   PORT le GRAND -
   117th Brigade R.F.A.   GRAND LAVIERS -
   M.T.M.Batteries.   SAILLY le SEC.
   D.A.C.
   Mobile Vet. Section.
   447th Company, Div.Train. (SAILLY le SEC).

A.C.Temperley.

Lieut.Colonel.
General Staff.
74th (Yeomanry) Division.

Issued at 0800.

Copies to:-
No.			No.	
1.	'G'		10.	Pioneer Bn.
2.	'Q'		11.	Machine Gun Bn.
3.	'Q'		12.	A.D.M.S.
4.	C.R.A.		13.	Div.Train.
5.	C.R.E.		14.	War Diary.
6.	Signal Company.		15.	War Diary.
7.	229th Inf.Bde.		16.	File.
8.	230th " "		17.	A.P.M.
9.	231st " "		18.	A.D.V.S.

Appendix B

SECRET.   Copy No...14

74th DIVISION ORDER No.59.

                                               19th May, 1918.

Reference 1:250,000 & Sheet 11. 1:100,000.

1.   The Division, less Artillery, will move by rail into the First Army Area on May 20th and to May 24th.

2.   Brigade Groups will be billetted as under:-

   229th Brigade Group - BUS-St.LEGER - HUMBERCOURT - COULLEMONT (F.4).

   230th Brigade Group - FOUFFLIN-RICAMETZ - BUNEVILLE Sub-areas. (E.2 and 3).

   231st Brigade Group - MAIZIERES Sub-area (F.3).

3.   Separate instructions will be issued by the A.A.&.Q.M.G.

4.   Divisional Headquarters will close in its present position at 2 p.m. on May 21st and open at ROELLECOURT (E.2) at the same hour.

5.   ACKNOWLEDGE.

                              a.c.Temperley.
                              Lieut.Colonel.
                              General Staff,
                              74th (Yeomanry) Division.

Issued at 2 p.m.

Copies to:-
   No. 1. 'G'   No. 11. Machine Gun Bn.
       2. 'Q'   12. A.D.M.S.
       3. 'Q'   13. Div.Train.
       4. C.R.A.   14. War Diary.
       5. C.R.E.   15. War Diary.
       6. Signal Company.   16. File.
       7. 229th Inf.Bde.   17. A.D.V.S.
       8. 230th Inf.Bde.   18. Reserve Army.
       9. 231st Inf.Bde.   19. First Army.
      10. Pioneer Bn.   20. Canadian Corps.

SECRET.   Copy No...16..

74th DIVISION ORDER No.60.

24th May 1918.

Reference LENS. Sheet 11. 1:100,000.

1. 74th Division, less Artillery, will move to areas tomorrow as under:-

    229th Brigade Group to LIGNEREUIL - LIENCOURT - GRAND RULLECOURT
                            - BEAUFORT.
        H.Q. - LIGNEREUIL.

    230th Brigade Group to PENIN - GIVENCHY-le-NOBLE - MANIN -
                            IZEL-lez-HAMEAU.
        H.Q. - IZEL-lez-HAMEAU.

    231st Brigade Group to TILLOY-les-HERMAVILLE - AVESNES-le-COMTE -
                            HAUTEVILLE - HERMAVILLE.
        H.Q. - AVESNES-le-COMTE.

    Div.H.Q. & Mobile)
        Vet.Section   )   Le GAUROY.

    The Machine Gun Battalion (now at TERNAS) will be transferred to 229th Brigade Group.

2. There is no restriction as to routes. Brigade Groups will not move East of the line COULLEMONT - GRAND RULLECOURT - AMBRINES - AVERDOINGT before 10 a.m.
    231st Brigade Group will be clear of the line MANIN - IZEL-lez-HAMEAU by noon.

3. Distances on the march will be maintained as under:-

        Between Battalions ...   .   500 yards.
            "   Companies   100   "
            "   Unit & its transport   ...   100   "
        When transport is Brigaded,
            between each Battn. transport ... 100   "

4. Administrative Instructions will be issued by the A.A.&.Q.M.G.

5. All moves will be completed by 1-30 p.m. B.G.s.C., Brigade Groups will report accordingly to Div. H.Q. by that hour.

6. Div. H.Q. will close at ROELLECOURT at 1 p.m. and open at Le GAUROY at the same hour.

7. ACKNOWLEDGE.

                                          (signed)
                                          Lieut.Colonel.
                                          General Staff.
                                          74th (Yeomanry) Division.

Issued at 12-30 p.m.

Copies to:-
    No.1. 'G'   No.11. A.D.M.S.
       2. 'Q'   12. Div.Train.
       3. 'Q'   13. Candn. Corps.
       4. C.R.A.   14. 1st Cav. Division.
       5. C.R.E.   15. War Diary.
       6. Signal Coy.   16.   "   "
       7. M.G.Battn.   17. File.
       8. 229th Inf.Bde.
       9. 230th "   "
      10. 231st "   "

Appendix D

SECRET.   Copy No. 15

74th DIVISION.
WARNING ORDER.

31st May 1918.

1. The 74th Division (completed with Div.Arty) is placed in G.H.Q. Reserve and will be held at 24 hours notice to move.

2. No Unit is to change location without sanction from Divisional Headquarters.

M M Pauy-jones Major
for Lieut.Colonel.
General Staff.
74th (Yeomanry) Division.

Issued at 1 p.m.

Copies to:-
No.					
1.	'G'	7.	M.G.Bn.	13.	Canadian Corps.
2.	'Q'	8.	229th Inf.Bde.	14.	Camp Commandant.
3.	'Q'	9.	230th " "	15.	War Diary.
4.	C.R.A.	10.	231st " "	16.	" "
5.	C.R.E.	11.	A.D.M.S.	17.	File.
6.	Signal Coy.	12.	Div.Train.		

D. D. & L., London, E.C.
(P6975) Wt.W11200/H2695 500,000 12/16 **W21** H16/580

COVER
FOR
BRANCH MEMORANDA.

Unregistered.

Referred to	Date	Referred to	Date

231st Infantry Brigade

Vol. 3.

General Staff,
74th Division.

June 1918

14

Army Form C. 2118

WAR DIARY
or
INTELLIGENCE SUMMARY
(Erase heading not required.)

74th Yeomanry Division
General Staff.
JUNE 1918

Instructions regarding War Diaries and Intelligence
Summaries are contained in F. S. Regs., Part II.
and the Staff Manual respectively. Title Pages
will be prepared in manuscript.

Place	Date	Hour	Summary of Events and Information	Remarks and references to Appendices
LE CAUROY	June 1st		Training continued. Inter Bde Tactical Exercise carried out in the LIGNEREUIL area. 229 Bde attacked 231 Bde less 2 Battalion in its defence. M.G. Bn cooperated also Bde and Battery Staffs R.A. Contact planes cooperated with advancing infantry. Scheme is attached.	APPENDIX I WD9
	2nd		Church Parade and Training	WD9
	3rd		Training continued throughout the Division. Bde Tactical Exercise carried out by 230 Bde in LIGNEREUIL area. 3 Battalion in the attack and 1 Battalion defending. 1 Coy. M.G. Bn cooperated, also Artillery F.O.O's	WD9

1875 Wt. W593/826 1,000,000 4/15 J.B.C. & A. A.D.S.S./Forms/C. 2118.

Army Form C. 2118

WAR DIARY
INTELLIGENCE SUMMARY
(Erase heading not required.)

Place	Date	Hour	Summary of Events and Information	Remarks and references to Appendices
LE CAUROY	June 4th		Training continued. Lecture to Officers at AVESNES LE COMTE on cooperation between Tanks and Infantry given by G.O.C. 1st Tank Bde.	Appx 79
	5th		Training Continued. 231 Bde carried out a Bde Tactical Exercise. Scheme attached. Army Command & Army present.	Appendix II
	6th		Training continued	Appx 79
	7th		Training continued. 228 Bde Brigade Tactical Exercise in LIGNEREUIL Area. 230 Bde practice in cooperation with Tanks. Information received that the 16th Bn. would probably relieve 1st Canadian Bn. of 1st Canadian Div.	Appx 79

1875. Wt. W593/825 1,000,000. 4/15 J.B.C. & A. A.D.S.S./Forms/C. 2118.

Army Form C. 2118

WAR DIARY
INTELLIGENCE SUMMARY
(Erase heading not required.)

Instructions regarding War Diaries and Intelligence Summaries are contained in F.S. Regs., Part II. and the Staff Manual respectively. Title Pages will be prepared in manuscript.

Place	Date	Hour	Summary of Events and Information	Remarks and references to Appendices
LE CAUROY	June 8th		Training. 229 Inf Bde practiced cooperation between Tanks and Infantry	App 17
	June 9th		231, 2 Inf Bde Tactical Exercise Advanced Guard and Attack 162 Funeral reports attack Enemy & opposed advances. Orders were received from Canadian Corps that the Division was to be held in G.H.Q. reserve ready to move at nine hours' notice.	App 17 App 6.
	June 10th		Training continued in vicinity of billets.	App 6.
	June 11th		Training continued in vicinity of billets. The nine hours' notice of move was extended to twelve hours' notice.	App 6.
	June 12th		Training continued in vicinity of billets.	App 6.

Army Form C. 2118

WAR DIARY
or
INTELLIGENCE SUMMARY
(Erase heading not required.)

Place	Date	Hour	Summary of Events and Information	Remarks and references to Appendices
LE CAUROY	June 13th		From midnight 12th/13th inst. the Division was held at 24 hours' notice to move.	App.6.
	June 14th		Training. Demonstration by 229th Inf. Bde of co-operation between Infantry and Tanks, breaching wire, advancing over trenches and shell holes, and consolidation.	App.6.
	June 15th		Training continued.	App.6.
	June 16th		Training. Arti. Brigade Field Day. 230th Inf. Bde in attack. 229th Inf. Bde in defence and counter-attack. M.G. Bn, Div. Arty. and anti-aircraft aeroplane co-operated.	App.6.
	June 17th		Training continued.	App.6.
			Training continued.	App.6.

WAR DIARY
or
INTELLIGENCE SUMMARY
(Erase heading not required.)

Army Form C. 2118

Instructions regarding War Diaries and Intelligence Summaries are contained in F. S. Regs., Part II. and the Staff Manual respectively. Title Pages will be prepared in manuscript.

Place	Date	Hour	Summary of Events and Information	Remarks and references to Appendices
LE CAUROY	June 18th		Training. Tactical exercise by 230th Inf. Bde. Co-operation of Tanks with Infantry in the attack. Air contact aeroplane co-operated.	J.P.G.
	June 19th		Training continued.	J.P.G.
	June 20th		Orders were received from Canadian Corps that the Division was to be reorganised on a nine battalion basis and that the 12th Norfolk Regt., 12th R. Scots Fus. and 2nd R. Welsh Fus. are to proceed on June 21st. to join the 31st Division, dismounted personnel by tactical train from TINCQUES to BLARINGHEM, horsed transport by road to BLARINGHEM staging at PERNES on night 21st/22nd. Orders for these moves were issued by the Division.	App. Ces 3 & 4 — J.P.G.
	June 21st		Training continued. The moves ordered above were carried out. Training continued.	J.P.G.
	June 22nd		Training. 229 Inf. Bde. Tactical exercise in the attack. 231 Inf. Bde. Attack in co-operation with Tanks.	J.P.G.
	June 23rd		Training continued.	J.P.G.

Army Form C. 2118

WAR DIARY
or
INTELLIGENCE SUMMARY
(Erase heading not required.)

Instructions regarding War Diaries and Intelligence Summaries are contained in F.S. Regs., Part II. and the Staff Manual respectively. Title Pages will be prepared in manuscript.

Place	Date	Hour	Summary of Events and Information	Remarks and references to Appendices
LE CAUROY	June 24th	9.58 a.m.	Warning Order was received from CANADIAN CORPS warning the Division to be prepared to move into the NORRENT FONTES area. This was subsequently confirmed by CAN CORPS O.O. No. 201. In accordance with this order 29th June 74th Div Order No. 63 was issued. The move to take place on 25, 26 & 29 June. Div mounted personnel & transport and Div Arty by road; dismounted personnel by rail; mounted personnel and transport staging one night. Destinations as follows:— 229th Bde Group — WITTERNESSE — MAZINGHEM area. 230th — do. — FLECHIN — ESTRÉE BLANCHE — ERNY ST. JULIEN area. 231st — do. — ST. HILAIRE — BOURECQ — LIÈRES area. Div Arty — FEBVIN — NÉDON — AMETTES — ANTES area. Training continued.	App. 5
	June 25th		Move of the Division to new Area commenced as ordered in 74th Div Order No 63. Training continued among units still in LE CAUROY area.	App.
LE CAUROY NORRENT FONTES	June 26th		Move to new area continued. Div HQ closed at LE CAUROY at 3 p.m. and opened at NORRENT FONTES same hour. At 6.30 p.m. 74th Div Ordr. No 64 was issued holding the Div. at 4 hours' notice for the purpose of relieving the XI or XIII Corps and at 24 hours' notice for that purpose or British G.H.Q. Troops. Also available battle stations in case of emergency, in rear of AIRE CANAL and the BUSNES — ST BEN BECQUE line to be rushed forenoon under command of B.G.C. 229th Inf Bde. Details in Appendix 6.	App. 6 Map 1/100,000 HAZEBROUCK 1/40,000 Sheet 3 A.

1875. Wt. W593/326 1,000,000 4/15 J.B.C. & A. A.D.S.S./Forms/C. 2118.

WAR DIARY or INTELLIGENCE SUMMARY

Army Form C. 2118

Place	Date	Hour	Summary of Events and Information	Remarks and references to Appendices
NORRENT FONTES	June 27th	5:30 p.m.	Move to new area complete. A conference of Bde. Majors was held at	A.54.
	June 28th		Some training was carried out in the vicinity of billets. In accordance with instructions received orders were issued for the move on the 29th inst. of 2 Bdes. 229 Fy. Bde. to work in forward area under XI Corps, as under:— Work Under 1. 1 Coy. 'A' Bt. — 61 Div. 2. 1 Coy. 'A' Bt. — do 3. 1 Coy. 'A' Bt. — 5 Div. 4. 1 Coy. 'B' Bt. — do 'B' Bt. — C.E. XI Corps Billets BUSNES ST. VENANT Camps J.19. J.25 do do	
	June 29th		16th Divnl and 123 Som. L.I. proceeded to work under XI Corps on advanced Reconnaissance & rear line of defence in XI Corps area above. parties of officers and O.Rs. from 229, 230 and 231 Fy. Bdes. and 74th Bn. M.G. troops attached. In accordance with instructions received the following further attachments for work on rear defences were ordered:— 1 Bn. 231 Fy. Bde. to replace Bn. of 4th Canadian Div. covering number XIII troops in vicinity of CHOCQUES 2 Sections R.E. do report to camps in J.19 for work under XI Corps. Both then move to take places on the 30th inst.	A.54.

Army Form C. 2118

WAR DIARY

INTELLIGENCE SUMMARY

(Erase heading not required.)

Place	Date	Hour	Summary of Events and Information	Remarks and references to Appendices
NORRENT FONTES	Jun 30th		Sunday Church Parade. "C" Sqn 74th Bn M.G.C. moved from GUERNES & FONTES. 74 Div. came under orders of the XIII Corps at CAUROY. The whole of the month of June was spent training in the Area. Training consisted of Musketry, Range practice, Section and other specialised training; A great many Battalion, Brigade Tactical exercises in open warfare were carried out; Tanks and Cadets partook co-operating. On the 26th June 1st Div. moved to the NORRENT FONTES Area and came into support of XI and XII Corps Order No. 64 and 65 issued.	Appendix 6 and 7.

Wm Campion Major
Gen. St. M.
74th Div.

APPENDIX I

Instructions for an Inter-Brigade and Tactical Exercise
to be held on 1st June 1918.

The 229th and 231st Infantry Brigades will take part in a Tactical Exercise being held on June 1st, scheme for which is attached.

1. The 229th Brigade will be assembled in H.36.d. by 10.15 a.m. ready to move forward at 11 a.m. No advance will take place before that hour.

2. The 231st Brigade, representing the enemy, will be in the position assigned to it in the scheme by 10.45 a.m.

3. O.C., M.G.Battalion will detail 1 M.G.Company to work with each of the above Brigades under direct orders of the G.Os.C. Brigades. G.Os.C., Brigades will issue necessary orders for these M.G.Companies to rendezvous.

4. The Artillery will not actually take part in the Exercise, but the C.R.A. will detail 1 Brigade and 3 Battery Commanders to each Infantry Brigade for liaison purposes and for practice in selecting Battery positions.

5. Only limbers carrying M.G. and L.G. will be on parade.

6. Haversack rations will be carried.

7. Care must be taken not to damage any crops outside the manoeuvre area.

8. Flares will be carried by the attacking Brigade.
   Arrangements are being made for a contact patrol to co-operate with the attack.
   Flares will be lit when called for but only by the most advanced troops of the attacking Brigade.

9. **Dress.** Battle Order.
   229th Brigade will wear steel helmets.
   231st Brigade, acting as enemy, will wear S.D. caps.

10. O.C., 74th Div. Signal Company will arrange with 229th Brigade to run a line from the Battle H.Q. of 229th Brigade to Div.H.Q. where messages and reports will be sent.

11. **Directing Staff.**
    G.O.C., 74th Division.
    G.S.O. 1. "   "
    O.C., 74th Bn. M.G.C.

    Umpires 229th Brigade.
    G.O.C., R.A.
    B.M., 230th Brigade.
    1 Lieut.Colonel, 230th Brigade.
    G.S.O. 2., 74th Division.

    Umpires 231st Brigade.
    G.O.C., 230th Brigade.
    B.M., R.A.
    1 Lieut.Colonel, 230th Brigade.
    G.S.O. 3., 74th Division.

All Umpires will wear White armbands on the left arm and will rendezvous at D.H.Q. at 10 a.m. June 1st to receive any necessary instructions from the G.O.C., 74th Division.

Reference Sheet 51(c) 1:40,000.

GENERAL IDEA.

The enemy (represented by 231st Brigade) has broken through the front system between COUTURELLE (U.11) and NOYELLETTE (J.18) and is advancing in a N.W. direction.

At 8 a.m. on 1st June the 74th, 15th and 3rd Divisions who have been moving forward with a view to counter-attacking are concentrated as follows:-

74th Division. 1 Brigade - LE CAUROY. 229th Brigade.
                1 Brigade - BERLENCOURT. 'B' Bde (imaginary)
                1 Brigade - ETREE WAMIN. 'C' "   ("   )

15th Division.   near BEAUDRICOURT.

3rd Division.   near AMBRINES.

The enemy are reported to hold the line COUTURELLE - GRAND RULLECOURT - BEAUFORT - NOYELLE - VION - NOYELLETTE.

Elements of a British Division which has already been heavily engaged hold the village of LIENCOURT and the BOIS DE ROBERMONT.

At 8.30 a.m. orders are received from W Corps ordering the 74th Division to attack the apex of the salient between GRAND RULLECOURT (exclusive) and BEAUFORT (inclusive). The 15th Division is at the same time ordered to co-operate on the Right and capture the line GRAND RULLECOURT - SOMBRIN both inclusive, while the 3rd Division on the left is ordered to capture the line BEAUFORT (exclusive) to NOYELLE - VION (inclusive).

Reference Sheet 51c 1/40,000.

SPECIAL IDEA "A".

G.O.C., 74th Division decides to attack the objective assigned to him with two Brigades keeping one Brigade in Reserve.

229th Brigade concentrated at LE CAUROY to attack enemy's line between GRAND RULLECOURT (exclusive) and APPEGREHEE (exclusive)

"B" Brigade (imaginary) concentrated at BERLENCOURT to attack the villages of APPEGREHEE and BEAUFORT.

At 9.30.a.m. the following message is received by the three Infantry Brigades and the C.R.A. of the 74th Division.

"G. A.B.C.   1st.

"The 74th Division will attack the enemy's position GRAND RULLECOURT (exclusive) - BEAUFORT (inclusive) aaa 15th Div and 3rd Div. co-operating on Right and Left Flanks respectively aaa 15th Div. will capture line SOMBRIN - GRAND RULLECOURT both inclusive aaa 3rd Div. will capture line BEAUFORT exclusive - NOYELLE VION inclusive aaa 74th Div will attack its objective with two Brigades in line and one in Reserve aaa 229th Brigade will attack on right 'B' Brigade on left aaa Dividing line between Brigades Road Junction I.25.c. - BLAVINCOURT to 'B' Brigade - APPEGREHEE to 'B' Brigade aaa C.R.A. will detail one Brigade R.F.A. to co-operate with each attacking Brigade aaa Artillery Brigade Commanders to report forthwith to respective Infantry Brigadiers aaa 'C' Brigade will move from ETREE to BERLENCOU and remain in Divisional Reserve aaa Infantry advance will commence 11 a.m. at which hour advanced D.H.Q. will open at LE CAUROY Chateau aaa Addressed 229, 'B' & 'C' Bdes, C.R.A. repeated 15th and 3rd Divis

Reference Sheet 51c 1/40,000.

SPECIAL IDEA "B".

231st Brigade (less 2 Battns) representing the enemy will take up a defensive position roughly on the line GRAND RULLECOURT (exclusive) - O.4. central - BEAUFORT (inclusive) and will be in position by 10.45. a.m.

The Brigade will retire as the attacking force pushes its attack home.

The flank not attacked will withdraw in compliance with the one attacked. The withdrawal will be towards AVESNES le COMTE.

Appendix II

BRIGADE FIELD EXERCISE.

Wednesday 5th June.

OPEN WARFARE.

BRIGADE IN THE ATTACK.

POINTS TO BE BROUGHT OUT.

1. The Fire fight.
2. Casualties with sequence of command and control.
3. Reorganisation.
4. Preparation to meet counter-attack.
5. Intercommunication.

NARRATIVE.

The enemy, having captured the villages of LATTRE ST QUENTIN and HAUTEVILLE, was on the morning of the 5th June, reported to be pressing forward.

Strength - about one brigade.

One Brigade of the Nth Division, lately holding the above named villages, has fallen back on GOUVES - HABARCQ.

231st Brigade, coming up from AGNEZ LEZ DUISANS, is ordered to counter-attack at once.

SITUATION at 9 a.m. on 5-6-18.

The head of the Brigade, marching from GOUVES has reached the bridge at K.21.b.4.9., the order of march being 24th R.W.F., 24th Welsh R., 25th R.W.F., 10th K.S.L.I. and 210th M.G.Coy.

Here the Brigadier is met by the Brigade Major of the Brigade lately fallen back from HAUTEVILLE, who informs him that the remains of his Brigade are holding the W.edge of the orchards round MONTENESCOURT.

The enemy appears to be consolidating the ridge N.E. of HAUTEVILLE digging strong points in the neighbourhood of les 4 vents farm, and making a general forward movement in small bodies under cover of snipers and patrols towards MONTENESCOURT.

On this information the Brigadier writes his order for the attack.

DETAIL.

1. Brigade attacks with 2 battalion in front line, one in support and one in reserve.
   Normal formation on a frontage of 500^x.

2. The fight will be controlled from the enemy's position by means of flags.

3. Casualties will be withdrawn at the following rates:-

	3500 to 3000	3000 to 2500	2500 to 2000	2000 to 1500	1500 to 1000	1000 tp 500
24/R.W.F.	0%	10%	10%	10%	15%	15%
24/Welsh R.	0	10	10	10	15	15

2.

	3500 to 3000	3000 to 2500	2500 to 2000	2000 to 1500	1500 to 1000	1000 to 500
25/R.W.F.	0%	5%	10%	5%	10%	10%
10/K.S.L.I.	0	0	5	5	10	10

4.   Lieut.Col the Lord KENSINGTON, D.S.O. will command the brigade with the Brigade Major and Signalling Officer.

The B.G.C., assisted by the following officers, will control the fight:-

Major J.P. HEYWOOD-LONSDALE	10th K.S.L.I.
Major H.J. HOWELL-EVANS	24th R.W.F.
Captain O. FISHER	24th Welsh R.
The STAFF CAPTAIN.	
Captain H.J. HODGES	24th R.W.F. attached B.H.Q.

App 3

SECRET.   Copy No. 14

74th DIVISION ORDER No.61.

20th June 1918.

1. Orders have been received that the Division will be reduced to nine battalions.

2. The 12th Bn. Norfolk Regt, 24th Bn. Royal Welsh Fusiliers and 12th Bn. Royal Scots Fusiliers will move on June 21st to 31st Division.
   Dismounted personnel will proceed by tactical train, transport will move by road.
   Battalions will take with them in each case their baggage and supply wagons.

3. ACKNOWLEDGE.

                          A. C. Temperley.
                                Lieut. Colonel.
                                General Staff.
                     74th (Yeomanry) Division.

Issued at 9 a.m.

Copies to:-
- No. 1. 'G'
- 2. 'Q'
- 3. 'Q'
- 4. C.R.A.
- 5. C.R.E.
- 6. Signal Coy.
- 7. M.G.Battn.
- 8. 229th Inf.Bde.
- 9. 230th " "
- 10. 231st " "
- No. 11. A.D.M.S.
- 12. Div. Train.
- 13. Canadian Corps.
- 14. War Diary.
- 15. " "
- 16. File.

SECRET.
Copy No. 11

App. 4

74th DIVISION ORDER NO 62.

20th June 1918.

Ref LENS 100,000. HAZEBROUCK. 100,000.

1. The 12th Norfolk Regiment, 12th Royal Scots Fusiliers, and 24th Royal Welsh Fusiliers accompanied by baggage and supply waggons will join the 31st Division on June 21st as follows:-

    (a) Dismounted personnel by rail, entrain TINQUES detrain BLARINGHEM.

    (b) Transport by road :-

Date.	Transport of	From.	To.	Starting point.	Remarks.
June 21st.	12th Royal Scots Fus:	GRAND RULLECOURT.	PERNES.	Cross roads VILLERS - SIRE - SIMON 10 a.m.	Stage night 21/22 PERNES. Billets from Town Major.
	12th Norfolk Regiment.	IZEL LEZ HAMEAU.	do	do 10.8.a.m.	Interval between transport of Battns 500 yards.
	24th Royal Welsh Fus:	HAUTEVILLE.	do	do 10.16 a.m	Route TINQUES - CHELERS - MONCHY le BRETON - VALHUON.
22nd	As above.	PERNES.	BLARINGHEM.	To be detailed by O.C. Column.	Location of respective units to be procured from Area Commandant, BLARINGHEM. Interval between transport of battns 500 yards. No restriction as to route.

2. 229th Brigade will detail a Field Officer or Senior Captain to be in command of the transport. This Officer will take over command at the starting point on 21st June.

3. 74th Division 'Q' will issue detailed instructions regarding Entrainment and Supplies.

actemperley.

Lieut Colonel.
General Staff.
74th (Yeomanry) Division.

Issued at 6. p.m.

Copies to No 1 'G'
    2 'Q'
    3 'Q'
    4 O.C. 74th Signals.
    5 229th Infantry Brigade.
    6 230th Infantry Brigade.
    7 231st Infantry Brigade.
    8 A.D.M.S.

No 9 O.C. 74th Div. Train.
    10 Canadian Corps.
    11 War Diary.
    12. War Diary.
    13 File.
    14 229 Brigade

"C" Form.
MESSAGES AND SIGNALS.

Army Form C. 2123.
(In books of 100.)

No. of Message 7

Prefix	Code	Words	Received.	Sent, or sent out	Office Stamp.
			From	At 25/VI 1 m.	
Charges to Collect			By 75	To	
Service Instructions.				By	

Handed in at ... Office 4.55 p. Received 5.15 p.m.

TO 231 Bde

Sender's Number.	Day of Month.	In reply to Number.	AAA
G557	26		

aaa
SG50 is cancelled, 231 Bde will be at 4 hours special notice until midnight June 27/28 aaa Thereafter 229 will be at special notice aaa 231 Bde to acknowledge added 231 Bde repeated 229 Bde mg Bolton
Q1

FROM 74 Divn
TIME & PLACE 4.30 pm

S.S.50

SECRET.

Headquarters.
    229th Infantry Brigade.
    230th Infantry Brigade.
    231st Infantry Brigade.
    C.R.A.
    C.R.E.
    A.D.M.S.
    'Q' Branch.
O.C. 74th Bn M.G.C.

1.   On arrival in the new area the Division again comes into G.H.Q. Reserve and is at 24 hours notice.

2.   The 229th Infantry Brigade will however be at the following special notice.
        Daily between 5.30 a.m. and 7.30 a.m. at 2 hours notice. Otherwise at 4 hours notice.

                                    Major.
                               General Staff.
25th June 1918.   74th (Yeomanry) Division.

App. 5

SECRET.   Copy No. 15

74th DIVISION ORDER NO 63.

24th June 1918.

1. The Division will move to NORRENT FONTES area in accordance with the attached table.

2. The Machine Gun Battalion will join 230th Brigade Group.

3. On arrival in the area 229th Brigade will detail two battalions to work under the orders of the XI Corps.

4. Instructions for entraining and billetting will be issued by A.A. & Q.M.G.

5. Divisional H.Q. will open at NORRENT - FONTES at 3 p.m. on June 26th, and close at LE CAUROY at the same hour.

6. ACKNOWLEDGE.

a C Temperley

Lieut Colonel,
General Staff.
74th (Yeo) Division.

Issued at 11.45 pm

Copies to:-
- No 1 'G'
- 2 'Q'
- 3 'Q'
- 4 C.R.A.
- 5 C.R.E.
- 6 Signal Coy.
- 7 M.G Battn.
- 8 229th Infantry Brigade.
- 9 230th Infantry Brigade.
- 10 231st Infantry Brigade.
- No 11 A.D.M.S.
- 12 Div. Train.
- 13 Canadian Corps.
- 14 3rd Canadian Div.
- 15 War Diary.
- 16 War Diary.
- 17 File.

MOVE TABLE.

Number.	DATE.	UNIT.	TO.	ROUTE.	REMARKS.
1.	June 25th	Dismounted personnel. 230th Bde Group.	FLECHIN - ESTREE - BLANCHE - ERNY ST JULIEN area.	From LIGNY ST FLOCHEL to AIRE.	BY RAIL.
2.	"	Dismounted personnel. 231st Bde Group.	ST HILAIRE - BOURECQ - LIERES area.	From TINQUES to AIRE.	BY RAIL.
3.	"	Mounted personnel and transport 230th Brigade Group.	TANGRY sub area.	Via CHELERS - MONCHY BRETON - VALHUON. Starting point TINQUES 10 a.m.	Under orders of respective O.C. Coys Dn TRAIN Billets from Sub area Commandant TANGRY.
4.	"	ditto. 231st Bde Group.	ditto.	ditto. Starting point 11 a.m.	
5.	June 26th	Dismounted personnel. 229th Brigade Group.	WITTERNESSE - MAZINGHEM area.	To AIRE.	BY RAIL.
6.	"	Mounted personnel and transport 229th Bde Group and Div. H.Q.	TANGRY sub-area.	Passing starting point 10 a.m.	Detail as for No 3 & 4.
7.	"	Divisional Artillery.	ditto.	Passing starting point 11 a.m.	Report for billets O.C. TANGRY sub-area.
8.	"	Mounted personnel and transport of 230th and 231st Brigade Groups.	Respective Brigade areas.	No restrictions.	Under orders of O.C. Coys. Div Train.

MOVE TABLE.

Number.	Date.	Unit.	To.	Route.	Remarks.
9.	June 27th	As in No 6.	Brigade Area.	Ditto.	Under orders to be issued by C.R.A.
10.	"	Div. Arty.	FEBVIN - NEDON - AMETTES - Ames area.	ditto.	

NOTE. Distances on the march in accordance with Divisional Standing Orders.

74.S.M.9/14.

Divisional Boundaries ———
Front Line Aug 20th ———

LESTREM

SECRET.

App.6
17
COPY NO...7....

74th DIVISION ORDER NO.64.

26th June 1918.

Reference Map Sheet 36.a.1/40,000.

1. The 74th Division will be at four hours notice for the purpose of reinforcing either the XI or XIII Corps.

    Arrangements are being made to carry out reconnaissances accordingly.

    S.G.50 is cancelled.

2. 74th Division will be at 24 hours notice for the purpose of G.H.Q.Reserve.

3. In case of emergency, from midnight June 27th/28th, B.G.C. 229th Infantry Brigade will command the nucleus garrison of the Switch along AIRE CANAL and the BUSNES - STEENBECQUE line in the XI Corps area. The garrison will consist of 229th Infantry Brigade, 1 M.G.Company, 1 Company 39th M.G.Battn.

    On receipt of the order to "MAN BATTLE STATIONS" 229th Infantry Brigade will move at once as follows and come into under the orders of G.O.C. 61st Division.

    > 1 Battalion to Canal Bank from drawbridge P.29.C.7.2 (inclusive) to drawbridge P.20 central (inclusive).
    > 2 Battalions and M.G.Company to BUSNES - STEENBECQUE line from drawbridge P.20 central to LYS Canal J.32 central.
    > Brigade Headquarters to House at O.36.a.8.8.
    > One Company 39th M.G.Battalion to AIRE Canal Bank from P.29.C.7.2. to P.20 central under orders to be issued by G.O.C. 61st Division.

    Reconnaissance of BATTLE STATIONS and routes to them will be carried out forthwith.

    Infantry, where possible, will make use of cross country tracks and routes along Canal banks.

4. ACKNOWLEDGE.

[signature] A.C.Tempserley

Lieut.Colonel,
General Staff,
74th (Yeomanry) Division.

Issued at... 6.30 pm

Copies to:-
No 1 'G'	No.11 A.D.M.S.
2 'Q'	12 Div.Train.
3 'Q'	13 Canadian Corps.
4 C.R.A.	14 XI Corps.
5 C.R.E	15 XIII
6 Signal Coy.	16 61st Division.
7 M.G.Battn.	17 War Diary.
8 229th Inf.Brigade.	18 War Diary.
9 230th Inf.Brigade.	19 File
10 231st Inf.Brigade.	

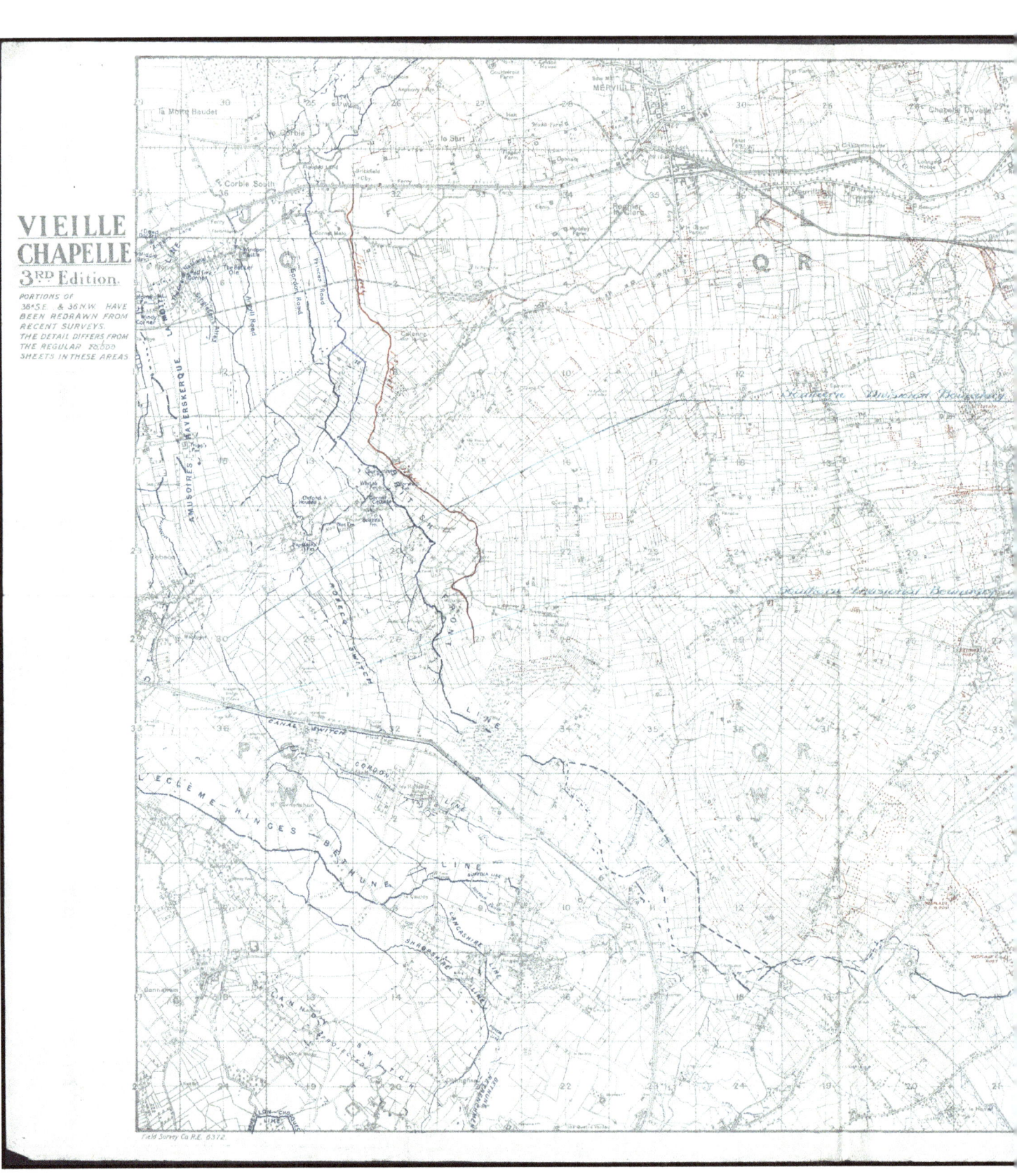

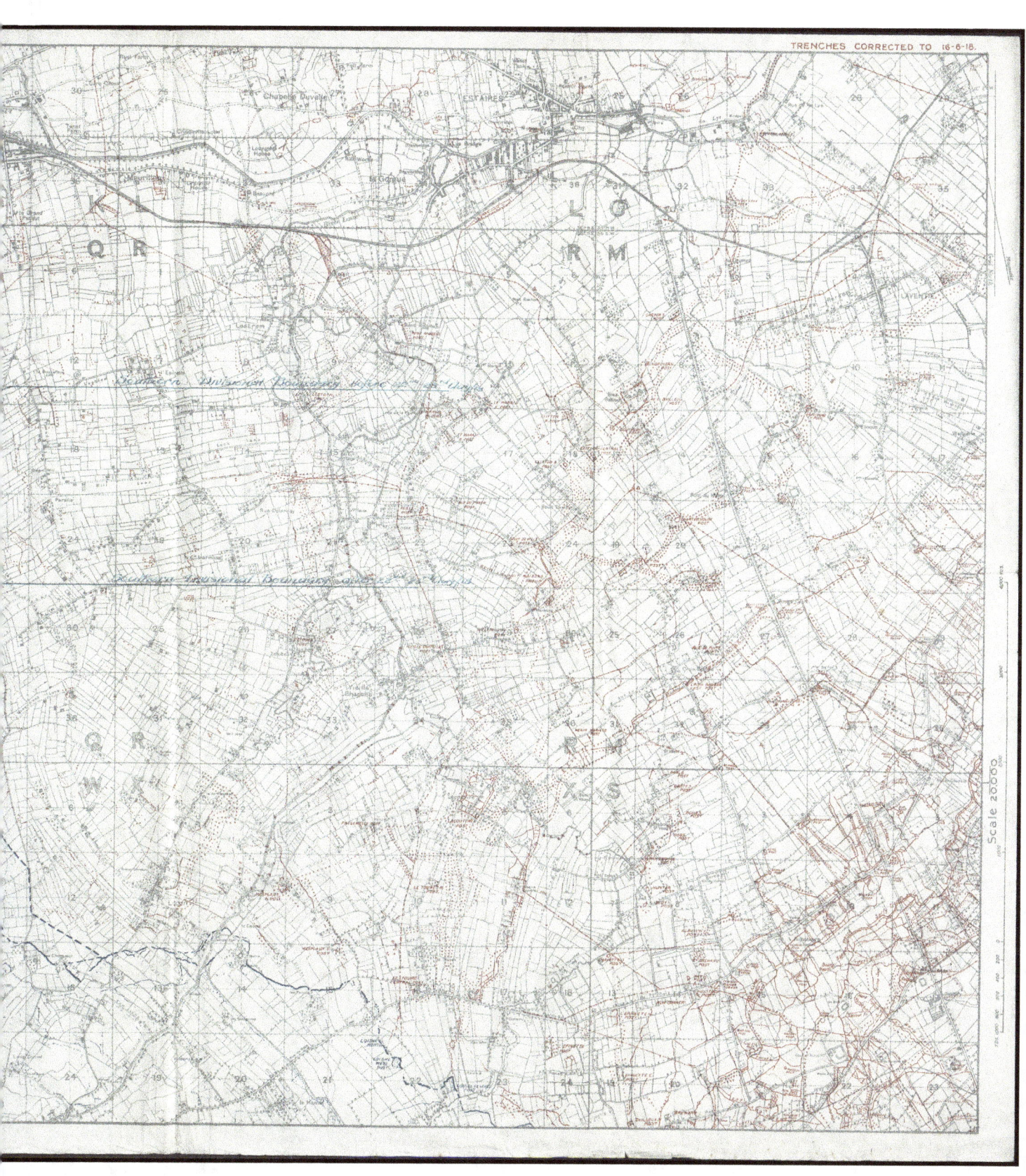

S.G.22/2.

S E C R E T.

Headquarters,
    231st Infantry Brigade.
C.R.E.
    4th Canadian Div.)
    Canadian Corps.   ) for information.
    XI Corps.   )
    XIII Corps.   )

Reference Sheet 44.b., 1/40,000.

1.   231st Brigade will detail one Battalion for work on rear def-ences in XIII Corps area.

2.   This Battalion will replace the 38th Battalion, 12th Canadian Brigade, on June 30th, and will take over Billets and Camps at present occupied by the 38th Battalion.

        Headquarters.   CHOCQUES.   D.5.d.6.5.
        Camps at E.1.c., E.7.c., and LA BEUVRIERE.

    Billets and Camps will be vacated by 38th Battalion by 3 p.m. 30th instant.

3.   231st Brigade will detail 2 officers to proceed today to CHOCQUES to take over details regarding work from 38th Canadian Battalion.

4.   C.R.E. will also get into touch with C.E., XIII Corps as regards details of work.

5.   74th Division 'Q' will notify supply arrangements.

6.   The Battalion at CHOCQUES must be prepared to rejoin the Division at very short notice in case of emergency. Should this Battalion be suddenly recalled, 74th Division 'Q' will arrange to send a lorry for the conveyance of surplus stores.

    ACKNOWLEDGE.

                                        Major,
                                  General Staff,
29th June 1918.   74th (Yeomanry) Division.

Copy to 'Q'.

Secret

Headquarters,
   229th Infantry Brigade,   C.R.E.
   230th Infantry Brigade.   O.C., 74th Div.Sigs.
   231st Infantry Brigade.-   O.C., 74th Bn.M.G.C.
C.R.A.   A.D.M.S.
                                     'Q'.

     The 74th Division will be transferred from the Canadian Corps to XI Corps at 12 noon, 30th June, and remains in G.H.Q. Reserve.

                                        Major,
                                  General Staff,
28th June 1918.   74th (Yeo) Division.

War Diary

SECRET.   S.G. 58

Amendment to

74th DIVISION ORDER NO. 65 of 29/6/18.
==

                                              1st July 1918.

para 4. for 61st Division read **XI** Corps.

                    M M Pany-Jones Major
                    for.
                           Lieut.Colonel,
                           General Staff,
                        74th (Yeomanry) Division.

Copies to:-
    'G'.
    'Q'   A.D.M.S.
    'Q'   Div. Train.
    C.R.A.   Canadian Corps.
    C.R.E.   XI Corps.
    Signal Coy.   XIII Corps.
    M.G. Battn.   61st Division.
    229th Inf Brigade.   War Diary.
    230th Inf Brigade.   War Diary.
    231st Inf Brigade.   File.

Appendix 7

SECRET.   COPY NO. 18

74th DIVISION ORDER NO. 65.

29th June 1918.

Reference sheet 36.a.1/10,000.

1.   Divisional Order No.64 is cancelled.

2.   74th Division will be at four hours notice for the purpose of reinforcing either the XIth Corps or the XIIIth Corps.

3.   74th Division will be at twenty-four hours notice for the purpose of G.H.Q. Reserve.

4.   In case of emergency, 229th Infantry Brigade and one Machine Gun Company is placed at the disposal of G.O.C. 61st Division.   They will not be used without reference to the First Army.

5.   (a).   On receipt of order to "MAN BATTLE STATIONS", the 229th Infantry Brigade will concentrate in one of three localities, from which it can man, or supply nucleus garrisons for the BUSNES - STEENBECQUE Line.
        These localities will be as follows, and will be such that the Right, Centre, or Left of the Line can be manned as the tactical situation develops.

     Right, Area. LE CORNET BRASSART - LE CORNET BOURDOIS - LA MIQUELLERIE all inclusive.
     Centre, Area. TREIZENNES - LA LACQUE - ISBERGUES all inclusive.
     Left, Area.   BOESEGHEM - STEENBECQUE - THIENNES - all inclusive.

     (b).   The telegram or message to "MAN BATTLE STATIONS" will be worded as follows to indicate in which area the Brigade is to concentrate, and will be repeated to 5th and 61st Divisions.
        e.g. "MAN BATTLE STATIONS" - CONCENTRATE RIGHT, CENTRE, or LEFT, as the case may be.

6.   Lorries will, if available, be provided for the move of the Battalion in FONTES area and the Machine Gun Company to the Left Concentration Area but units will be prepared to move by march route.

7.   Reconnaissances will be carried out by 229th Infantry Brigade and Machine Gun Company in the following order of priority:-

     (a). BUSNES-STEENBECQUE Line, South of LYS CANAL.
     (b).   "   "   " North of LYS CANAL.
   * (c). AMUSOIRES-HAVERSKERQUE-LA MOTTE Line-S.of LA MALADERIE (J.34.)
   * (d).   "   "   "   "   -N.of LA MALADERIE.
     (e). LILLERS-STEENBECQUE Line.

   * (Arrangements for these will be made by Divisional H.Q. with 5th and 61st Divisions).

8.   Infantry wherever possible will make use of cross-country tracks and routes along Canal Banks, and the shortest routes to the BUSNES - STEENBECQUE Line, from the concentration areas.
        These tracks and routes will be reconnoitred and marked by the formations and units concerned.

9.   B.G.C. 229th Infantry Brigade will prepare a scheme and have orders issued down to Companies for the action to be taken on receipt of the order to "MAN BATTLE STATIONS" in any one of the concentration areas.

10.   5th and 61st Divisions will be responsible for warning the Units of 229th Infantry Brigade now working in their respective areas of the receipt of the order to "MAN BATTLE STATIONS". These Units will then march to the concentration area ordered, in accordance with the plan of B.G.C. 229th Infantry Brigade.

11.   ACKNOWLEDGE.

A.C. Temperley
Lieut.Colonel,
General Staff,
74th (Yeomanry) Division.

Issued at.. 11.p.m.

Copies to:-
- No.1 'G'
- 2 'Q'
- 3 'Q'
- 4 C.R.A.
- 5 C.R.E.
- 6 Signal Coy.
- 7 M.G. Battn.
- 8 229th Inf. Brigade.
- 9 230th Inf. Brigade.
- 10 231st Inf. Brigade.
- 11. A.D.M.S.
- 12 Div. Train.
- 13 Canadian Corps.
- 14 XI Corps.
- 15 XIII Corps.
- 16 61st Division.
- 17 5th Division.
- 18 War Diary. ✓
- 19 War Diary.
- 20 File.

CONFIDENTIAL. Vol 4

WAR DIARY
OF
GENERAL STAFF, 74th (YEO) DIVISION
FROM 1st JULY 1918 TO 31st JULY 1918

WAR DIARY or INTELLIGENCE SUMMARY

Army Form C. 2118

Gen. H.W. 74th (Yeomanry) Div.

JULY 1918

Place	Date	Hour	Summary of Events and Information	Remarks and references to Appendices
NORRENT FONTES	JULY 1st		One section of 439 Field Coy. R.E. ordered to move from J.19 to Aigham. ST. VENANT under arrangements to be made by C.R.E. Training continued.	R.G.
	JULY 2nd		Warning order issued to move on 3rd inst. of the Pioneer Bn to camp in BOIS D'AMONT. Accordingly, under orders of XI Corps, the move was postponed until July 4th. Training continued.	R.G.
	JULY 3rd		Training continued	R.G.
	JULY 4th		Pioneer Bn moved from FANCQUENHEM to BOIS D'AMONT. Training continued.	R.G.
	JULY 5th		XI Corps Commander met the 3 B.G.'s C. Inf/Bdes, C.R.A. and C.R.E. at Div. H.Q. at 11 a.m. Training continued.	R.G.
	JULY 6th		Training continued. B.G.'s C. Inf/Bdes., C.R.E. C.R.A., O.C.T.G.Bts, G.S.O.1 and G.S.O II reconnoitred the BERNENCHON-HINGES ridge with a view to a counter-attack by the 74th Div in the event of the enemy gaining this ridge.	R.G.
	JULY 7th		Nothing to report.	R.G.

Army Form C. 2118

WAR DIARY
or
INTELLIGENCE SUMMARY
(Erase heading not required.)

JULY

Place	Date	Hour	Summary of Events and Information	Remarks and references to Appendices
NORRENT FONTES	JULY 8th		XI Corps No 370 was received to the effect that 74th Div would be relieved from G.H.Q. reserve on July 10th and would relieve 61st Div in line, relief by infantry by 10/11th and 11th/12th, of artillery on nights of 12/13th and 13/14th. Columns and to pass to 74th Div at 10 a.m. July 11th. Later XI Corps Ordr No 371 giving further details concerning the relief was received. In accordance with these orders 74th Div Ordr No 66 was issued at 11 p.m. 230th Inf Bde to relieve 182nd Inf Bde in Right Bde Sector. 231st Inf Bde to relieve 183rd Inf Bde in Left Bde Sector. 229th Inf Bde to be in Divisional Reserve concentrated in HAM-EN-ARTOIS — GUARBECQUE — MIQUILLERIES area. Training continued.	A/y/1*
	JULY 9th		Reconnaissances of the 61st Divl sector continued in view of impending relief. Training continued.	
	JULY 10th		All "B" teams of Infantry Brigades, Pioneer Battn, 74th Battn M.G.C. & L.T.M.B's moved to 74th Divl Reception Camp at WITTERNESSE, with exception of B team of 24th WELSH REGT. Relief of 61st Div was begun in accordance with 74th Divl Order No 66.	A/y/3
	July 11th		"B" team of 24th WELSH REGT moved to Divl Reception Camp, WITTERNESSE. Relief of 61st Div continued in accordance with 74th Divl Order No 66.	A/y/5

Army Form C. 2118

WAR DIARY
or
INTELLIGENCE SUMMARY

(Erase heading not required.)

JULY

Place	Date	Hour	Summary of Events and Information	Remarks and references to Appendices
NORRENT FONTES	JULY 12th		Relief of Div: Artillery begun in accordance with 74th Div: Order No 66	
	JULY 13th		Visit of Army Commander at 11.30 a.m. Relief of Div: Artillery continued.	
LILETTE CHATEAU Hd Qrs. Relieved XI Corps front	JULY 14th		74th Div: Headquarters closed at NORRENT FONTES at 10 a.m. and opened at LILETTE CHATEAU at the same hour, when G.O.C. 74th Div: took over command 74th Div: front. Orders received from XI Corps to the effect that 331st Bde R.F.A. would be withdrawn into reserve in WARNE-GLOMENGHEM area on the nights 16th/17th and 17th/18th July, but would continue to be administered by 74th Division. In accordance with these orders, 74th Div: Artillery Order No 67 was issued, also 74th Div: Artillery Order No 32, which warned "C" & "D" Btys 117 Bde R.F.A. that they would move to Left Group under orders to be issued later. Quiet day on Div: front.	Appx. II
	JULY 15th		Conference at 5 p.m. at Div: Headquarters, attended by B.G.R.A., C, Bde Majors, C.R.E. C.R.A & D.A.A.G. Orders received from XI Corps that 66th Div: Artillery would be completely withdrawn	Appendix III

Army Form C. 2118

WAR DIARY
or
INTELLIGENCE SUMMARY
(Erase heading not required.)

JULY

Place	Date	Hour	Summary of Events and Information	Remarks and references to Appendices
LILETTE CHATEAU	JULY 20th		74th Div Order No 69 was issued at 12 noon, ordering the relief of the 230th Infantry Bde by the 229th Infantry Bde on the night of 23rd/24th July. Quiet day on the Div front.	App. V /SS
	JULY 21st		Successful raid was carried out at midnight 21st/22nd July by 1 Off. + 20 O.R. of the 16th Sussex Regt on enemy position in Q8c8.8. Two enemy were killed & three (O.R) were captured. Our casualties were 2 wounded. Prisoners belonged to 1st Coy 102 R.I.R. Quiet day on Div front.	/SS
	JULY 22nd		25th R.W.F were relieved by the 10th K.S.L.I. during the night 22nd/23rd July in the right subsector of the left sector. Quiet day on the Div front.	/SS
	JULY 23rd		229th Infy Bde relieved 230th Infy Bde during the night in the right sector, 19th S.L.I. on the right, 16th Devons on the left and 14th Rl Highlanders in Brigade Reserve. Considerable increase in hostile shelling during the night, including a considerable number of Yellow Cross gas shells around AMUSOIRES.	/SS
	JULY 24th		74th Divl Reception Camp was moved from WITTERNESSE to LINGHEM. Quiet day in the line.	/SS

Army Form C. 2118

WAR DIARY
or
INTELLIGENCE SUMMARY
(Erase heading not required.)

JULY

Place	Date	Hour	Summary of Events and Information	Remarks and references to Appendices
LIETTE CHATEAU	JULY 15th (Cont'd)		from the line, and that one Brigade of the 5th Div'l Artillery would cover part of the 74th Div'l front. 74th Div'l Order No. 68 accordingly issued. This relief took place night 15th/16th July, when 27th Bde R.F.A. relieved the 66th Div'l Artillery.	Appx. to IV A/45
	JULY 16th		10th K.S.L.I. were relieved by the 24th WELSH Regt in the left subsector of the left sector. Quiet day on the Div'l front.	A/45
	JULY 17th		One prisoner (O.R.) captured by 25th R.W.F. in the right subsector of the left sector. Prisoner belonged to 9th Coy of the III/392 E.I.R. Quiet day on the Div'l front.	A/55
	JULY 18th		Visit of Army Commander, who inspected the defences in forward area. One M.G. captured by 25th R.W.F. Rifle fire of the Div'l Artillery assisted in successful raid by 4th Division. Quiet day in the line.	A/55
	JULY 19th 2pm		1 Sgt & 8 ORs of 25th R.W.F. successfully raided a hostile post and captured 5 prisoners (O.Rs) belonging to 11th Coy III/392 E.I.R. Quiet day in the line. During night 19th/20th July, several harassing fires were directed against the sector held by 392.I.R. in views of a suspected inter-battalion relief.	

Army Form C. 2118

WAR DIARY
INTELLIGENCE SUMMARY
(Erase heading not required.)

JULY 1918.

Place	Date	Hour	Summary of Events and Information	Remarks and references to Appendices
LILETTE CHATEAU	JULY 25th		At 2 a.m. an enemy bombing aeroplane was forced to land a short distance behind the front line in the Right sector. The occupants – 3 officers – were captured and marched away from the aeroplane. At 8.15 a.m. a raid was attempted by about 40 enemy on the front in Q.1.3.6. This was easily repulsed by Lewis gun and rifle fire. Casualties were inflicted on the raiding party. H.Q. R.E. moved to LILETTE CHATEAU.	A/S
	JULY 26th		Quiet day in the line.	1/W/S
	JULY 27th		A successful daylight raid was made by 10th K.S.L.I which resulted in the capture by 4 prisoners (O.R.S.) 392 I.R. In addition three enemy were killed. Although M.G fire was opened by the enemy, the officers succeeded in getting all his party of 13 or so back to our lines without casualties. In order to test the means of communication other than telephone a telegram, all telephonic & telegraphic communication was suspended for 2½ hours from 8 a.m. Urgent messages were sent by Power Buzzer, Wireless, Lobcatur? and pigeon.	A/S

1875 Wt. W593/326 1,000,000 4/15 J.B.C. & A. A.D.S.S./Forms/C. 2118.

WAR DIARY
or
INTELLIGENCE SUMMARY
(Erase heading not required.)

Army Form C. 2118

JULY

Place	Date	Hour	Summary of Events and Information	Remarks and references to Appendices
LILETTE CHATEAU	July 28th		Quiet day in the line. 25th R.W.F. relieved the 24th Welch Regt in the left subsection of the Pt FLORIS Rd Section.	A.A. G.
	29th		"B" Coton of MG Battalion moved from the Div. Recup Ctre Camp and rejoined their Unit. These men however to continue training and not to be used in the line. Enemy raiding party about 30 strong attempting to raid a post of the 10th K.S.L.I. at 4.30 a.m. An surprise bying into front observed them coming and allowed the enemy to come within 15 yds before killing them. The sentry was then given warning & the post alarm was taken and the garrison of the post engaged the enemy with L.G. and rifle fire. At least four Germans were observed and there is reason to believe that further casualties were inflicted.	A.A. 7.

Army Form C. 2118

WAR DIARY
or
INTELLIGENCE SUMMARY
(Erase heading not required.)

July

Place	Date	Hour	Summary of Events and Information	Remarks and references to Appendices
LILETTE CHATEAU	July 30th		A quiet day in the line. Increase of shelling during night of 29th/30th however, a total of 350 gas shell being reported.	M.M 17.
	July 31st		B. Coy. 74th Bn. M.G.C. relieved the Res. gun of the Right and Left Groups from by 'C' Coy. 74th Bn. M.G.C. in the right subsection of 14th Regt at Hooft relieved the 1st R.F.F. in the Rubecque Bals Sector. Quiet day in the line.	M.M 17.

M M Gans-Iam Major
Gen. Stoff
74th Div.

SECRET.

Headquarters.
  229th Infantry Brigade.   O.C. 74th Bn. M.G.C.
  230th Infantry Brigade.   O.C. Div. Train.
  231st Infantry Brigade.   O.C. Signal Coy.
  C.R.A.   A.D.M.S.
  C.R.E.   'Q' Branch.

WARNING ORDER.

The Division will commence relieving the 61st Division in the line on July 10th.

No further details at present, but 231st and 230th Brigades will be the Brigades in the line.

G.744 is cancelled

[signature]

Lieut Colonel.
General Staff.
74th (Yeo) Division.

8th July 1918.

War Diary App. 1

SECRET. COPY NO. 18

74th DIVISION ORDER NO. 66.

8th July 1918.

Reference Sheet 36.A.1/40,000.

1. The 74th Division will relieve the 61st Division in Right Divisional Sector XI Corps commencing July 10th in accordance with attached table.

2. The 230th Infantry Brigade will relieve 182nd Infantry Brigade in the Right Brigade Sector, and the 231st Infantry Brigade will relieve the 183rd Infantry Brigade in the Left Brigade Sector.
All details will be arranged direct between Brigadiers concerned.
229th Infantry Brigade will be in Divisional Reserve concentrated in the HAM-EN-ARTOIS - GUARBECQUE - MIQUELLERIE area.

3. On arrival in the 61st Divisional Area all troops will come under command of G.O.C. 61st Division until completion of relief.

4. The 74th Divisional Artillery will relieve the 61st Divisional Artillery on the nights 12/13th and 13/14th.
The D.A.C. will relieve on night 12/13th.
All details direct between C.R.A's.

5. Field Ambulances will be relieved under arrangements to be made between A.D.M.S.' concerned.

6. All details as regards relief of Machine Gun Battalions will be arranged between Os.C. Machine Gun Battalions.

7. The Command of the Sector passes from G.O.C. 61st Division to G.O.C. 74th Division at 10 a.m. July 14th at which hour 74th Divisional H.Q. closes at NORRENT FONTES and opens at MOLINGHEM.

8. Completion of all reliefs will be wired to this H.Q.

9. ACKNOWLEDGE.

A C Temperley
Lieut Colonel.
General Staff.
74th (Yeomanry) Division.

Issued at 11pm

Copies to:-
- No 1 'G'
- 2 'Q'
- 3 'Q'
- 4 C.R.A.
- 5 C.R.E.
- 6 Signal Coy.
- 7 M.G.Battn.
- 8 229th Inf. Brigade.
- 9 230th Inf. Brigade.
- 10 231st Inf. Brigade.
- 11 A.D.M.S.
- No 12. DIV Train.
- 13. 4th Division.
- 14. XI Corps.
- 15. XIII Corps.
- 16. 61st Division.
- 17. 5th Division.
- 18. War Diary.
- 19. War Diary.
- 20. File.

TABLE TO ACCOMPANY 74th DIVISIONAL ORDER NO 66.

No.	Date.	Unit.	From.	To.	Remarks.
1.	July 9th.	231st Inf. Brigade. Right Bn. Left Bn.	Bde Area. " "	HAM-EN-ARTOIS. GUARBECQUE.	Route HAM-EN-ARTOIS. Stage night 9/10th July.
2.	July 10th	230th Inf. Brigade. Right Bn. Left Bn. Reserve Bn.	Bde Area. " " " "	MIQUELLERIE. GUARBECQUE. HAM-EN-ARTOIS.	Becomes Div.Reserve 61st Div. night 10/11th. By bus.Details later Bde H.Q. HAM-EN-ARTOIS. Billets will be occupied in HAM-EN-ARTOIS and GUARBECQUE until 231 Bde move forward to relieve.
3.	July 10th	74th Bn. M.G.C.	LIGNY les AIRE.	GUARBECQUE.	Route Rd Junction O.3.c.1.8. Relieving personnel 61st Bn. M.G.C. there.
4.	July 10th	231st Inf. Bde. One Battn.	CHOCQUES.	HAMET BILLET. (P.14.a.)	Route - BUSNETTES - BUSNES. Not to reach BUSNES till 9.30 pm
5.	July 10,	12th(Pioneers) LOYAL NORTH LANCS.	J.19.c.	P.1.d.5.0.	Time of move depends on bussing arrangements for 61st Div. Relieve 61st Division Pioneer Battn under orders of C.R.E.
6.	July 10th	No 5 Coy R.M.R.E.	ESTREE BLANCHE.	Bivouacs at OBLOIS.	
7.	Night July 10/11th.	231st Inf. Bde. less 1 Battn.	HAM-EN-ARTOIS - GUARBECQUE area.	Left Bde Sector.	Relieving 183rd Brigade.
8.	July 11th.	229th Inf. Bde.	Billets.	Divisional Reserve.	Bde H.Q. HAM-EN-ARTOIS. 1 Battn do. 1 Battn GUARBECQUE. 1 Battn.MIQUELLERIE. To be clear of FONTES by 12 noon. 230th Inf. Bde. will be in area until it moves forward to Right Bde Sector.

P.T.O

FRANCE EDITION 5. A. (Local) SHEET 62°

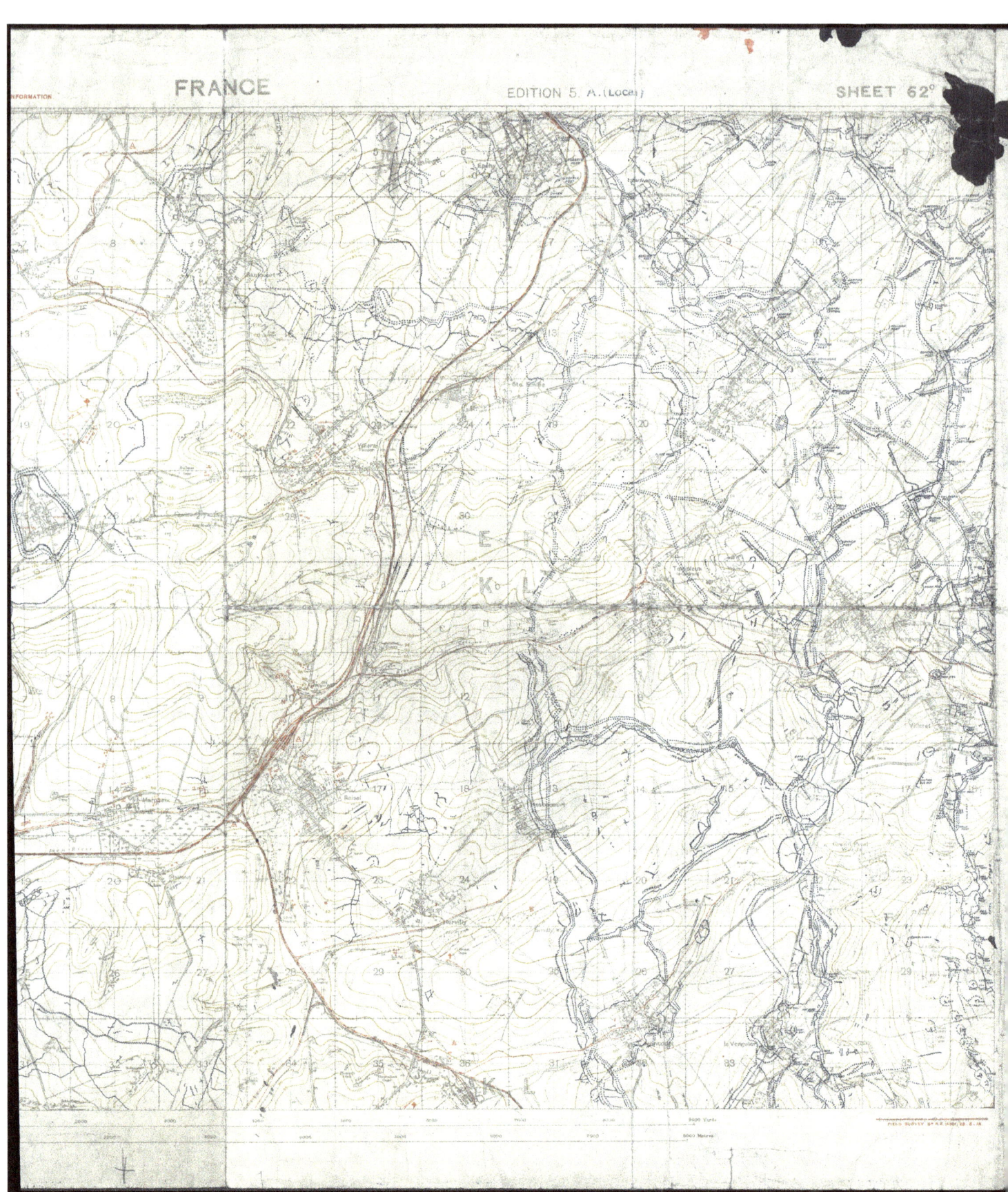

TABLE TO ACCOMPANY 74th DIVISIONAL ORDER NO 66. (Continued.)

No.	Date.	Unit.	From.	To.	Remarks.
9.	July 11th.	One Coy R.E.	Billets.	Relieve One forward Coy 61st Div.R.E.	
10.	Night July 11/12th.	230th Inf. Bde.	Reserve Area	Right Bde Sector.	Relieving 182nd Inf Brigade.
11.	Night July 11/12th.	74th Bn. M.G.C.	GUARBECQUE.	To relieve M.G.Group in Left Bde sector.	
12.	July 12th.	1 Coy R.E.	Billets.	To relieve one forward company 61st Div. R.E.	
13.	Night July 12/13th.	74th Bn. M.G.C.	GUARBECQUE.	To relieve M.G.Group in Right Bde sector.	
14.	July 13th	439th Field Coy. R.E.	TREIZENNES.	MOLINGHEM.	

Divisional Artillery.

No.	Date.	Unit.	From.	To.	Remarks.
15.	July 12th.	74th D.A.C.	NED ON.	HAM-EN-ARTOIS.	Time to be notified Div.H.Q. Route LILLERS.
16.	Night July 12/13th	One section per Bty 74th Div. Arty.	AMES Area.	Line.	Relieve equivalent 61st Div. Arty.
17.	Night July 13/14th.	74th Div. Arty (less one section per Bty and D.A.C.)	AMES area.	Line.	To be clear of AMES area by 12 noon 13th July.

Identification Trace for use with Artillery Maps.

Objective

Infantry Forming up Line

Northern Div Bdy

Southern Div Bdy

36 O

36 U

Reference Sheet 36 SW 1/20000

NOTE.—(1). These traces are intended to facilitate the communication of information as to the position of targets, which have been located on a squared map.
(2). The squares on this trace are 500 yards in length on the 1/10,000 scale, 1,000 yards in length on the 1/20,000 scale, and 2,000 yards in length on the 1/40,000 scale.
(3). The squares on the trace are fitted to the squares of the map showing the targets, which are then drawn on the trace. Sufficient letters and numbers must also be added to enable the recipient to place the trace in the correct position on his own map. A little detail may also be traced, but this is not essential. The name and scale of the map to which the trace refers must be always given. The trace can be used for the 1/10,000, 1/20,000, or 1/40,000 scale.

G.S.G.S. 3025.

Tracing taken from Sheet _____

of the 1 _____ map of _____

Signature _____ Date _____

War Diary

SECRET.

S.G.16/2/9

AMENDMENT TO 74TH DIVISION ORDER NO 66.

Para 7, Third Line, for MOLINGHEM read CHATEAU, LILETTE.

ACKNOWLEDGE.

A. Galloway Capt
for Lieut Colonel.
General Staff.
74th (Yeomanry) Division.

11th July 1918.

Copies to all recipients of 74th Division Order No 66.

"C" Form.
MESSAGES AND SIGNALS.

Army Form C. 2123.
(In books of 100.)

No. of Message _____

Prefix ___ Code ___ Words ___	Received.	Sent, or sent out.	Office Stamp.
£ s. d.	From ___	At ___ m.	
Charges to Collect	By ___	To ___	
Service Instructions		By ___	

Handed in at _____ JD _____ Office Noon m. Received 1231 m.

TO 221 Bde

Sender's Number	Day of Month	In reply to Number	A A A
G 876	13		
D067 is		Cancelled	

FROM
PLACE & TIME 74 Div

* This line should be erased if not required.

War Diary

App. II

SECRET.

COPY NO. 17

74th DIVISION ORDER NO. 67.

16th July 1918.

Reference Sheet 36.A. 1/40,000.

1. One Brigade 66th Divisional Artillery will be withdrawn into Corps Reserve on the nights 16/17th and 17/18th July under orders of C.R.A., 74th Division.

2. This Brigade will be located at WARNE and GLOMENGHEM (West of AIRE), and will be available to reinforce the front of either the 5th or 74th Division.
   Orders for reconnaissance and training are being issued by G.O.C., R.A., XI Corps.

3. The Brigade selected will continue to be administered by 74th Division.

4. 74th Division 'Q' will issue instructions as regards billets.

5. Proposed dispositions of the remaining Brigades of R.F.A. in the line, and amended schemes for S.O.S. barrage will be forwarded in duplicate to Divisional Headquarters.

6. ACKNOWLEDGE.

M M Pany-Jones Major
for
Lieut-Colonel,
General Staff,
74th (Yeomanry) Division.

Issued at 8 a.m.

Copies to:-
No 1	'G'.		No 11.	Div Train.
2	'Q'.		12.	4th Division.
3	'Q'.		13.	XI Corps.
4	C.R.A., 74th Divn.		14.	66th Divisional Arty.
5	C.R.E. "		15.	G.O.C. R.A. XI Corps.
6	Signal Coy.		16.	5th Division.
7	229th Inf. Brigade.		17.	War Diary.
8	230th Inf. Brigade.		18.	War Diary.
9	231st Inf. Brigade.		19.	File.
10	A.D.M.S.			

SECRET.

Headquarters.
   229th Infantry Brigade.
   230th Infantry Brigade.
   231st Infantry Brigade.
   C.R.A.
   C.R.E.
   O.C. 74th Bn. M.G.C.
   'Q' Branch.

War Diary

MINUTES OF CONFERENCE HELD AT DIVISIONAL HEADQUARTERS
JULY 15th 1918.

PRESENT.

G.O.C.	C.R.E.
G.S.O. (1)	Lieut-Col SPENCE JONES.
G.S.O. (2)	Bde Major, R.A.
B.G.C. 229th Inf. Bde.	Bde Major 229th Inf. Bde.
B.G.C. 230th Inf. Bde.	Bde Major 230th Inf. Bde.
B.G.C. 231st Inf. Bde.	Bde Major 231st Inf. Bde.
C.R.A.	

AGENDA.

RELIEFS.	SCREENING.
POLICY OF WORK.	TRAMWAYS.
DISTRIBUTION OF TROOPS.	TRAINING.
CO-OPERATION BETWEEN ARTILLERY AND INFANTRY.	SALVAGE.
	DRAINAGE.
RAIDS.	SELECTION OF HEADQUARTERS OF BATTALIONS.
AGGRESSIVE ATTITUDE.	
EMPLOYMENT OF TRENCH MORTARS.	REINFORCEMENTS.
	OFFICERS.

1. **RELIEFS.**

    Decided that Brigade Reliefs should be arranged so that each Brigade should be 24 days in the line and 12 days in Divisional Reserve. Decided that 230th Brigade should be relieved by 229th Brigade on the night 23/24th July.

2. **WORK.**

    Decided that the Battalion in Brigade Reserve should supply 100 men per company every other night, (i.e. 200 men per Brigade every night) for work under C.R.E. No party being provided from this Battalion on nights reliefs are carried out.

    Necessity for garrisons working on the lines they occupy was emphasised.

    The priority of work will be as follows :-

    (i) Cutting crops where necessary in two belts on either side of the wire, about 20 feet inside and 15 feet outside.

    (ii) To make a continuous breastwork along the Support line to facilitate communication.

    (iii) Construction of defended localities in the Support line with flank defences.

    (iv) Construction of shelters for the Infantry and Artillery.

- 2 -

2. WORK. (continued)

(v) Siting of one and eventually two communication trenches per Brigade Sector.
(vi) Wiring will be continued and improved.

3. DISTRIBUTION OF TROOPS.

So as to economise troops in the front system. It was decided for forward Battalions to hold the front according to attached diagram.

4. CO-OPERATION BETWEEN ARTILLERY AND INFANTRY.

(i) Decided that S.O.S. barrage consist of Artillery and Machine Gun fire sandwiched together. The actual S.O.S. barrage and details to be worked out between Artillery and Machine Gun Group Commanders, O.C. Machine Gun Battalion assisting to ensure co-ordination. This to be taken in hand at once.

(ii) Liaison between Infantry and Artillery to be carefully preserved.

5. RAIDS.

Plans for possible raids to be prepared, often these raids are required at very short notice.
Company and Platoon Commanders must be encouraged to give this matter careful thought.

6. AGGRESSIVE ATTITUDE.

It is essential to keep the upper hand. An aggressive attitude must be encouraged on all occasions.

7. SCREENING.

Infantry Brigadiers and C.R.A. to consult with the C.R.E. as to which roads and localities need screening. Proposals to be submitted as soon as possible.

8. TRAMWAYS.

Decided to put in hand at once the Tramway Scheme proposed by the 61st Division. One company of Pioneer Battalion to be employed on this work.

9. TRAINING.

Reserve Brigade to centralise on Training. If avoidable no work parties will be taken from the Reserve Brigade.
Decided that 'B' Teams of the Reserve Brigade should rejoin their Units.
On the order to "Man Battle Stations" being received, "B" Teams will proceed at once to the Reception Camp.
It was decided that "B" Teams from the Pioneer Battalion should at once rejoin their unit.

10. SALVAGE.

Every effort must be made to collect all possible salvage. O.C. Salvage Company to go into this matter thoroughly.

11. DRAINAGE.

C.R.E. to take up the question of the drainage of the CLARENCE and HOG Rivers. Proper tools required for this purpose.

12. BATTALION HEADQUARTERS.

Any change in Battalion H.Q. must be decided at once, suggestions to be submitted. When once decided upon locations must be adhered to.
Battalion H.Q. generally to be made more secure.

- 3 -

13. **REINFORCEMENTS.**
Drafts will not go up to Brigades in the line unless especially asked for. They will remain at the Reception Camp.

14. **OFFICERS.**
Officers are inclined at times to do work that should be performed by N.C.Os. N.C.Os must be encouraged to perform their own duties, taking the necessary responsibility.

15. **TRENCH MORTARS.**
3" and 6" Stokes to co-operate in S.O.S. Barrage. Details need working out by Brigadiers, Artillery and Machine Gun Battn.

16. **REQUIRED FROM BRIGADES.**
  (a) Proposed siting of C.T's.
  (b) Proposed redistribution of troops.
  (c) Proposed new Battalion H.Q.
  (d) Proposals for screening.
  (e) Proposals for Artillery, M.G. and T.M. Barrage.

16th July 1918.
           Major.
         General Staff.
        74th (Yeomanry) Division.

War Diary

App. IV

SECRET.   COPY NO. ...17..

74th DIVISION ORDER NO. 68.

15th JULY 1918.

Reference Sheet 36.A. 1:40,000.

1. 74th Division Order No. 67 is cancelled.

2. 66th Divisional Artillery, attached 74th Division, will be withdrawn from action to-night to their wagon lines, under orders to be issued by C.R.A. 74th Division, and will be prepared to move to-morrow to join Second Army under orders being issued by XIth Corps.

3. One Brigade R.F.A., covering 5th Division will be withdrawn from present position to-day and will go into action in relief of 66th Division Artillery. Relief to be completed by 12 midnight July 15/16th.

4. All details of relief to be arranged between C.R.A's concerned.

5. Completion of relief to be reported by wire to Divisional H.Q.

6. ACKNOWLEDGE.

                                                                                 Lieut-Colonel,
                                                                               General Staff.
Issued at............   74th (Yeomanry) Division.

Copies to :-
        No 1 'G'   No 11 Div. Train.
          2   'Q'   12 4th Division.
          3   'Q'   13 XI Corps.
          4   C.R.A. 74th Divn.   14 66th Divisional Arty.
          5   C.R.E. "   "   15 G.O.C., R.A. XI Corps.
          6   Signal Coy.   16 5th Division.
          7   229th Inf. Brigade. 17 War Diary.
          8   230th Inf. Brigade. 18 War Diary.
          9   231st Inf. Brigade. 19 File.
         10   A.D.M.S.

War Diary   App V

SECRET.   Copy No. 16

74TH DIVISION ORDER NO 69.

20th July 1918.

1. The 229th Infantry Brigade will relieve the 230th Infantry Brigade in the ROBECQ SECTION on the night 23rd/24th July.

2. All details will be arranged between B.G.C's concerned.

3. On relief the 230th Infantry Brigade comes into Divisional Reserve, and will be concentrated in the HAM-EN-ARTOIS GUARBECQUE - MIQUELLERIE Area.

4. Defence instructions, aeroplane photographs and Special Maps will be handed over.

5. On July 23rd "B" Teams of the 229th Infantry Brigade will proceed to the Divisional Reception Camp, WITTERNESSE.
"B" Teams of the 230th Infantry Brigade will move to the Reserve Brigade Area on the same day.
74th Division 'Q' will notify transport arrangements.

6. Completion of relief will be wired to Divisional H.Q.

7. ACKNOWLEDGE.

ACTemperley.

Lieut-Colonel.
General Staff,
Issued at 12 noon.   74th (Yeomanry) Division.

Copies to :-

No		No	
1	'G'	11	Div. Train.
2	'Q'	12	4th Division.
3	'Q'	13	XI Corps.
4	C.R.A. 74th Division.	14	5th Division.
5	C.R.E.	15	O.C. Reception Camp.
6	Signal Coy.		
7	229th Infantry Brigade.	16	War Diary.
8	230th Infantry Brigade.	17	War Diary.
9	231st Infantry Brigade.	18	File.
10	A.D.M.S.		

General Staff
with Appendices
14 (Yeomanry) Division
August 1918

August 1918
Army Form C. 2118.

WAR DIARY

INTELLIGENCE SUMMARY

(Erase heading not required)

General Staff.
74th (Yeomanry) Division.

Place	Date	Hour	Summary of Events and Information	Remarks and references to Appendices
LILETTE CHATEAU. H.Q. Right Div. XIth Corps.	Aug. 1st.		74th Division holding Right Divisional Sector, XIth Corps Front. Division on Right, the 4th Division of XIII Corps. Division on Left, the 5th Division of XI Corps. 229th Infantry Brigade holding Right Brigade Section, 231st Infantry Brigade holding Left Brigade Section, 230th Infantry Brigade in Divisional Reserve.	
			A quiet day in the line. General Sir I. MAXSE, Inspector General of Training, held a conference at LINGHEM Camp. Representatives from all Divisions in the Army were present. The general scheme for training of Army in France was discussed. The following attended from the Division :- G.O.C. B.G.C. 230th Infantry Brigade. As many C.Os as could G.S.O. (1) Brigade Major. 229th Inf. Bde. be spared. G.S.O. (2) Brigade Major. 231st Inf. Bde.	
	2nd.		Quiet day in the line, nothing to report.	
	3rd.		Quiet day in the line. G.O.C. proceeded to England on leave. Brigadier-General A.A. KENNEDY, C.M.G. took over command of the Division.	
	4th.		A quiet day in the line. A warning order issued to the effect that the 27th Brigade, R.F.A. at present covering the ST FLORIS Section would shortly be relieved by a Brigade of the 61st Divisional Artillery.	Appendix. i.

Army Form C. 2118.

WAR DIARY
INTELLIGENCE SUMMARY

General Staff.
74th (Yeomanry) Division.

(Erase heading not required.)

Place	Date	Hour	Summary of Events and Information	Remarks and references to Appendices
LILLETTE CHATEAU	Aug. 5th		On the night 4th/5th 230th Infantry Brigade relieved the 231st Infantry Brigade in the ST FLORIS SECTION, in accordance with Divisional Order No 70 issued on 31st July. Relief complete by 4.20 a.m. News was received from the 4th Division on the Right that the enemy trenches on their right had been found unoccupied, in consequence of this, special patrols were sent out from this Division. The enemy lines, however, were found to be held as usual opposite this front.	Appendix. II.
	Aug. 6th	4.30 p.m.	229th Infantry Brigade reported that a patrol of the Devons had entered the enemy trench at Q.14.a.35.40. and had proceeded along the trench to Q.14.a.6.2. killing one enemy and capturing another, also a Machine Gun. Later, a patrol of the 14th Royal Highlanders entered the enemy line between the CLARENCE RIVER and the ROBECQ - CALONNE Road capturing three prisoners. These reconnaissances proved that the enemy was on the verge of withdrawing from his line. Order to maintain touch with enemy issued.	APPENDIX III
		7.55 p.m.	14th Royal Highlanders had occupied a line from Q.14.a.7.2. to Q.14.d.7.5. with a post established at Q.14.b.7.1. where one enemy was killed and one more prisoner taken. Touch was established with the Left Brigade of the Division on the Right. No further advance took place by the Right Brigade, and there was no sign of withdrawal by the enemy opposite the Left Brigade.	
	Aug. 7th	8.15 a.m.	Right Battalion of Left Brigade (10th Buffs.) reported they were unable to advance except by a general attack owing to enemy M.G. fire. A post was established at Q.8.a.5.2. in touch with 229th Infantry Brigade.	

Army Form C. 2118.

WAR DIARY
INTELLIGENCE SUMMARY

(Erase heading not required.)

General Staff.
74th (Yeomanry) Division.

Instructions regarding War Diaries and Intelligence Summaries are contained in F. S. Regs., Part II. and the Staff Manual respectively. Title pages will be prepared in manuscript.

Place	Date	Hour	Summary of Events and Information	Remarks and references to Appendices
BILLETS CHATEAU	Aug. 7th.	(Ctd)	10th K.S.L.I. were moved up in Support of the Right Brigade to the Front and Support lines of the AMUSOIRES - HAVERSKERQUE system.	[illegible]
		12.15. p.m.	Orders issued to 230th Infantry Brigade to advance Northwards along enemy Front Line from Q.8.a.7.4. and that next bound for Division will be road from Q.15.b.10.5. - Q.9.d.4.6. - CALONNE Village in Q.9.a., thence back to our lines as far N. as 230th Infantry Brigade had been able to reach. Boundary between Brigades to Road Junction Q.9.a.60.95. - Q.3.d.5.5. - Old River LYS to Q.4.d.30.95. all inclusive to 229th Infantry Brigade.	Appendix IV.
		12.15. p.m.	O.C. Machine Gun Battn was ordered to get up his limbers so as to be able to move his guns forward with 229th Infantry Brigade.	Appendix V.
		3.45. p.m.	Orders issued to 229th and 230th Infantry Brigades that Brigade Groups would be immediately formed.	Appendix VI.
		4.p.m.	230th Infantry Brigade tried to advance in accordance with the above orders but were unable to do so owing to enemy opposition.	
			Orders were issued to 229th and 230th Infantry Brigades that harassing fire by M.G's and artillery was to be maintained during the night in rear of enemy lines.	Appendix VII.
		7.p.m.	Right Battn of Right Brigade (14th Royal Highlanders) had reached second objective and were pushing on to the QUENTIN Road, in accordance with orders issued in order to get in touch with 4th Division. 229th Inf. Brigade moved their H.Q. to CARVIN.	Appendix VIII.
		10.20. p.m.	10th Buffs entered enemy trenches at Q.8.a.8.4. and occupied them from that point N. to Railway at Q.2.c.1.9. with posts established on the road 300 yards east. During the night the Left Battn (16th Sussex) of the Left Brigade occupied the line Q.2.a.1.1. - Q.1.b.90.10. - K.31.d.7.5. - K.31.b.8.1. The Right Brigade advanced to within 200 yards W. of QUENTIN Road in Q.16.a. and Q.10.c. Both Brigades were in touch with their flank Brigades. 7 P/W and 1 M.G. were captured during the night by the Right Brigade.	

Army Form C. 2118.

WAR DIARY
INTELLIGENCE SUMMARY
General Staff.
74th (Yeomanry) Division.

(Erase heading not required.)

Instructions regarding War Diaries and Intelligence Summaries are contained in F.S. Regs., Part II. and the Staff Manual respectively. Title pages will be prepared in manuscript.

Place	Date	Hour	Summary of Events and Information	Remarks and references to Appendices
LILETIE CHATEAU.	Aug. 8th.	4.30. a.m.	Unsuccessful ruse attempted by the enemy to capture one of our posts.	AR
"		6. a.m.	Left Brigade continued their advance, their objective being Q.3.c.9.1. - Q.3.central - line of Old River LYS in Q.3.b. and K.33.d.	Appendix. VIII a.
"		11. a.m.	Orders issued that when the above line has been reached, 229th Infantry Brigade will advance to line of TURBEAUTE Stream.	Appendix. IX.
"		5. a.m.	Relief of 27th Bde R.F.A. by 306th Bde R.F.A. as detailed in Divisional Order 71 completed.	Appendix X.
"		11.15a.m.	Orders issued to 231st Infantry Brigade to move two rear battns to HAMET BILLET and LA PIERRIE, and its Brigade H.Q. to P.7.c. during the afternoon.	Appendix XI.
"		12.noon.	230th Infantry Brigade H.Q. opened at P.11.a.9.2. During the afternoon 12th S.L.I. relieved the 16th Devons in left sub-section of Right Brigade.	
"		4.p.m.	Right Battn, Left Brigade was counter attacked by party of 100 enemy from Q.4.c.central. and fell back to line Q.3.c.6.0. to Q.3.a.8.4.	
"		4.50. p.m.	Brigades were ordered not to advance beyond East bank of TURBEAUTE and old LYS but to consolidate there.	Appendix XII.
"		10.p.m.	Division had reached line of TURBEAUTE Stream from Q.17.a.1.7. to LE PETIT PACAUT, thence along old River LYS to K.33.b.2.1. Touch with Divisions on both flanks was established.	MM M
"	Aug. 9th.	1.45. a.m.	Warning Order issued to both Brigades that enemy would, according to prisoners statements, probably continue to hold present line and that patrols must be sent out to test the strength of their line.	Appendix. XIII.
"			This was confirmed by Divisional Order No 72 issued at 10. a.m.	Appendix. XIV.

Army Form C. 2118.

WAR DIARY
~~INTELLIGENCE SUMMARY~~

(Erase heading not required.)

General Staff.
74th (Yeomanry) Division.

*Instructions regarding War Diaries and Intelligence Summaries are contained in F. S. Regs., Part II. and the Staff Manual respectively. Title pages will be prepared in manuscript.

Place	Date	Hour	Summary of Events and Information	Remarks and references to Appendices
LILLERS CHATEAU.	Aug. 9th. (ctd)	5.p.m.	No change in the line held by the Division. 2 P/W were captured by the left Brigade during the afternoon. Our Front Line was freely shelled during the day.	Initials
		5.25. p.m.	Warning order issued that 230th Infantry Brigade would take over line held by 229th Infantry Brigade on the night 10th/11th August.	Appendix. XV.
		6. p.m.	This was confirmed by Divisional Order No 73.	Appendix. XVI.
	Aug. 10th.	5. a.m.	Situation was unchanged. Some shelling of the Forward area of Left Sector with Yellow Cross Gas took place during the night.	
		6.a.m.	A post on the TURBEAUTE in Q.10.d. was attacked by the enemy, but the attack was easily repulsed.	
			The King passed through the Divisional Area in the afternoon. The G.O.C. met the King at BOURECQ.	
		8.p.m.	Situation unchanged. Enemy artillery was active during the day against the Left Sector. During the night the 230th Infantry Brigade took over the front held by the 229th Infantry Brigade in accordance with Divisional Order No 73. 229th Infantry Brigade were withdrawn to Support.	Initials
	Aug. 11th.		No change in Situation. During the night ST FLORIS and vicinity of LA HAYE was heavily shelled. CARVIN Area was heavily shelled during the day.	Initials

Army Form C. 2118.

WAR DIARY

INTELLIGENCE SUMMARY

General Staff.
74th (Yeomanry) Division.

(Erase heading not required.)

Instructions regarding War Diaries and Intelligence
Summaries are contained in F. S. Regs., Part II.
and the Staff Manual respectively. Title pages
will be prepared in manuscript.

Place	Date	Hour	Summary of Events and Information	Remarks and references to Appendices
LILLERS CHATEAU.	Aug. 11th. (ctd)	2.p.m.	Divisional Order No 74 was issued in accordance with instructions from Corps. This order pointed out that although the Division on our left had failed to reach its objective, it made it clear that the enemy was holding the present line in considerable force and had to keep reserves in this area which no doubt were urgently required elsewhere. Consequently, small local operations of a surprise nature must be attempted.	Appendix. XVII.
	Aug. 12th.		Situation unchanged. CARVIN and ROBECQ areas were again shelled by the enemy.	
		9.30. p.m.	A minor enterprise was carried out by the 10th Buffs on the left of the front. An attempt was made to occupy the enemy posts in K.33.d. and K.34.c. and Q.4.a. These posts, however, were found to be strongly held by M.G's and no advance was possible without suffering serious casualties.	
	Aug. 13th.		No change in situation. Hostile artillery continued active against ST FLORIS and CARVIN. Q.8.b. & d. Q.14.b. & d., ... and P.6.d. were subjected to gas shelling, the latter place with Yellow Cross gas.	
	14th	4 pm	Situation unchanged. Slight hostile shelling on St.FLORIS during night. Div.Order No.75 issued ordering the relief of the 230th Brigade by the 231st Brigade on the night of 16th/17th August, 231st to go into support and 229th Brigade to go into Divl.Reserve at HAM-EN-ARTOIS.	App XVIII
	15th		Quiet day in the line. St.FLORIS and LA HAYE shelled during the night with 5.9's. and a small quantity of blue Cross Gas.	
	16th		Situation unchanged - usual shelling of St.FLORIS and CARVIN Areas with H.E. and slight amount of gas. Nothing of further interest to report.	

Army Form C. 2118.

WAR DIARY
INTELLIGENCE SUMMARY.
(Erase heading not required.)

Place	Date	Hour	Summary of Events and Information	Remarks and references to Appendices
LILSTTE Chateau.	Aug. 17th		Situation unchanged. Enemy artillery unusually quiet. One prisoner of 142 Regt. gave himself up to one of our posts. He had lost his way and wandered into our lines. During the night 16/17th, 231st Brigade relieved 230th Brigade in the line with 25th R.W.F. on left and 24th Welsh on right, 10th K.S.L.I. in Brigade Reserve. 230th Brigade on relief moved into Divl.Support and the 229th Brigade into Divl.Reserve.	
	18th	5 am 12-45pm	Sunday, the Army Commander attended the Church Parade of the 229th Inf.brigade. Situation normal after a quiet night. The 231st Brigade was ordered to push out patrols as the enemy was thought to be retiring. (wire No. G.549 sent). 231st Brigade selected as their next objective the line Q.11.c.5.9. - WOLF TRACK - WOOKEY Farm - junction of Road and Canal at K.24.a.1.2.	App. XIX
		4 pm. 4-45 pm 8-40 pm	Fires seen in Q.11 and Eastward, explosions also heard. 25th R.W.F. reported enemy seen retiring through K.34.d. 231 Brigade reached and consolidated the objective. Patrols pushed out to keep in touch with the enemy. During the day 4 prisoners captured, 6 enemy killed and one M.G. captured. "M" Special Coy, R.E. had arranged to project gas on the enemy in Q.11.b. Order No.78. This was however cancelled owing to the withdrawal of the enemy.	App.XX
	19th	5 am.	The Corps Commander inspected the 14th Royal Highlanders in the morning and the 16th Devons in the afternoon. The Divl. front was unchanged at 5 a.m. but during the day the line was advanced and by 4-30 p.m. ran approximately along the road N.E. through Q.11.a and thence Northward through Q.5.d and b. and just West of the LYS River in K.35.d, during this advance 2 O.R. of the 4th Coy, 322 Inf.Regt were captured also 1 M.G. Further advance brought the Brigade by 9-40 p.m. to the line Q.12.d.2.8. - Q.6.a.3.0. - Q.6.b.5.0. thence along the road to K.36.Central, patrols being pushed forward to keep in touch with the enemy.	

Army Form C. 2118.

WAR DIARY
or
INTELLIGENCE SUMMARY.
(Erase heading not required.)

Instructions regarding War Diaries and Intelligence Summaries are contained in F.S. Regs., Part II. and the Staff Manual respectively. Title pages will be prepared in manuscript.

Place	Date	Hour	Summary of Events and Information	Remarks and references to Appendices
LILLETTE Chateau.	Aug. 20th		At 5-30 a.m. the line was unchanged. there was some gas shelling on whole Divisional Front during the night. During the morning patrols of the 24th Welsh were advanced to EPINETTE and N.E. as far as R.7.b. Slight M.G. fire was experienced. One prisoner was captured - belonged to 2nd Coy, 102 R.I.R.	
		4-45 pm	231st Brigade received Warning Order to take over portion of front held by 4th Division. Our line was established as follows, R.7.c.0.7. - Q.6.b.5.0. thence along road to K.36.Central. 231st Brigade was ordered to push on patrols to line of LAWE River in conjunction with an advance being made by 61st Division on their left.	App. XXI. App. XXII.
		5-20 pm	Patrols reached road running through R.1.b and L.31.d, where they were held up by M.G. fire from either side of the railway. The Corps Commander inspected the 12th S.L.I.	
	21st		Situation unchanged. Patrol of 24th Welsh located enemy post of about 40 at L.31.c.3.9. 231st Brigade H.Q. moved to Q.19.a.7.6. Redistribution of Coys of M.G.Bn ordered to take place on 23rd instant. 230th Brigade H.Q. ordered to move from BUSNES to LA HAYE on 22nd inst. 23⁰th Brigade also ordered to take over portion of Reserve line from 11th Inf.Bde (4th Div) by 3 p.m. on August 22nd.	App. XXIII App. XXIV App. XXV
		11 pm	A patrol of 4 men of 24th Welsh which had gone out the previous day returned in the evening. It was unable to return before, owing to heavy M.G. fire and was away for a period of about 30 hours. A congratulatory telegram was sent by the G.O.C. to the patrol leader. 231st Brigade were ordered to co-operate if conditions suitable with the advance of the 61st Division on their left.	App. XXVI
	22nd	8 am.	In accordance with the above order patrols were pushed forward and little opposition was experienced. On reaching line R.7.a. - R.1.c. and a and L.31.Central patrols were counter-attacked after a heavy barrage of H.E., shrapnel and T.M.s and were forced back to their original line. Considerable casualties were incurred.	
		7-15 pm.	Warning Order issued that 229th Bde would relieve the 231st Bde on night 24/25th.	App. XXVIII

Army Form C. 2118.

WAR DIARY
or
INTELLIGENCE SUMMARY.
(Erase heading not required)

Place	Date	Hour	Summary of Events and Information	Remarks and references to Appendices
LILLETTE Chateau	Aug. 23rd.		During night 22/23rd in accordance with Div. Order No.77 231st Brigade took over the line held by left Brigade of 4th Division. The new Southern Divisional Boundary being the southern grid line of squares Q.23,24 and R.19. Front line was intermittently shelled during the day and the normal gas shelling was experienced at night.	App XXIX
	24th.	5-40 am.	Situation unchanged. Div.H.Q. moved to BUSNES Chateau and opened there at 12 noon.	App XXX
		11-30 pm	Warning Order issued that Division would be relieved by 59th Div. on night 26/27th inst. 2 Battns, 1st Portuguese Inf. Bde were attached to the Division to be employed on work on Reserve line.	App XXXI App XXXII
BUSNES Chateau	25th	5-40 am.	Situation quiet. During night 24/25th 229th Brigade relieved 231st Brigade in the front line, the 231st Bde becoming Bde in support and the 230th Bde in Divisional Reserve in accordance with Div.Order No.78.	App XXXIII
	26th		Quiet day in the line. During the afternoon 231st Brigade was relieved by 177th Inf.Bde (59th Div) and proceeded by bus to LA LACQUE - MAZINGHEM - LAMBRES area. Later in the afternoon 230th Bde was relieved by 176th Bde and marched to St.HILAIRE - BOURECQ Area.	App XXXIV
	27th	6 pm	Command of Sector passed to G.O.C., 59th Division at which hour 74th Div. H.Q. opened at NORRENT FONTES.	

Army Form C. 2118.

WAR DIARY

INTELLIGENCE SUMMARY

General Staff.

74th (Yeomanry) Division.

(Erase heading not required.)

Instructions regarding War Diaries and Intelligence Summaries are contained in F.S. Regs., Part II. and the Staff Manual respectively. Title pages will be prepared in manuscript.

Place	Date	Hour	Summary of Events and Information	Remarks and references to Appendices
NORRENT FONTES.	Aug. 28th.	4.30	Relief of 229th Brigade by 177 Bde (59th Division) was completed by 2.20 a.m. and 229th Brigade proceeded by bus to HAM-EN-ARTOIS Area. Brigade Groups were formed and Division began moving by rail to 4th Army Area in accordance with Divisional Order No 80.	App 35. Appendix 36.
BEAUCOURT CHATEAU.	Aug. 29th.	3. p.m.	Division continued entraining for 4th Army area. D.H.Q. closed at NORRENT FONTES at 3. p.m. and opened at BEAUCOURT CHATEAU at same hour being in G.H.Q. Reserve administered by III Corps. Shortly afterwards, the first two trains arrived. Orders were issued that Brigade Groups would be billeted in accordance with amendment to 74th Division Order No 80 issued at 4.30 p.m.	
	Aug. 30th.		The Division continued to arrive during the day and were accommodated as follows :- Divisional H.Q. at BEAUCOURT CHATEAU, Divisional Artillery BONNAY, 229th Brigade Group BEHENCOURT and LA HOUSSOYE, 230th Brigade Group HEILLY, 231st Brigade Group RIBEMONT. (Ref. 1/40,000 Sheet 62D).	Appendix 37.
	Aug. 31st.	10.10 a.m.	The detrainment of the Division in the new area was completed by 8. a.m. Warning Order sent out for relief of 58th Division in the line.	Appendix 38.
		1.30 p.m.	Divisional Order No 81 issued. 74th Division to relieve 58th Division night of August 31st/Sept 1st. Infantry Brigade Groups to move up by Battalions. Artillery relief to take place later. The relief was postponed for 24 hours.	Appendix 39.
		6.p.m.	The three Infantry Brigade Groups moved by bus in accordance with Divisional Order No 81 to 58th Division area, debussing at MARICOURT, coming under orders of 58th Division Commander. 229th and 230th Brigade Groups bivouacked in valley South of LE FOREST (B.22.c. & B. 28.a.) Sheet 62D. 231st Brigade Group bivouacked in TRIGGER WOOD (A.35.b. Sheet 62C). Orders received from III Corps ordering move of Divisional Artillery from BONNAY to Valleys South of MARICOURT. Divisional Artillery ordered to comply. Move to take place on September 1st.	Appendix 40.

[signed] Br Gen / Maj Gen Staff 74th Division

COPY.

SECRET.

Headquarters.
    230th Infantry Brigade.
    231st Infantry Brigade.
C.R.A.
Q.

WARNING ORDER.

The 27th Brigade, R.F.A. at present covering part of the ST FLORIS Section is being relieved by a Brigade of the 61st D.A. within a few days.

                      (Signed) M.M. Parry Jones.
                                 Major.
                           General Staf f.
4th August 1918.   74th (Yeomanry) Division.

App. II

SECRET.   Copy No. 17

74th DIVISION ORDER NO 70.

31st July 1918.

1.   The 230th Infantry Brigade will relieve the 231st Infantry Brigade in the ST FLORIS Section on the night 4th/5th August.

2.   All details will be arranged between B.G.C's concerned.

3.   On relief, the 231st Infantry Brigade comes into Divisional Reserve, and will be concentrated in the HAM-EN-ARTOIS - GUARBECQUE - MIQUELLERIE Area.

4.   Defence instructions, aeroplane photographs and Special Maps will be handed over.

5.   On August 4th, "B" Teams of the 230th Infantry Brigade will proceed to the Divisional Reception Camp, LINGHEM.
"B" Teams of the 231st Infantry Brigade will move to the Reserve Brigade Area on the same day.
74th Division 'Q' will notify transport arrangements.

6.   Completion of relief will be wired to Divisional H.Q.

7.   ACKNOWLEDGE.

M M Pany-Jones Major
for

Lieut Colonel.
General Staff.
74th (Yeomanry) Division.

Issued at 10 p.m.

Copies to :-
```
    No 1  'G'                           No 11 A.D.M.S.
       2  'Q'                              12 Div Train.
       3  'Q'                              13 4th Division.
       4  C.R.A. 74th Division.            14 XI Corps.
       5  C.R.E.                           15 5th Division.
       6  Signal Coy.                      16 O.C. Reception Camp.
       7  229th Infantry Brigade.          17 War Diary.
       8  230th Infantry Brigade.          18 War Diary.
       9  231st Infantry Brigade.          19 File.
      10. M.G. Battn.
```

"A" Form.
MESSAGES AND SIGNALS.

Prefix	Code	m	Words	Charge	This message is on a/c of:	Recd. at ... m.
Office of Origin and Service Instructions.			Sent			Date
copy			At ... m.		Service.	From
			To			
			By		(Sig. of "Franking Officer.")	By

TO:
- 230 Bde
- 229 Bde
- CRA
- 61 Div
- 4 Div
- 11 Corps

Sender's Number	Day of Month	In reply to Number	AAA
T.1	8		

230 Bde now advancing to line of Old L/S in K.33.d. and Q.3.b. aaa When 230 Bde has reached objective 229 Bde will advance to line of TURBEAUTE stream keeping touch with the right of 230 Bde on Bde boundary and with 4th Div on right aaa 230 229 reptd CRA 61st and 4th Divs 11 Corps.

From 74 Div
Place
Time 11. am

The above may be forwarded as now corrected. (Z) Lt. M M Parry Jones

MESSAGES AND SIGNALS.

Army Form C. 2121.
(In pads of 100.)

This message is on a/c of: Appendix VIII

TO: 229 Bde, 230 Bde, CRA, 4 Div

Sender's Number: G333
Day of Month: 7

4th Div continuing to advance to line of QUENTIN Road their left to join ours at Q16a85.40 aaa Advance of own right Div to join 4th on this objective

From: 74 Div

A C Temperley M[?]

MESSAGES AND SIGNALS.

Priority to
230, 229.
(Sgd) Act.

TO 230 Bde   M.G. Bn
   229 ---   C.R.A.

Sender's Number: G.334   Day of Month: 7

Maintain as much harassing fire as possible with machine guns and artillery in rear of present enemy lines tonight.

From 7th Divn
Time ?

(Sgd) AC Tembesley
Lt Col

"A" Form.
MESSAGES AND SIGNALS.

Army Form C.2121.
(In pads of 100.)

This message is on a/c of: Append VI

TO:
229 Bde	CRE	MG Bn
230 - -	ADMS	
231 - -	74 Train	

Sender's Number.	Day of Month.	In reply to Number.	AAA
G.322	7		
The	following	groups	will
be	formed	forthwith	for
active	operations	aaa	229
Bde	Group	composed	of
229	Inf. Bde	1 MG Coy	R.M.
Fd Coy RE	448 Coy	Div. Train	detachment
229	Fd Amb.	aaa	230
Bde	Group	composed	of
230	Inf. Bde	1 MG Coy	R Ang
Fd Coy RE	449 Coy	Div. Train	detachment
230	Fd Amb	aaa	O.C
these	units	will	report
forthwith	to	Brigadier	concerned
aaa	Addressed	all	concerned
	copies to	CRA	
		Q	
		War Diary.	

From: 74 Div
Place:
Time: 3.45 pm

Sd. M.H. Parry-Jones

"A" Form.
MESSAGES AND SIGNALS.

Prefix	Code	m	Words	Charge	This message is on a/c of:	Recd. at m.
Office of Origin and Service Instructions.		Sent				Date
Copy		At m.			Service.	From
		To				
		By			(Sig. of "Franking Officer.")	By

TO { Prior / M.G. Bn

Sender's Number	Day of Month	In reply to Number	AAA
*G.313	7		

Send	up	limbers	to Right
Machine	Gun	Group	and
be	prepared	to	send
limbers	to	left	group
at	short	notice	add
a	number	of	guns
in	right	group	will
move	forward	as	soon
as	limbers	can	arrive

From 7th DW
Place
Time 12.15

The above may be forwarded as now corrected. (Z) R C Temperley Lt Col

Censor. Sig. of Addressor or person authorised to telegraph in his name.

"A" Form.
MESSAGES AND SIGNALS.

TO	229 Bde	CRA	Q	5 Div
	230 "	CRE	XI Corps	61 Div
	231 "	M.G. Bn	4 Div	OC Sig Coy

Sender's Number: G.312
Day of Month: 7
AAA

229 Bde is now making good line Q.15.d.0.6 (where it is in touch with 4th Div) — Q.15.a. central Q.8.d.7.5. Its patrols are now in Q.15.b. central and pushing on towards Road Junction at Q.9.d.4.6. aaa 230 Bde will advance northwards along enemy front line from Q.8.a.7.4 aaa Next bound for Division will be road from Q.15.b.10.5 — Q.9.d.4.6. — CALONNE Village in Q.9.a. thence back to our line as far northward as 230 Bde has been able to reach aaa Boundary between Brigades present Bde boundary — Road Junction Q.9.a.60.95. — Q.3.d.5.5 — old River b/s to Q.4.d.30.95 (all inclusive to 229 Bde) aaa. 230 Bde will be responsible for forming a defensive flank from CALONNE Village (exclusive) westward

From: 74 Div.
Place:
Time: 12.15 pm

(Z) Sd. A. Temperley Lt Col
G.S.

"A" Form.
MESSAGES AND SIGNALS.

Army Form C. 2121.
(In pads of 100.)

Prefix... Code... m	Words.	Charge.	This message is on a/c of:	Rec'd. at ...m.
Office of Origin and Service Instructions. Copy	Sent At ...m. To... By...		Appendix III ...Service. (Signature of "Franking Officer.")	Date... From... By...

TO { 229 Bde
       CRA

Sender's Number.	Day of Month.	In reply to Number.	
G285	6	SC17	A A A

send	fresh	patrols	into
enemy	line	to	move
North	and	South	till
touch	with	enemy	is
regained	aaa	also	patrol
to	eastward	of	enemy
line	for	same	purpose
aaa	occupy	enemy	line
by	posts	with	lewis
guns	and	be	prepared
to	support	post	as a
arrange	S.O.S	barrage	to
cover	post	when	in
position			

added 229 Bde:
rptd CRA

From: 74 DIV
Place:
Time: 4.30 pm

The above may be forwarded as now corrected. (Z)

Censor. Signature of Addressor or person authorised to telegraph in his name.

* This line should be erased if not required.

SECRET.

Headquarters,
   229th Infantry Brigade.
   230th Infantry Brigade.
   231st Infantry Brigade.
   C.R.A.

Reference XIth Corps SS.24 (XIth Corps Policy).

Offensive Attitude to be adopted by the Corps.

At the present moment the enemy opposite this Divisional front is holding his front line in strength and the defences are properly constituted with a continuous front line. All information shows that each Regiment holds its front line with a battalion with all four companies in the line. Should the enemy attitude change, the policy ordered by the Corps Commander will immediately be adopted. For the meantime everything must be done by raids and strong patrols, especially by day, to test the strength of his defences and his method of holding his line. Under no circumstances must the enemy be allowed any rest. In this connexion see this office G.1054 of July 23rd in reference to patrol activity.

Action to be taken in the event of the enemy withdrawing.

The action to be taken by Company, Battalion and Brigade Commanders is fully discussed in the Corps Memorandum.

Brigadiers in the line will ensure that:-

(a) definite schemes by Company and Battalion Commanders are drawn up.

(b) they are handed over on relief.

(c) material for consolidation is at hand in every Company Dump.

Lieut. Colonel.
General Staff.
74th (Yeomanry) Division.

4th August 1918.

SECRET.
Appendix
Copy No. 18
4th August 1918.

74th DIVISION ORDER NO 71.

1. The 61st Division is relieving the 5th Division in the line. Relief will be completed by 6 a.m. on August 7th, except that of the Divisional Artillery which will be completed by 10 a.m. on August 8th.

2. The relief of the 5th Divisional Artillery by 61st Divisional Artillery, (including the 27th R.F.A. Brigade now covering the front of the ST FLORIS Sector) will be carried out on the nights of August 6th/7th and 7th/8th, one section per battery relieving on August 6th/7th and remainder on August 7th/8th.

3. Arrangements for relief of 27th Brigade R.F.A. will be made between C.R.A's concerned.

4. Completion of relief will be reported by wire.

5. ACKNOWLEDGE.

A C Temperley
Lieut Colonel.
General Staff.
74th (Yeo) Division.

4th August 1918.

Issued at 8pm

Copies to :-

No		No	
1	'G'	11	A.D.M.S.
2	'Q'	12	Div Train.
3	'Q'	13	XI Corps.
4	'Q'	14	5th Division.
5	C.R.A.	15	61st Division.
6	C.R.E.	16	G.O.C,R.A.XI Corps.
7	229th Infantry Bde.	17	War Diary.
8	230th Infantry Bde.	18	War Diary.
9	231st Infantry Bde.	19	File.
10	M.G.Battn.	20	Signal Coy

"A" Form.
MESSAGES AND SIGNALS.

Army Form C. 2121.
(In pads of 100.)

Copy

TO: 231 Bde, 229 Bde, CRE, Q, 230 Bde, MGBn, CRA, Signal

Sender's Number: T.2
Day of Month: 8
AAA

231 Bde will move as follows aaa 2 rear battns to HAMET BILLET and LA PIERRIERE Bde H.Q. to P.T.C. this afternoon addsd all concerned.

From 74 Dw
Time 11.15 am

(Z) Sd MM Parry Jones

"A" Form.
MESSAGES AND SIGNALS.

Army Form C. 2121.

Office of Origin and Service Instructions: Urgent Operation priority to 230 +229 fd. A.C.T.

This message is on a/c of: Copy

TO:
- 230 Bde
- 229 Bde
- CRA
- 61 Dv
- 4 Dv
- 11 Corps

Sender's Number: G 368
Day of Month: 8

objective on east bank of TURBEAUTE and old LYS will be consolidated aaa there will be no further advance tonight except by patrols.

added 230 Bde
229 Bde
reptd CRA
61 Dv
4 Dv
11 Corps

From: 74 Dv
Time: 4.50 pm

(Z) fd AC Temperley

"A" Form.
MESSAGES AND SIGNALS.

Appendix XIII

Office of Origin and Service Instructions: **copy**

TO: 229 Bde / 230 Bde / CRA

Sender's Number: G.377
Day of Month: 9
AAA

Information from prisoners and captured map indicates enemy will probably continue to hold line PARADIS (Q.18.c) Q.4.d.central – K.34.c.0.0. – CANAL at K.34.a.0.2 – K.22.d.2.4. during 9th and possibly 10th August aaa. Bdes will endeavour by employing small forces to test strength of opposition in this line aaa. If enemy shows any sign of withdrawal or weakening troops concerned will press forward at that point and exploit any success aaa ACKNOWLEDGE aaa added all concerned

From 74 DW
Time 1.45 am

(Z) A Craig Lt fr

Append XIV

SECRET.   Copy No. 17

74th DIVISION ORDER No. 72.

9th August 1918.

1. From information received from prisoners, which is confirmed by a captured map, it appears probable that the enemy will continue to hold the line PARADIS (Q.18.c.) - Q.4.d.Central - K.34.c.0.0. - Canal at K.34.a.0.2. - K.22.d.2.4. - K.17.d.4.2. - thence road running North through K.17.d. & b. and K.11.d. during 9th and possibly 10th August.

2. Brigadiers will endeavour by the employment of small forces to test the strength of the opposition in this line in every way possible.

3. The 61st Division will also endeavour to establish a bridgehead including PURESBECQUES and SINBAD FARM across the PLATE BECQUE, so as to be prepared when ordered to advance South East to envelop MERVILLE from the North.

4. If the enemy shows any sign of withdrawal from the line given in para 1. above or any weakening of his defence of that line the troops concerned will press forward at that point and exploit any success.

5. The present operations may last some time, it is important for commanders of all formations to husband their reserves as much as possible, so that at a later stage the necessary reserves of fresh troops may be available.

6. ACKNOWLEDGE.

                                    A.C.Temperley
                                    Lieut.Colonel.
                                    General Staff.
                                    74th (Yeomanry) Division.

Issued at 10 a.m.

Copies to:-
No. 1.	'G'	No. 11. A.D.M.S.
2.	'Q'	12. Div. Train.
3.	'Q'.	13. XIth Corps.
4.	C.R.A.	14. 4th Division.
5.	C.R.E.	15. 61st Division.
6.	229th Inf.Bde.	16. War Diary.
7.	230th Inf.Bde.	17. " "
8.	231st Inf.Bde.	18. File.
9.	M.G.Bn.	
10.	O.C., Signals.	

"A" Form.
MESSAGES AND SIGNALS.

Army Form C. 2121.
(In pads of 100.)

Office of Origin and Service Instructions: Copy

This message is on a/c of: Appendix Service.

Date XV

TO: 230 Bde / 229 Bde / Q

Sender's Number: G 389
Day of Month: 9
AAA

Warning Order aaa 230 Bde will take over front now held by 229 Bde on night 10/11th aaa Order follows

From: R. Divn
Time: 5.25 pm

(Z) A.C. Temperley Lt-Col

Append XVI

SECRET. Copy No. 17

74th DIVISION ORDER No. 73.

9th August 1918.

1. The enemy's position along the right bank of the BOURRE River and thence Southwards to the MERVILLE-PARADIS Road appears to be well organised and held in some strength, probably with the object of covering the completion of a more permanent line which has been located by aeroplane photographs and extends from the West side of NEUF BERQUIN through L.13, 19, 25 to 31 and thence West of LESTREM and the LAWE.

2. The further progress of the 74th Division depends upon the progress made by the two flank Divisions. The present front line will be organised as a strong outpost position. Patrolling will be very active and every endeavour will be made to discover any weakening of the enemy's defence, in accordance with Div. Order No. 72.

3. The Division will be organised in depth.
On the night 10/11th August, 230th Brigade Group will take over the front now held by 229th Brigade Group and will become the Advanced Guard Brigade of the Division.
229th Brigade, to which 'C' Coy, M.G.Bn will continue to be attached, will take over the Reserve line, which remains the Line of Retention of the Division. The Brigade will be disposed in the Reserve and AMUSOIRES lines with a Reserve Battn. in the AMUSOIRES line.
R.M.Field Coy, R.E. and detachment of the Field Ambulance attached to 229th Brigade Group will revert to the command of the C.R.E. and A.D.M.S. respectively.
The 231st Brigade will remain in Divisional Reserve in its present billets North of BUSNES.

4. Every effort will be made by frequent relief of the most advanced troops, and by development of pack transport, to keep the troops fresh for future operations and avoid using up Reserves.

5. Precautions must be taken to guard against road mines, booby traps and delay action mines in cellars and dug-outs. 1 Officer and 12 men of the Tunnelling Coy who have had previous experience in looking for these mines have been placed under the orders of B.G.C., 230th Inf. Brigade for this purpose.

6. ACKNOWLEDGE.

A.C.Temperley.

Lieut. Colonel.
General Staff.
74th (Yeomanry) Division.

Issued at 6 p.m.

Copies to:-
- No. 1. 'G'
- 2. 'Q'
- 3. 'Q'
- 4. 'Q'
- 5. C.R.A.
- 6. C.R.E.
- 7. 229th Inf. Bde.
- 8. 230th " "
- 9. 231st " "
- 10. M.G.Battn.
- No. 11. A.D.M.S.
- 12. Div. Train.
- 13. Div. Signal Coy.
- 14. XIth Corps.
- 15. 4th Division.
- 16. 61st Division.
- 17. War Diary.
- 18. " "
- 19. File.

SECRET. Copy No. 9

74th DIVISION ORDER No. 74.

Appendix XVII

11th August 1918.

1. The operation carried out today by 61st Division though unsuccessful in forming a bridgehead on Left bank of PLATE BECQUE, has been most useful.
    First by discovering that the enemy is holding his position in strength and is not yet withdrawing in this area.
    Secondly by making him anxious regarding future possible attacks and thus compelling him to keep reserves in this area which no doubt are urgently required elsewhere.

2. This offensive policy on the part of the Corps will be maintained.
    The 61st Division will do its utmost to establish posts on the Left bank of the PLATE BECQUE by local operations of a surprise nature: and will then endeavour to enlarge the position on the Left bank especially as regards the capture of the RENNET Farm locality.

3. The 230th Inf. Brigade by small local operations of a surprise nature, especially to the area S. of the OLD LYS, will endeavour to capture small posts of the enemy. Thus slowly advancing the line with the double object of helping the Division on the Right and maintaining the closest possible touch with the enemy so as to discover any signs of withdrawal.

4. These enterprises should be assisted if possible by one or two Field Guns specially brought up for the purpose.

5. The Companies in the front line must necessarilly be relieved frequently, but these reliefs must not interfere with the local operations described above.

6. B.G.C., 230th Brigade will draw up schemes in accordance with the above and will communicate them as soon as possible to Div. H.Q.

7. ACKNOWLEDGE.

Parry-Jones Major
for.

Lieut. Colonel.
General Staff.
74th (Yeomanry) Division.

Issued at.... 2 pm.

Copies to:-
          No. 1. 'G'.
              2. 229th Inf. Bde.
              3. 230th   "   "
              4. 231st   "   "
              5. C.R.A.
              6. C.R.E.
              7. M.G.Battn.
              8. 'Q'.
           9-10. War Diary.
             11. File.

SECRET.   Copy No. 19

                    74th DIVISION ORDER No. 75.
                    ----------------------------   Appendix XVIII

                                                              14th August 1918.

1.   The 231st Brigade will relieve 230th Brigade in the
     line on the night August 16/17th.

2.   On relief 230th Inf.Bde will take over responsibility
     for the Reserve line from 229th Inf.Bde and will be
     located as under:-

            Brigade H.Q.   ...   ...   LABIETTE FARM.
            2 Battns   ...   ...   Reserve and
                                                AMUSOIRES Lines.
            1 Battn   ...   ...   HAMET BILLET.

     'C' Coy, M.G.Battn at present attached to 229th
     Brigade will come under the orders of B.G.C., 230th
     Brigade.

3.   On night August 16/17th, 229th Inf.Bde will be with-
     drawn to Div. Reserve and will be located as under;-

            Brigade H.Q.   ...   ...   HAM EN ARTOIS.
            'A' Battn   ...   ...   HAM EN ARTOIS.
            'B' "   ...   ...   MIQUELLERIE.
            'C' "   ...   ...   GUARBECQUES.

4.   The Detachment Field Ambulance at present under
     B.G.C., 230th Brigade will come under the orders of
     the A.D.M.S.
        The Field Company, R.E. in the forward area will
     remain affiliated to the Front line Brigade but will
     come under the orders of the C.R.E.

5.   Defence Instructions, aeroplane photographs and
     special maps will be handed over.

6.   "B" Teams, 229th Inf.Bde will move to Reserve Brigade
     area on August 16th.
        A.A.&.Q.M.G. will arrange transport.

7.   All details will be arranged direct between Brigades
     concerned.

8.   Completion of relief will be wired to Div.H.Q.

9.   ACKNOWLEDGE.

                                                Lieut.Colonel
                                                General Staff.
                                                74th (Yeomanry) Divis.

Issued at 4 p.m.

Copies to:-
     No. 1. 'G'.   No. 12. A.D.M.S.
         2-4. 'Q'.   13. Div.Train.
         5. C.R.A.   14. XIth Corps.
         6. C.R.E.   15. 4th Division.
         7. O.C. Signal Coy.   16. 61st Division.
         8. 229th Inf.Bde.   17. O.C. Reception Camp.
         9. 230th   "   "   18-19. War Diary.
        10. 231st   "   "   20. File.
        11. M.G.Battn.

"A" Form
MESSAGES AND SIGNALS.

Army Form C. 2121
(In pads of 100)

Urgent Operation Priority
Sd. A.C. Temperley
Lt Col. GS

This message is on a/c of:
APP. XIX

TO: 231 Bde
230 Bde
CRA

Sender's Number.	Day of Month.	In reply to Number.	AAA
G549	18		
In	view	of	information
received	push	out	patrols
at	once	to	ascertain
if	enemy	still	holding
front	line	aaa	Acknowledge
Added	231	Bde	reptd
230	and	CRA	

From: 74 BW
Time: 12.45 pm

(Z) Sd. A Galloway
Capt. GS

SECRET.

App XX
Copy No. 17

74th DIVISION ORDER No. 78.

17th August 1918.

Ref. Map. Sheet 36.A.
and sketch map attached 1:20,000.

1. 125 drums C.G., will be fired from projectors to inflict casualties.

2. **FIRING POSITIONS.**
   Projectors installed at Q.10.d.1,8.

3. **TARGETS.**
   Posts and area in Q.11.b.

4. **PROGRAMME.**
   Projectors to be fired simultaneously at a zero during the night. Hour to be communicated later.

5. **WIND LIMITS.**
   S.S.W. to W.N.W. through W.

6. **CODE.**
   Operation will not take place tonight. .... JERICHO.
   Operation will take place at - ... JERUSALEM....
   followed by a number which will represent the number of minutes after 11.0 p.m. that the operation will take place.

   Thus:- JERUSALEM 80 = 11 p.m. plus 80 mins. = 12.20 a.m.
          JERUSALEM 120 = 11 p.m. plus 120 " = 1.0 a.m.

   Operation cancelled (after circulation of JERUSALEM)
   ...... DAMASCUS.
   Operation complete .... JORDAN.

7. The Infantry Company Commander of the Sector concerned will send a runner to report to the Officer of "M" Special Coy, R.E. at Q.10.d.1.8. 30 minutes before zero to carry back messages of completion or cancellation of the Operation.

8. Troops will be cleared from the area shaded in red on attached map one hour before zero.

9. Troops in the area shaded blue will wear Box Respirators from zero minus 5 minutes until ordered by an Officer to remove them.

10. The final decision in accordance with local conditions to project gas or not will rest with the Officer of "M" Special Company, R.E. in charge of the Operation.

11. ACKNOWLEDGE.

ACTemperley.
Lieut-Colonel,
General Staff,
74th (Yeomanry) Division.

Issued at R.Er.

Copies to:- No. 1. 'G'   8. "M" Spec. Coy R.E.
            2. 'Q'   9. 4th Division.
            3. C.R.A.   10. 61st Division.
            4. C.R.E.   11. XIth Corps.
            5. 231st Inf. Bde.   12-13. War Diary.
            6. 230th "   14. File.
            7. M.G. Battn.

"A" Form
MESSAGES AND SIGNALS.

Army Form C. 2121
(In pads of 100)

This message is on a/c of:

App. XXI .Service.

TO: 231 Inf Bde.

Sender's Number.	Day of Month.	In reply to Number.	AAA
* G. 579	20		
Warning	Order	aaa	231
Bde	will	take	over
portion	of	4th	Div
line	on	night	22nd/23rd
aaa	details	later	aaa
in	view	of	this
BAQUEROLLES	Farm	is	more
suitable	for	your	new
H.Q.			

From: 7th Div
Place:
Time: 8.45 a.m.

(Sd) A.C. Temperley Lt Col
CS

"A" Form
MESSAGES AND SIGNALS.

Army Form C. 2121 (In pads of 100)

URGENT OPERATION
PRIORITY to 231 Bde.
(Sd) M.M. Parry Jones
Lt.Col. ?? Major

App XXII

TO	231 Bde.	C.R.A.	Signals	61 Div
	229 — " —	C.R.E.	'Q'	II Corps
	230 — " —	M.G.Bn	H D V	

Sender's Number: G.591
Day of Month: 20
AAA

Information as to position to which enemy has decided to withdraw is uncertain aaa advanced guard to which the 439 Fld. Coy will be attached will push forward boldly until touch with enemy is firmly established and will endeavour to get patrols on to line of River LAWE today aaa 61 Div is sending forward advanced guard Bde which will endeavour to get patrols on to line CHAPELLE

"A" Form
MESSAGES AND SIGNALS.

Army Form C. 2121 (In pads of 100)

Prefix	Code	Words	Charge	This message is on a/c of:	Recd. at ......m
		Sent At ......m To ...... By		......Service (Signature of "Franking Officer.")	Date ...... From ...... By ......

TO		2.		
Sender's Number	Day of Month	In reply to Number		AAA
DUVELLE	—	NEUF	BERQUIN	
aaa	Keep	touch	on	
flanks	forming	defensive	flanks	
when	necessary	aaa	If	
enemy	is	not	encountered	
on	above	line	advanced	
guard	Bde	will	continue	
forward	movement	aaa	231	
Bde	to	acknowledge		
aaa	Addsd	231	Bde	
reptd	all	concerned		

From: 7th Div
Place:
Time: 4.15 pm

The above may be forwarded as now corrected.

(Sd) H. M. Parry Jones
Major
for Lt Col J.S.

Signature of Addresser or person authorised to telegraph in his name.

* This line should be erased if not required.

"A" Form
MESSAGES AND SIGNALS.

Army Form C. 2121
(In pads of 100)

This message is on a/c of: App XXIII Service.

TO: 230 Bde M.G. Bn. Q.

Sender's Number: G.620
Day of Month: 21

Following moves will take place on Aug 23 aaa M.G. Bn H.Q. to LABIETTE Farm aaa one and a half Coys into ROBECQ area aaa ½ Coy into ST FLORIS area aaa M.G. Bn will arrange for accommodation direct with 230 Bde. aaa Addsd M.G. Bn reptd 230 Bde Q.

From: 1/4 Div
Time: 4 pm

"A" Form
MESSAGES AND SIGNALS.

Army Form C. 2121
(In pads of 100)

This message is on a/c of:

App. XXIV Service.

TO: 230 Bde. / 231 — " — / Q. Camp Comdt

Sender's Number.	Day of Month.	In reply to Number.	AAA
G.613	21		

Your Bde H.Q. will move from BUSNES to LA HAYE tomorrow aaa Addsd 230 Bde reptd 231 Bde Q Camp Comdt

From: 7/H Div

(Sgd) H S Sharp Capt

"A" Form
MESSAGES AND SIGNALS.

Army Form C. 2121
(In pads of 100)

This message is on a/c of: App XXV Service.

TO: 230 Bde
4 Div

Sender's Number.	Day of Month.	In reply to Number.	AAA
G. 608	21		

Reference Div Order para 3 aaa new portion of Reserve line will be taken over from 11th Inf Bde by 3 Bn on Aug 22nd aaa Addsd 230 Bde repld 4th Div.

From 74 Div
Time 9 am

(Sd) A.C. Temperley

"A" Form
MESSAGES AND SIGNALS.

Army Form C. 2121

This message is on a/c of: App XXVI

To: 231 Bde.

Sender's Number: G.635
Day of Month: 21

AAA

61 Div has reached line L.31.a.5.5 L.19.central L.13.d.1.0 L.7.c.8.2 aaa Push on to co-operate with them if conditions on your front make it possible aaa in any case secure liaison with them on Divisional boundary.

From: 74 Div
Time: 11 am.

(Z) Sd. H.L. Sharp Capt

"A" Form
MESSAGES AND SIGNALS.

Army Form C.2121
(In pads of 100)

This message is on a/c of: app XXVII Service

TO: 231 Bde.

Sender's Number	Day of Month	In reply to Number	AAA
* G.634	21		

G.O.C. is extremely pleased to hear of the safe return of the missing patrol of 2/4 Welsh and wishes his congratulations to be conveyed to the patrol leader and his men, aaa please render account of their experiences.

From: 7th Div

(Sgd) W.S. Sharpe Lt Col

"A" Form
MESSAGES AND SIGNALS.

Army Form C. 2121 (in pads of 100).

This message is on a/c of: Copy
Appendix XXXVIII

Sender's Number	Day of Month	In reply to Number	AAA
G658	22		

231 Bde will be relieved as advanced Guard Bde by 229 Bde on night Aug 24/25 aaa On relief 231 Bde will become Support Bde and 230 Bde will go into Div Reserve aaa Details follow

Addressed 229 230 231 Bdes repeated "Q"

From 74 Div
Time 7.15 pm

Sd A L Temperley Lt Col

SECRET.   Copy No...17...

74th DIVISION ORDER No. 77.

20th August 1918.

1.   The 74th Division will extend its front on the night 22/23rd August to the South grid line of map squares Q.23, Q.24, R.19, R.20, etc Eastwards.
       The Divisional Southern Boundary will then run as shown on attached map.

2. (a) The 231st Infantry Brigade will take over the Outpost system as far South as this new boundary.

    (b) Completion of relief will be wired to Div.H.Q.

    (c) Command of this portion of the Divisional Front will pass to G.O.C., 74th Division ~~on completion of the Infantry relief.~~ at 6 a.m. on August 23rd.

    (d) The Artillery relief will be arranged direct between C.R.A.s concerned. The 4th Div. Artillery will cover the new front until 10 a.m. on August 23rd.

3. (a) 230th Infantry Brigade will take over responsibility for the Reserve line as far South as the new Divisional Boundary.
       The C.R.A. will arrange to cover the new portion of the Reserve line, which remains the Line of Retention.

    (b) The Reserve line will be held by a series of nucleus garrisons, consisting of 4 platoons in each Battalion Sector. The remainder of the two Battalions now in the Reserve and AMUSOIRES lines will be billetted in ROBECQ and St.FLORIS.

4.   ACKNOWLEDGE.

                                              A.C. Tempsley
                                              Lieut.Colonel,
                                              General Staff,
                                              74th (Yeomanry) Division.

Issued at...8 p.m...

Copies to:-
   No. 1. 'G'   No.12. A.D.M.S.
      2-4. 'Q'   13. Div.Train.
       5. C.R.A.   14. XIth Corps.
       6. C.R.E.   15. 61st Division.
       7. O.C. Signal Coy.   16. 4th Division.
       8. O.C. M.G.Battn.   17-18. War Diary.
       9. 229th Inf.Bde.   19. File.
      10. 230th   "   "
      11. 231st   "   "

SECRET.
Copy No. 9

74th DIVISION ORDER No. 77.

20th August 1918.

1. The 74th Division will extend its front on the night 22/23rd August to the South grid line of map squares Q.23, Q.24, R.19, R.20, etc Eastwards.
    The Divisional Southern Boundary will then run as shown on attached map.

2. (a) The 231st Infantry Brigade will take over the Outpost system as far South as this new boundary.

    (b) Completion of relief will be wired to Div.H.Q.

    (c) Command of this portion of the Divisional Front will pass to G.O.C., 74th Division on completion of the Infantry relief.

    (d) The Artillery relief will be arranged direct between C.R.A.s concerned.

3. (a) 230th Infantry Brigade will take over responsibility for the Reserve line as far South as the new Divisional Boundary.
    The C.R.A. will arrange to cover the new portion of the Reserve line, which remains the Line of Retention.

    (b) The Reserve line will be held by a series of nucleus garrisons, consisting of 4 platoons in each Battalion Sector. The remainder of the two Battalions now in the Reserve and AMUSOIRES lines will be billetted in ROBECQ and St. FLORIS.

4. ACKNOWLEDGE.

BM162

[signature]

Lieut. Colonel,
General Staff,
74th (Yeomanry) Division.

Issued at.. 8pm..

Copies to:-
    No. 1. 'G'   No. 12. A.D.M.S.
       2-4. 'Q'   13. Div. Train.
        5. C.R.A.   14. XIth Corps.
        6. C.R.E.   15. 61st Division.
        7. O.C. Signal Coy.   16. 4th Division.
        8. O.C. M.G.Battn.   17-18. War Diary.
        9. 229th Inf.Bde. ✓   19. File.
       10. 230th   "   "
       11. 231st   "   "

S E C R E T.

Headquarters.
  231st Infantry Brigade.
    C.R.A.
    'Q' Branch.

            Reference Divisional Order No 77.

(1)   Para 2 (c) cancel "on completion of the Infantry relief" and substitute "at 6. a.m. on August 23rd".

(2)   Para 2 (d) add "The 4th Division Artillery will cover the new front until 10. a.m. on August 23rd."

                                                Lieut Colonel.
                                          General Staff.
20th August 1918.   74th (Yeomanry) Division.

Copies to 4th Division.
         XIth Corps.

SECRET.

Copy No. 19

22nd August 1918.

Divisional H.Q. will close at LILETTE CHATEAU and open at BUSNES CHATEAU. P.31.c.4.5. (Sheet 36A) at 12 noon August 24th.

[signature]
Lieut Colonel.
General Staff.
74th (Yeomanry) Division.

Issued at 2. p.m.

Copies to :-

No		No	
1	'G'	12.	A.D.M.S.
2-4	'Q'	13	Div Train.
5	C.R.A.	14	XIth Corps.
6	C.R.E.	15	61st Division.
7	O.C. Signal Coy.	16	4th Division.
8	O.C. M.G. Battn.	17.	C. Commandant.
9	229th Inf. Bde.	18-19	War Diary.
10	230th Inf. Bde.	20	File.
11	231st Inf. Bde.	21	19th Division.

"A" Form
MESSAGES AND SIGNALS.

Army Form C. 2121 (in pads of 100).

This message is on a/c of:
Copy
Appendix

TO	229 Bde	CRA	ADMS	Q
	230 Bde	CRE	MG Bn	19 Div
	231 Bde	Signals	Div Train	61 Div

Sender's Number	Day of Month	In reply to Number	AAA
G/709	25		

Warning order aaa 74 Div will be relieved by 59 Div nights 26/27 and 27/28 August aaa Details later aaa addressed all concerned.

From 74 Div
Place
Time 11.30 pm

Sgd M.M. Parry Jones G/O

"A" Form
MESSAGES AND SIGNALS.

Army Form C.2122
(In pads of 100)

Appendix XXXII

TO: 1st Portuguese Inf Bde
British Mission attd 1st Port. Div.
CRE

Sender's Number.	Day of Month.	In reply to Number.	
G.695	24		AAA

Your two Battalions and less one company will be employed on work in Reserve line under arrangements to be made direct with CRE 74 Div aaa please send an officer to make these arrangements to report to CRE at BUSNES at 8.30 am Tomorrow aaa ~~addressed to~~ report numbers available aaa acknowledge addressed 1st Portuguese Inf Bde repeated British Mission

CRE

From: 74 Div
Place:
Time: 3.40 pm

S E C R E T.

64/67

Headquarters.
—231st Infantry Brigade.
230th Infantry Brigade.
M.G.Battn.

1. On the night August 22nd/23rd, 231st Infantry Brigade relieves 11th Infantry Brigade in the line as far South as the new Division boundary.
   At the conclusion of relief on August 23rd, the 10th Infantry Brigade will be the Brigade on the right flank of the Division with one outpost Battn in the line.   Brigade H.Q. V.12.b.2.6.

2. During the night 23rd/24th August the 10th Infantry Brigade will be relieved by the 58th Infantry Brigade of the 19th Division with one outpost Battn in the line.
   Brigade H.Q. will be at HINGES. probably at W.10.a.1.0.

Lieut Colonel.
General Staff.
74th (Yeo) Division.

21st August 1918.

SECRET.

Appendix XXXIII

Copy No. 7

74th DIVISION ORDER No.78.

23rd August 1918.

Reference Map. 1:10,000 Sheet 36A.

1. The 229th Inf.Bde will relieve the 231st Inf.Bde as Advanced Brigade on the night 24th/25th August. Troops of 229th Inf.Bde will march early on the 24th and will bivouac for the day in or West of the AMUSOIRES Line preparatary to moving forward to relief that night.

2. On completion of relief the 231st Inf.Bde will become the Brigade in Support and will be distributed as follows:-

   Brigade H.Q.
   One Battn. ... ... LA HAYE.
   "   "   ... ... St.FLORIS.
   "   "   ... ... ROBECQ.
              ... ... Asylum, St.VENANT.

   Nucleus garrisons in the Reserve Line will be found as at present by the Support Brigade.

3. On the same night the 230th Inf.Bde will move into Divisional Reserve and will be distributed as follows:-

   Brigade H.Q.
   One Battn. ... ... P.7.c.
   "   "   ... ... HAMET BILLET.
   "   "   ... ... LA PIERRIERE.
              ... ... BUSNES.

4. All details of relief will be arranged between Brigadiers concerned.

5. 230th Inf.Bde will not move into Divisional Reserve until Battns of the 229th Inf.Bde have moved forward of the AMUSOIRES Line.

6. The Artillery Bde, Field Coy, R.E. and the Company of the 11th Cyclist Battn at present attached to 231st Inf.Bde will come under orders of B.G.C., 229th Inf.Bde on relief.

7. Command of the Advanced Brigade Area will pass to B.G.C., 229th Inf.Bde on completion of relief.

8. 'B' Teams, 229th Inf.Bde will move to the Reception Camp. 'B' Teams, 230th Inf.Bde to the Reserve Brigade Area on the 24th instant. The A.A.& Q.M.G. will arrange transport.

9. Defence Instructions, aeroplane photographs and special maps will be handed over.

10. M.G.Companies at present attached to the Advanced and Support Brigades will come under orders of B.G.C., 229th Inf.Bde and B.G.C., 231st Inf.Bde respectively.

11. Completion of relief will be wired to Divisional H.Q.

12. ACKNOWLEDGE.

Lieut.Colonel,
General Staff,
74th (Yeomanry) Division.

Issued at 8 a.m.

Copies to:-

No. 1. 'G'
2-4. 'Q'
5. C.R.A.
6. C.R.E.
7. O.C., 74th Div. Signal Company.
8. O.C., 74th Bn. Machine Gun Corps.
9. 229th Infantry Brigade.
10. 230th Infantry Brigade.
11. 231st Infantry Brigade.
12. A.D.M.S.
13. 74th Divisional Train.
14. XIth Corps.
15. 61st Division.
16. 19th Division.
17-18. War Diary.
19. File.

SECRET.   Copy No. 20

74th DIVISION ORDER No. 79.

Appendix XXXIV

25th August 1918.

1. 74th Division will be relieved in its present sector by 59th Division in accordance with attached Table. All details will be arranged direct between Brigadiers.

2. All troops of 59th Division on arrival in the 74th Division Area will come under the command of G.O.C., 74th Division until command passes.

3. 59th Divisional Artillery will relieve 74th Divisional Artillery, in accordance with orders issued by G.O.C., R.A. All details direct between C.R.A.s.

4. All details as to relief of Field Companies, Pioneer Battn and Field Ambulances will be made direct between C.O.s concerned.

5. O.C., Machine Gun Battalion will arrange all details of relief of Machine Gun Companies, except that of the Company attached to 229th Infantry Brigade.

6. Command of the Sector will pass to G.O.C., 59th Division at 6 p.m. on August 27th; at which hour 74th Div.H.Q. closes at BUSNES and opens at NORRENT FONTES.

7. Details from the Divisional Reception Camp, including 'B' Teams will join their units on their arrival in the new areas. Those of the 229th Infantry Brigade will proceed to the new area on August 27th.

8. Completion of all reliefs will be reported by wire to Divisional Headquarters.

9. ACKNOWLEDGE.

A.C.Tempersley.

Lieut. Colonel,
General Staff,
74th (Yeomanry) Division.

Issued at ...R.6ns...

Copies to:-
```
    No. 1.  'G'                       No.12.  A.D.M.S.
     2-4.  'Q'                          13.  Div.Train.
       5.  C.R.A.                       14.  XIth Corps.
       6.  C.R.E.                       15.  61st Division.
       7.  O.C., Signal Coy.            16.  19th Division.
       8.  O.C., M.G.Battn.             17.  59th Division.
       9.  229th Infantry Bde.          18.  O.C. 74th Reception Camp
      10.  230th Infantry Bde.      19-20.  War Diary.
      11.  231st Infantry Bde.          21.  File.
```

RELIEF TABLE.

SERIAL NUMBER.	DATE.	UNIT.	FROM.	TO.	RELIEVED BY.	REMARKS.
1.	Aug. 26th	177th Inf.Bde.	LAMBRES Area.	Support Bde Area.		By Bus.
2.	"	231st Inf.Bde.	Support Bde Area.	LA LACQUE - MAZING-HEM - LAMBRES - WITTERNESSE Area.	177th Inf.Bde.	By Bus.
3.	"	176th Inf.Bde.	St.HILAIRE Area.	Reserve Bde Area.		
4.	"	230th Inf.Bde.	Reserve Bde Area.	St.HILAIRE - COTTES - LESPESSES - BOURECQ Area.	176th Inf.Bde.	March not to commence before 3 p.m.
5.	"	M.G. Company. (59th Div)	ESTREE BLANCHE.	Forward Area.		relieve night 26/27th August.
6.	"	59th M.G.Battn. (less 1 Coy)	"	LABIETTE Farm.		relieves 74th M.G.Bn less 1 Coy.
7.	"	74th M.G.Battn. (less 1 Coy)	LABIETTE Farm.	GUARBECQUE & BERGUETTE.	59th M.G.Battn.	Probably by bus
8.	Aug. 27th.	1 Coy,74 M.G.Coy.	Line.	"	Coy, 59th M.G.Bn.	
9.	"	Field Coys.R.E. & Pioneer Bn, 59th Division.	ESTREE BLANCHE.	74th Div.Area.	—	By Bus.
10.	"	Pioneer Battn.	74th Div.Area.	OBLOIS Wood in N.18.c.	59th Pioneer Bn.	
	"	Field Coys,R.E.	"	Respective Bde Groups.	Field Coys, 59th Div.	as detailed by C.R.E.

SERIAL NUMBER.	DATE.	UNIT.	FROM.	TO.	RELIEVED BY.	REMARKS.
11.	Aug. 27th/28th	178th Inf.Bde.	HAM Area.	Support Brigade Area.		Arrive by bus 8 p.m.
12.	" "	177th Inf.Bde.	Support Bde Area	Line.		
13.	" "	229th Inf.Bde.	Line.	HAM - HARQUEVILLE - MOLINGHEM - CORNET BOURDOIS Area.	177th Inf.Bde.	By Bus.

Headquarters.
　229th Infantry Brigade.
　231st Infantry Brigade.
　'Q' Branch. (for information.)

Reference Divisional Order No 79 and Serial Nos of attached Relief Table as under :-

1.　Serial No 2.

　　Embussing points for 231st Brigade :-

　　(a) For Bde H.Q. and 2 Battalions - head of convoy P.9.b.8.9.

　　(b) For One Battalion - head of convoy at Road Junction P.23.c.8.3.

2.　Serial No 13.

　　Embussing points for 229th Brigade - as in para (1) above.

for Lieut Colonel.
General Staff.
25th August 1918.　74th (Yeomanry) Division.

"A" Form
MESSAGES AND SIGNALS.

Army Form C. 2121
(In pads of 100)

Prefix......Code......m.	Words.	Charge.	This message is on a/c of:	Recd. at..........m.
Office of Origin and Service Instructions				Date..................
	Sent At......m.		................Service.	From..................
	To........			By....................
	By........		(Signature of "Franking Officer.")	

TO { 229 Bde.   C.R.A.   A.D.M.S.   5 Corps.
     230 Bde   C.R.E.   Div. Train.
     231 Bde.   ....Signal Co.

Sender's Number.	Day of Month.	In reply to Number.	AAA
G.774	29		

Amendment 74 Divl Order No 80 aaa Bde Groups as stated in para 2 of above order will now be billetted as under aaa 229 Bde Group FRANVILLERS LAHOUSSOYE area aaa 230 Bde Group HEILLY area aaa 231 Bde Group MERICOURT L'ABBE - RIBEMONT area aaa R.A. Group BONNAY area aaa Div will be held ready to move Eastwards at short notice tomorrow 30th inst aaa ACKNOWLEDGE aaa Addressed all concerned.

HJR 1030

From 74 Div.
Place
Time

The above may be forwarded as now corrected.   (Z) A. [signature]   Capt GS
                              Censor.   Signature of Addressor or person authorised to telegraph in his name.

* This line should be erased if not required.

"C" Form.   Army Form C.2128.
MESSAGES AND SIGNALS.   No. of Message 120

| Prefix....Code....Words | Received. From Inf 10 By | Sent, or sent out. At...........m. To........... By | Office Stamp. |

Charges to Collect
Service Instructions

Handed in at Hqd   Office ...m. Received 6.30 m.

TO   231 Bde

Sender's Number.	Day of Month.	In reply to Number.	AAA
G7/1	28		
Ref	Div	order	no 80
ada	amend	grouping	of
field	coys	as	follows
aaa	439	Field	Coy
to	229	Coy	aaa
R&RE	231	Group	added
229	and	231.	Bde
C&RE	Q		

FROM
TIME & PLACE

SECRET.   Copy No. 17

74th DIVISION ORDER No.80.

Appendix XXXV

28th August 1918.

Reference 1:100,000 Sheets 11 & 17.

1. 74th Division is moving by rail to the Fourth Army area. Administrative Instructions have been issued by the A.A.&.Q.M.G.

2. Brigade Groups will be formed.
   The Division will be billetted in the new area as under:-

   Div.H.Q.   BEAUCOURT SUR L'HALLUE (Sheet 17 F.1)

   229th Brigade Group.)
     229th Inf.Bde   )
     R.A.R.E.   ) BEAUCOURT - MONTIGNY Area.
     74th Bn.M.G.C.   )
     No.2 Coy. Div.Train.)
     229th Field Amb.   )

   230th Brigade Group.)
     230th Inf.Bde   )
     R.M.R.E.   ) BAVELINCOURT - BEHENCOURT Area.
     No.3 Coy. Div.Train.)
     230th Field Amb.   )

   231st Brigade Group.)
     231st Inf.Bde   )
     439 Field Coy. R.E.) CONTAY Area. (F.6. Sheet 11).
     12th L.N.Lancs.Rgt.(P))
     No.4 Coy. Div.Train.)
     231st Field Amb.   )

   R.A. Group.   FRECHENCOURT.

3. Divisional H.Q. will close at NORRENT FONTES at 3 p.m. on August 29th and open at BEAUCOURT at the same hour.

4. ACKNOWLEDGE.

                                    A C Temperley
                                    Lieut.Colonel.
                                    General Staff.
                                    74th (Yeomanry) Division.

Issued at 5 P.M.

   Copies to:-
     No.1. 'G'   12. A.D.M.S.
      2-4. 'Q'   13. Div. Train.
        5. C.R.A.   14. XIth Corps.
        6. C.R.E.   15. IIIth Corps.
        7. O.C., Sig.Coy.   16-17. War Diary.
        8. O.C., M.G.Bn.   18. File.
        9. 229th Inf.Bde.
       10. 230th "   "
       11. 231st "   "

"A" Form
MESSAGES AND SIGNALS.

Army Form C. 2121 (in pads of 100).

229 Bde	CRA	ADMS	3 Corps	
230 Bde	CRE	Div Train	Q	
231 Bde	MGBn	Signal Coy		

TO:

Sender's Number	Day of Month	In reply to Number	AAA
G 774	29		

Amendment 74 Div Order No 80 aaa Bde Groups as stated in para 2 of above order will now be billeted as under aaa 229 Bde Group FRANVILLERS LAHOUSSOYE area aaa 230 Bde Group HEILLY area aaa 231 Bde Group MERICOURT L'ABBE – RIBEMONT area aaa RA ready to move Eastwards at short notice tomorrow 30th inst aaa ACKNOWLEDGE aaa Addressed all concerned.

From: 74 Div
Place:
Time: 4.30 pm

(Sgd) A Galoway Capt

"A" Form.
MESSAGES AND SIGNALS.

Army Form C. 2121.
(In pads of 100,)

app XXXVII

TO: 229 Bde Signals. "Q" Train.
231 Bde C.R.E. A.D.M.S. AAA

G. 798 31

74 Div is relieving 58 Div in line to-night aaa 229 and 230 Bde groups will move up by bus aaa Details later

From: 74 Div

10.10. a.m.

Lt Col. GS.

SECRET.

XXXVIII

Copy No.....1...

74th DIVISION ORDER No.81.

31st August 1918.

1. 74th Division is relieving 58th Division.

    Groups will be formed as under:-

    229th Brigade Group.
    229th Inf.Bde.
    2 M.G.Companies.
    439 Field Coy. R.E.
    229th Field Amb.

    230th Brigade Group.
    230th Inf.Bde.
    1 M.G.Company.
    R.M.R.E.
    231st Field Amb.

    231st Brigade Group.
    231st Inf.Bde.
    R.A.R.E.
    1 M.G.Company.
    230th Field Amb.

2. Dismounted personnel will move by bus.
    B.G.C., 229th Inf.Bde will be responsible for moving M.G.Battn to MARICOURT; thence the Coy will join their respective Brigade Groups. M.G.Battn H.Q. will relieve that of 58th M.G.Battn.
    231st Inf.Bde will be responsible for moving Pioneer Battn to MARICOURT area where they will bivouac.

3. 229th Inf.Bde will relieve the Brigade in the line.
    230th Inf.Bde will relieve the Support Brigade.
    231st Inf.Bde will be in Reserve West of MARICOURT.

4. Busses will be detailed as under:-

    Busses for 800 men will arrive at cross-roads S.W. of FRANVILLERS at 2 p.m. for 229th Bde.
    Busses for 6,000 men will arrive at same place at 3-30 p.m. whence they will be despatched by Div.Staff Officer as required, (i) to cross roads in J.13.a for 230th Inf.Bde (ii) MERICOURT Church for 231st Inf.Bde (iii) remain at FRANVILLERS cross roads for 229th Inf.Bde.
    They will proceed to MARICOURT where guides for 230th and 229th Brigades will meet them.

    The 2nd Echelon of busses of 229 Bde will leave FRANVILLERS at 6 p.m. proceed direct to CLERY.

5. Transport will march as under:-

    229th Bde via ALBERT - FRICOURT and will be clear of FRICOURT at 6 p.m.
    230th Bde South of the ANCRE via MEAULTE and will not pass FRICOURT before 6 p.m.
    231st Bde will follow 230th Bde.

6. Artillery relief will take place later.

7. The hour of command passing to G.O.C., 74th Division has not yet been fixed, probably 10 a.m. on Sept.1st.

8. ACKNOWLEDGE.

                                        A C Temperley
                                        Lieut.Colonel,
                                        General Staff,
                                        74th (Yeomanry) Division.

Issued at 1.30 p.m.

Copies to:-

No. 1.	"G"	12.	A.D.M.S.
2-4.	"Q"	13.	Div. Train.
5.	C.R.A.	14.	III Corps.
6.	C.R.E.	15.	58th Divn.
7.	O.C., Sig. Coy.	16-17.	War Diary.
8.	O.C., 74th Bn. M.G.C.	18.	File.
9.	229th Inf. Brigade.		
10.	230th Inf. Brigade.		
11.	231st Inf. Brigade.		

SECRET.

S.G. 16/3/1.

Reference 74th DIVISION ORDER No.81.

1. The relief is postponed.

The concentration of the Brigade Groups in the 58th Divisional Area will continue and they will bivouac in 58th Div. Area.

All other arrangements hold good except that;-

(a) 2nd Echelon of busses of 229th Brigade will not proceed to CLERY and will move as soon as they are loaded to MARICOURT.

(b) 2nd Echelon of busses for 231st Brigade (the returning busses for 800 men which carried 1st Echelon of 229th Bde) will be met at BRONFAY FARM (F.29.b) by Reserve Brigade, 58th Division to whom they will be handed over. 231st Brigade personnel in these busses will then march to MARICOURT. It may be necessary for some of the busses of 230th Bde to be handed over also.

2. In para. 4 of Div.Order No.81 for "J.13.a." read "J.13.b."

[signature]

Lieut.Colonel.
General Staff.
74th (Yeomanry) Division.

31st August 1918.

To all recipients of 74th Div.Order No.81.

SECRET.
******

Headquarters.
III Corps.

No RA/2255.

74th Division. (2 copies)
****

Reference Map Sheet 620.

1. The 74th Divisional Artillery will march from BONNAY Area to Valleys in A.20., A.21., A.26., and A.27., South of MARICOURT on the morning of the 1st September.

2. There are no restrictions as to times or routes.

3. There are water troughs at MOULIN DE FARGNY.

4. The 74th Divisional Artillery will be moved into action under the orders of the 74th Division on the 2nd September.

5. 74th Division to acknowledge to IIIrd Corps R.A.

                          (Signed) M.H.Dendy.
                                Major. G.S.
31/8/18.   for B.G., G.S. III Corps.

Copies to :- 'G'
            'Q'
            58th Division (2 copies)
            47th Division. (2 copies)
            18th Division. (2 copies)
            A.D. Signals.
            C.E.

Headquarters.
   229th Infantry Brigade.
   230th Infantry Brigade.
   231st Infantry Brigade.
   O.C. Signals.

     Every indication points to the fact that the Division will very shortly be engaged in the battle South of ARRAS.
     The chief failures in our recent advance require immediate attention and these failures must be brought home to all concerned without delay.

    (a)   Ignorance of contact patrol work. Flares were rarely lit at all. Those that were lit were usually lit when an artillery machine came over.
         The use of contact aeroplanes is fully explained in S.S.135 Appendix 'B'. Flares are lit when called for by contact aeroplanes which send the letter 'A' on a klaxon horn.
         All contact aeroplanes have special markings.

    (b)   Failure to use alternative means of communications. When lines were cut, runners only were usually employed. Pigeons were hardly ever used. The O.C. Pigeon Lofts reports that birds were neglected and badly treated owing to the fact that pigeon men were constantly being changed while no birds were used for proper messages. Practically no use was made of visual, or power buzzer. Some C.Os complained that they had not time to code messages for the Power Buzzer and therefore they did not use it.

     It is unnecessary to labour the points mentioned in either (a) or (b). Failures under either of these headings may lead to serious loss of life and imperil the success of operations.

     The G.O.C. directs that immediate steps be taken to bring these failures home to every one.

                                        Lieut Colonel.
                                        General Staff.
27th August 1918.   74th (Yeomanry) Division.

BELGIUM 1:100 000   TOURNAI

TOURNAI

2ND EDITION

SECRET

Headquarters.
   229th Infantry Brigade.
   230th Infantry Brigade.)
   231st Infantry Brigade.)
   C.R.A.   )   for information.
   O.C. 74th Bn. M.G.C.)
   'Q' Branch.   )

        The G.O.C. considers it desirable that you should be placed in possession of his policy before taking over the Front Line.

INFORMATION REGARDING THE ENEMY.

1.   Information points to the fact that the enemy main line is approximately R.8.central - BEAUPRE (L.32.central).
     In front of this line an outpost position strong in Machine Guns along ABBEY Road - EPINETTE - about L.31.central. At present the enemy is prepared to fight hard for the retention of his outpost line and to counter attack if necessary.

INTENTION OF G.O.C.

2.   It is not the intention of the G.O.C. to attempt to force the enemy back. His object is to keep close touch with the enemy, to test constantly the strength of his defences by active patrolling, to capture isolated posts in front of his line, to follow him closely if he shows signs of withdrawing, and to avoid casualties.

METHOD OF ADVANCING.

3.   If patrols or other sources of information discover the enemy is withdrawing, the method to be adopted is as follows :-
     Patrols will follow the enemy closely to some definite objective selected by you. When the patrols are on this objective platoons will be sent forward to make it good. Once the objective has been made good, a fresh advance by patrols will be made and the same procedure followed.
     The enemy is watchful and will counter attack if he considers the pressure too great. Such counter attacks if Lewis Guns are well handled, should prove particularly expensive for him.

METHOD OF HOLDING THE LINE.

4.   The line should be held on the principles laid down in the amended Defence Scheme (a) a line of observation of section posts, (b) a line of supports consisting of platoon posts with some forward machine guns, (c) and outpost line of resistance held by Battn Reserves with Rear Machine Guns.
     No elaborate defences should be constructed in the forward area. In case of hostile shelling, positions of posts should frequently be changed.

/5. Preparation

- 2 -

PREPARATION IN CASE OF AN ADVANCE.

5.   It will be important to bring up your Battn 1st Line Transport and the transport of M.G.Coy at once to enable them to get forward.

The transport of the L.T.M's must be provided from your Brigade resources. Some forward M.G's and L.T.M's are very important on reaching a new line.

The most advanced troops, in case of a forward movement, must always be in possession of (a) Aeroplane flares, (b) S.O.S. rockets, (c) a few message carrying rockets.

The Divisional Train must be made to deliver your rations well forward if you are advancing otherwise the 1st Line Transport will be compelled to deposit their loads and go long distances to draw rations while your men will be worn out by parties at night carrying the material which should be brought up by the 1st Line Transport.

ARTILLERY.

6.   The 117th Bde R.F.A. is supporting the Infantry very closely, with F.O.O's in or close to the Front Line. They can engage any target such as a hostile machine gun or T.M. at once.

Please ensure close personal liaison between Company Commanders and Artillery.

SIGNALS.

7.   When lines are cut, Company and Battn Commanders have shown considerable reluctance to use any other means of communication but that of runners. This is slow, costly in life, and very wearing to the men. Pigeons, power buzzer and visual have rarely been used.

FIELD COMPANY.

8.   The Field Company is at present entirely under your orders. Should the line remain stationary, it will be transferred to the command of the C.R.E. but will remain affiliated to your Brigade.

Lieut Colonel.
General Staff.
74th (Yeomanry) Division.

24th August 1918.

SEEN BY:-
G.O.C.........
G.S.O.I.......
G.S.O.II......
G.S.O.III.....
....

S E C R E T.
****

Headquarters,
III Corps.

No. RA/2255.

74th Division. (2 copies).
****

Reference Map, Sheet 62C.

1. The 74th Divisional Artillery will march from BONNAY Area to Valleys in A.20., A.21., A.26., and A.27., South of MARICOURT on the morning of the 1st September.

2. There are no restrictions as to times or routes.

3. There are water troughs at MOULIN DE FARGNY.

4. The 74th Divisional Artillery will be moved into action under the orders of the 74th Division on the 2nd September.

5. 74th Division to acknowledge to IIIrd Corps R.A.

M.H. Dendy

31/8/18.

Major G.S.,
for B.G., G.S., III Corps.

Copies to :- G.
              Q.
              58th Division. (2 copies).
              47th Division. (2 copies).
              18th Division. (2 copies).
              A.D. Signals.
              C.E.

Copy sent to CRA

14th
Division
General Staff
September
1918

Confidential

D.A.A.G.

Herewith war diary for October along with narrative of Operations on the Somme which was not completed when September war diary was sent away –

A Cunningham
B.
6/x/s.

Army Form C. 2118

WAR DIARY
or
INTELLIGENCE SUMMARY

(Erase heading not required.)

Instructions regarding War Diaries and Intelligence Summaries are contained in F. S. Regs., Part II. and the Staff Manual respectively. Title Pages will be prepared in manuscript.

Place	Date	Hour	Summary of Events and Information	Remarks and references to Appendices
	Sept 1st		Divisional Headquarters closed at BEAUCOURT CHATEAU at 11 a.m. and opened at New Headquarters at H.3.b.central, Sheet 62.c. at 4 p.m. The relief of 58th Division by 74th Division was completed in accordance with 74th Division Order No 81 and the command passed to G.O.C., 74th Division at midnight Sept 1st/2nd. Orders were received from III Corps that the attack would be continued on September 2nd by 74th Division on the Right, 47th Division in the centre, and 18th Division on the left. The 2nd Australian Division were to co-operate on the right of the 74th Division. 74th Division Order No 82 was issued, detailing 229th Brigade as the Attacking Brigade. 230th Brigade as Support, and 231st Brigade as Reserve.	App. I.
	Sept 2nd	6.25 a.m.	229th Brigade reported that the relief was carried out successfully and that when our Barrage started at 5.30 a.m. the enemy put down a barrage on road in G.20.	
		8.15 a.m.	229th Brigade reported that their Left Battalion had been held up by Machine Gun fire from MOISLAINS but was reported to be advancing again.	
		8.45 a.m.	Troops of 229th Brigade reported to have crossed Canal du NORD in G.24 and later were counter-attacked from direction of MOISLAINS.	
		8.55 a.m.	230th Brigade report that Australian attack is making good progress up slope from Canal to PERONNE - NURLU Road. One Battalion 230th Brigade being moved forward to establish touch with Australian left flank and to seize high ground along line of PERONNE - NURLU Road from Australian left flank to junction of road D.20.d.0.5.	
		9.5 a.m.	Wire sent to III Corps that 229th Brigade had crossed the Canal and were counter attacked from MOISLAINS, but were again going forward. One Battery 77 mm guns was reported captured.	
		9.50 a.m.	2nd Australian Division report their troops are on line of road I.6.d.9.4. to I.6.d.3.0. and in touch with both flanks.	
		11.0 a.m.	Wire sent to III Corps, that advanced troops 229th Brigade reported to have reached D.14, but reported to have been driven back to area OPERA Trench. Right Battalion 229th Brigade reported to be in touch with 2nd Australian Division and advancing towards high ground in D.19 at 9 a.m.	

Army Form C. 2118

WAR DIARY
or
INTELLIGENCE SUMMARY
(Erase heading not required.)

Instructions regarding War Diaries and Intelligence Summaries are contained in F. S. Regs., Part II. and the Staff Manual respectively. Title Pages will be prepared in manuscript.

Place	Date	Hour	Summary of Events and Information	Remarks and references to Appendices
	Sept 2nd	4.35 p.m.	Situation wire sent to Corps and usual addresses. 230th Brigade in touch with 2nd Australian Division in C.5.b. thence line runs West North-West to SCUTARI Trench. Thence along SCUTARI and BROUSSA Trenches to 47th Division about C.18.d.5.0. Men of mixed units in trench about C.32.d.central to C.17.central. Many Australians and men of 47th Division in BROUSSA and ANGORA Trenches. 229th Brigade now reorganizing in old line.	App. II.
		5.0 p.m.	Wire sent out ordering 230th Brigade to hold line between 2nd Australian Division and SCUTARI TRENCH. 229th Brigade to hold from Left of 230th Brigade Northwards along old line to Point where 47th Division is holding. Boundary between 229th and 230th Brigades to be arranged between Brigades concerned. Brigades to reorganize as soon as possible and get their Machine Guns in depth. 230th Brigade will be in Divisional Reserve and will occupy high ground with Machine Gun Company on line B.24, B.18. 231st Brigade to be prepared to move to fresh bivouac about B.22.b.9.0. and B.23.a. during the evening.	
		7.40 p.m.	229th and 230th Brigades ordered to advance their line at dusk to approximately C.28.d. - ANSPACH TRENCH - MOISLAINS TRENCH, as far as Divisional Boundary and to relieve troops of 47th Division in C.17.b. & d. Line to be held as Outpost Line and troops to be economised as much as possible. Divisional NORTHERN Boundary grid line between C.11 and C.17.	App. III.
		8.0 p.m.	Wire received from 229th Brigade giving Boundary between 229th and 230th Brigades as East and West grid line through C.22.central, inclusive to 229th Brigade.	
		8.15 p.m.	Wire received from III Corps ordering consolidation and reorganization in depth. 74th Division to take over from 47th Division the defence of all trenches including MOISLAINS Trench South of East and West Grid line through C.10.d.0.0. After consultation with 2nd Australian Division 74th Division may withdraw during the night all troops South of CANAL DU NORD. 74th Division to establish a joint liaison post with Australians in vicinity of Canal and inform Corps Headquarters of its location.	
		3.50 p.m.	Situation wire received from 230th Brigade reporting that about 100 Gas shells (Yellow Cross) fell in area C.27.a. since 12 noon. 12 low flying Enemy aeroplanes flew over 230th Brigade line at 5.30 p.m. but were driven off by Lewis Gun fire.	

Army Form C. 2118

WAR DIARY
or
INTELLIGENCE SUMMARY
(Erase heading not required.)

Instructions regarding War Diaries and Intelligence
Summaries are contained in F.S. Regs., Part II.
and the Staff Manual respectively. Title Pages
will be prepared in manuscript.

Place	Date	Hour	Summary of Events and Information	Remarks and references to Appendices
	Sept 2nd	10.50 p.m.	Late air reconnaissance 7.30 to 7.45 p.m. reported trenches between BUSSU WOOD and NURLU - AIZECOURT Road and trench round EAST of AIZECOURT full of enemy. Many gun flashes seen from GURLU and BUIRE WOODS and Woods South of BUSSU.	
		About 9 p.m.	Australian Division asked to release one Battalion of 230th Brigade South of CANAL DU NORD in time to allow it to be withdrawn to locality C.28.c. before dawn unless withdrawal possible by daylight.	
	Sept 3rd.	5.50 a.m.	229th Brigade report quiet night with some gas shelling. Relief quickly effected. Large fire burning in direction of NURLU.	
		5.55 a.m.	230th Brigade report situation unchanged. Some gas shelling during night. Enemy aircraft bombed and machine gunned front line twice during the night.	
		6.0 a.m.	Situation wire from III Corps. Fairly quiet night. Fully confirmed that enemy still holding on and no signs of withdrawal.	
		6.10 a.m.	Wire sent to III Corps, that relief of 47th Division in C.17.b. & d. completed. Situation report. Quiet night with some gas shelling. Large fire burning in direction of NURLU.	
		8.15 a.m.	Telephone message from Corps. Aeroplanes report at 6.15 a.m. that many villages in front of our line are on fire probably indicating a withdrawal.	
		8.30 a.m.	229th and 230th Brigades informed of indications of enemy withdrawal and ordered to push out mounted and infantry patrols to find out the situation.	
		9.30 a.m.	Wire sent to 229th Brigade, that No. 2 Company 22nd Corps Cyclist Battalion will be attached 229th Brigade and will be bivouaced in MARRIERES WOOD, C.19.a. The Company is in need of rest and orders were given that it was not to be employed without reference to Divisional Headquarters.	

1875 Wt. W593/826 1,000,000 4/15 J.B.C. & A. A.D.S.S./Forms/C. 2118.

Army Form C. 2118.

WAR DIARY
or
INTELLIGENCE SUMMARY.
(Erase heading not required.)

Instructions regarding War Diaries and Intelligence Summaries are contained in F. S. Regs., Part II. and the Staff Manual respectively. Title pages will be prepared in manuscript.

Place	Date	Hour	Summary of Events and Information	Remarks and references to Appendices
	Sept 3rd	10.20 a.m.	Wire sent out ordering 229th Brigade in co-operation with Left Brigade 2nd Australian Division to advance the lines to approximately L.30.central, C.24.central, thence back to the old line about C.17.central. When line established 230th Brigade to remain in SUPPORT. Method of advancing to be by patrols which will establish post. The line then to be made good.	App. IV.
		10.40 a.m.	Divisional Order 83 issued. In case of advance 230th Brigade to act as Advanced Guard. Right Divisional Boundary C.29.central, C.30.central, thence Eastwards. Left Divisional Boundary Grid line eastwards between C.11 and C.17.	App. V.
		10.45 a.m.	Wire received from III Corps. The 2nd Life Guards M.G. Battalion less two Companies at present under 47th Division to be transferred to 74th Division on night 3rd/4th September. Present location A.19.b.5.2.	
		10.45 a.m.	Wire received from III Corps giving Divisional and Corps Boundaries in case of enemy withdrawal. Southern Corps Boundary through C.29.central. Between Right and Centre Divisions through C.19.d.9.0.	
		1.10 p.m.	230th Brigade reported that one of their patrols on reaching Canal in C.23.d. was sniped from C.24.d., and that another patrol was shelled immediately it moved from the line N.E. of HAUT ALLAINES and was fired on from MIDINETTE Trench and AIZECOURT.	
		2.30 p.m.	229th Brigade reported that one of their patrols reached LA TORTILLE River in C.24.d. and followed the river to within 200 yards of MOISLAINS where they were fired on from MOISLAINS. A second patrol proceeded East through C.5.c. and d. None of our infantry were found East of line through C.5.central and C.11.central. SORROWITZ Trench and MONASTIR Trench in C.6.c. were unoccupied, but MONASTIR Trench in C.12.b. was occupied by enemy who also had a post in C.6.d.9.3.	
		12.29 p.m.	230th Brigade informed that "B" Squadron, NORTHUMBERLAND HUSSARS would be located in area to be selected by O.C., Squadron about B.30. O.C., Squadron to report to B.G.C., 230th Brigade on arrival. Exact location notified later at H.6.a.5.3.	

Army Form C. 2118

WAR DIARY
or
INTELLIGENCE SUMMARY
(Erase heading not required.)

Instructions regarding War Diaries and Intelligence Summaries are contained in F. S. Regs., Part II. and the Staff Manual respectively. Title Pages will be prepared in manuscript.

Place	Date	Hour	Summary of Events and Information	Remarks and references to Appendices
	Sept 3rd.	5.9 p.m.	230th. Brigade Report. One patrol which left our lines at 11 a.m. reached D 25 a 2.4. Considerable sniping from slopes in D 25 a and b and M.G. fire from COUTURAS COPSE was encountered. Enemy work in D 25 a was unoccupied. Nine enemy posts all occupied were observed on S.W. slopes of ridge through D 19 Central. Enemy M.G. was observed while being withdrawn into strip of wood in D 19 c. A second patrol starting at the same time reached D 19 c 34 were four enemy posts were encountered, one of which was attacked, but coming under enfilade Machine Gun fire from MOISLAINS and WOOD in D 19 D, the patrol was forced to withdraw.	
		6.30 p.m.	229th. Brigade reported that patrols returned at 4.30 p.m, having reached C 17 d 6.4, C 17 d8.4 and C 17 b 4.8 being held up at those points by Machine Gun fire from MOISLAINS.	
		6.45 p.m.	230th.Brigade reported snipers S.E. bank of Canal from C 28d to C 24a 6.5 and several M.Gs, on WEST side of MOISLAINS.	
		8.10 p.m.	Telephone conversation with Brigade Major 230th.Brigade. Orders given to form a Liaison post with Left Australian Div. at C 28d 8.5.	
		8.45 p.m.	229th.Brigade patrol 1 Off. and 3 O.Rs, returned with information that SLAG HEAP near Canal Lock in C 24a held by enemy with several M.Gs at 5 p.m. Patrol was fired on by M.Gs from S, of MOISLAINS and was unable to get beyond C 30a Central. 229th.Brigade were unable to advance by day to the line laid down in wire sent out at 10.20 a.m., but are to carry out the operation during the night Sept. 3/4th.	
		7.40 p.m.	Warning order sent out by wire. On night Sept 4th/5th Division will side slip Southwards. Boundaries not definitely fixed but will probably on the Right, I.10.central - I.12.central Eastwards. On the Left, grid line between C.17 and C.23. Dividing line between Brigades grid line between C.29 and I.5. Eastward. 230th Brigade will take over Right sector. 231st Brigade Left Sector. 229th Brigade will be withdrawn to Divisional Reserve. Reconnaissance to be carried out on Sept 4th for attack in conjunction with flank Division Eastward by 230th and 231st Brigades upon three systems of trenches contained by squares J.1., J.4., D.22., D.19. The battalion of the 230th Brigade South of CANAL DU NORD was not withdrawn by dawn on Sept 3rd and it was not found possible to withdraw the Battalion during the day. The Battalion spent the day in a trench running through I.5.a. & b. and were withdrawn to North of Canal after dark on night Sept 3rd/4th.	

Army Form C. 2118

WAR DIARY
or
INTELLIGENCE SUMMARY

(Erase heading not required.)

Instructions regarding War Diaries and Intelligence Summaries are contained in F. S. Regs, Part II and the Staff Manual respectively. Title Pages will be prepared in manuscript.

Place	Date	Hour	Summary of Events and Information	Remarks and references to Appendices
	Sept 4th	5.20 a.m.	229th Brigade reported that their right Battalion had made good the new line from C.24.central Southwards towards C.30.central. No report received from Right Company of Right Battalion. No reports received from Left or Centre Battalions owing to communication being broken. Enemy shelling more intense during night, and C.25.b. and C.21. shelled with Blue Cross gas shells during the night.	
		5.30 a.m.	The above situation wired to III Corps.	
		6.0 a.m.	Telephone message from 229th Brigade to say that Centre Battalion established on line C.17.d. 8.4. to C.24.central.	
		6.10 a.m.	Situation wire sent to Corps giving position of Centre and Right Battalions on line C.17.d.8.4. to C.24.central, thence Southwards in direction of C.30.central. Position of Left Battalion not yet known.	
		8.15 a.m.	Location 230th Brigade as follows :- 15th Suffolks C.28.d.4.0., along SCUTARI TRENCH to C.22.c. 4.0. thence 10th Buffs to C.16.c.7.4. 2 sections of Machine Gun in this line. 16th Sussex in C.23.c. and North part of I.2.d. 1 section Machine Guns in YASSA Trench.	
		10.35 a.m.	Situation wire to Brigades and Divisional troops giving 229th Brigade line as follows - C.30.d.6.0. - C.24.c.7.8. thence just in rear of trench cutting sunken road at C.17.d.4.8. thence MOISLAINS Trench to Divisional Boundary.	
		10.49 a.m.	Air report from III Corps. No signs of occupation of NURLU - TEMPLEUX LA FOSSE line.	
		11.50 a.m.	Divisional Order No. 84 sent out ordering side slip Southwards of 74th Division night 4th/5th. Divisional Boundaries laid down. The 231st and 230th Brigades to take over Right and Left sectors respectively, and not as ordered in Warning order issued 7.40 p.m. September 3rd.	App. VI.
		12.35 p.m.	229th Brigade report one prisoner taken at D.1.c.0.3. at 10.30 a.m.	

Army Form C. 2118.

WAR DIARY
or
INTELLIGENCE SUMMARY.
(Erase heading not required.)

Instructions regarding War Diaries and Intelligence Summaries are contained in F. S. Regs., Part II. and the Staff Manual respectively. Title pages will be prepared in manuscript.

Place	Date	Hour	Summary of Events and Information	Remarks and references to Appendices
	Sept 4th	1.45 p.m.	Situation wire to III Corps reporting that right of 229th Brigade definitely in touch with troops of 2nd Australian Division. Mounted patrol reported to have crossed Canal at C.6.d.9.3. where bridge is blown up. Bridges across Canal at C.18.b., C.24.a., C.23.d. also destroyed. Water in canal North of Bridge C.6.d.9.3. but to South of this Canal is dry as the water is diverted into the TORTILLE RIVER.	
		2.16 p.m.	229th Brigade reported heavy gas shelling in area C.22.a., C.22.b., 7 a.m. to 10.30 a.m. with Yellow and Blue Cross. 160 Yellow Cross shells fell in C.26.a. and b. from 8.30 to 10.30 a.m. 140 Green Cross in C.21.d. at 3 a.m.	
		2.30 p.m.	III Corps informed that patrols of 229th Brigade now on line of canal in C.18. Devons and Royal Highlanders moving forward to make good line of canal as far as Divisional Boundary, with patrols pushing forward to OPERA TRENCH.	
		3.20 p.m.	229th Brigade ordered to push forward patrols immediately to regain touch with enemy. R.A.F. report no enemy on TEMPLEUX - NURLU Ridge. 47th Division pushing forward on North of 229th Brigade.	
		5.7 p.m.	Situation wire from 229th Brigade reporting C.17.d., C.21.c.6.8., C.16.d. heavily shelled at intervals since 11.30 a.m. Large number enemy aircraft 10.30 a.m. to 12.45 p.m.	
		6.30 p.m.	47th Division reported that their patrols had been through MOISLAINS and found the village quite clear of enemy.	
		8.17 p.m.	229th Brigade reported patrol of Corps Cavalry just returned, they were fired on by enemy machine guns at 7.25 p.m. from posts about D.19.d.2.7., D.25.a.8.5. and J.1.a.8.8.	
		9.5 p.m.	Mounted patrol report sent on to III Corps.	
		10.21 p.m.	Dusk air patrol report large number of fires S.E. PERONNE. Enemy seen in D.8.c.	

Army Form C. 2118.

WAR DIARY
or
INTELLIGENCE SUMMARY.
(Erase heading not required.)

Instructions regarding War Diaries and Intelligence Summaries are contained in F. S. Regs., Part II. and the Staff Manual respectively. Title pages will be prepared in manuscript.

Place	Date	Hour	Summary of Events and Information	Remarks and references to Appendices
	Sept 4th	11.25 p.m.	230th Brigade as Advanced Guard Brigade (Divisional Order No.83) is ordered to push on with greatest boldness in event of enemy trenches in front of Divisional front being found unoccupied by enemy.	App. VII.
		8.22 p.m.	47th Divisional Order received. 142nd Brigade will relieve left of 229th Brigade.	
		11.36 p.m.	229th Brigade reported two weak patrols proceeded via Slag dumps to junction of trench D.13.c.7.1. thence up hill to D.13.b.7.5. They met no opposition and returned owing to darkness.	
		10.30 p.m.	47th Division reported that post had been established at D.7.c.7.6., D.7.c.5.2., D.13.a.2.8.	
	Sept 5th	12.5 a.m.	Wire to Corps reporting that command of new Sector passed to G.O.C., 74th Division.	
		12.10 a.m.	Wire to Corps and flank Divisions reporting two weak patrols proceeded via C.24.central to junction of trench D.13.c.7.1. thence up hill to D.13.b.7.5. They met no opposition and returned owing to darkness.	
		12.35 a.m.	Left Battalion, 2nd Australian Division established posts at I.6.a.5.8., C.30.c.8.7., C.30.c.5.3. in close touch with right of 74th Division.	
		2 a.m.	2nd Australian Division wire that command of sector North of East and West grid line through I.12.central passed to G.O.C., 74th Division.	
		5.35 a.m.	47th Division reported heavy gas shelling in Squares C.11 and C.15 at 2.15 a.m. MOISLAINS shelled earlier with all calibres up to 8 inch and with gas.	
		6.10 a.m.	230th Brigade reported relief of left portion of line completed by 2 a.m. Patrols report that MIDINETTE Trench held by enemy about D.19.d.	

WAR DIARY or INTELLIGENCE SUMMARY

(Erase heading not required.)

Army Form C. 2118

Place	Date	Hour	Summary of Events and Information	Remarks and references to Appendices
	Sept 5th	7.45 a.m.	231st Brigade reported relief of two Battalions in front line completed.	
		9.45 a.m.	47th Division definitely reported they have reached line D.9.a.0.6. - Quarry in D.15.a. - OAT COPSE and are advancing Eastwards.	
		9.30 a.m.	Telephone message from 47th Division to report that their Advance Guard Brigade have reached D.9.central - Quarry in D.15.d. - D.15.central.	
		10.35 a.m.	231st Brigade order received. 25th R.W.F. and 10th K.S.L.I. to push on and make every effort to clear up AIZECOURT and occupy LARRIS and MESERITZ TRENCH.	
		11.15 a.m.	231st Brigade ordered to form defensive flank along Spur on J.8.a. and b., J.7.b. and c. as the 230th Brigade continues to advance.	
		11.30 a.m.	Wire to III Corps reporting that our troops are reported to have reached MIDINETTES TRENCH in D.19.d. at 11 a.m.	
		12.15 p.m.	231st Brigade operation order received. 231st Brigade to be in Support to 230th Brigade who are pushing on. One Battalion of 230th Brigade will pass through 231st Brigade. 25th R.W.F. will be responsible for protection of Right flank in case 230th Brigade advances more quickly than Australian Division Left.	
		12.20 p.m.	Wire received from III Corps reporting that there is every indication that the enemy is about to continue his retirement on the whole Fourth Army Front. Divisions to follow up the enemy energetically with advance guards.	
		12.40 p.m.	Wire sent to 230th and 231st Brigades ordering 230th Brigade to push on across NURLU - PERONNE Road to next objective J.4.central - D.28.central - D.22.c. and a. 231st Brigade to form defensive flank along Ridge in J.7.c. and b., J.8.a. and b. This Order had been previously given verbally to B.G.C., 230th Brigade and B.G.C., 231st Brigade by the G.O.C. at about 10 a.m.	App. VIII.

Army Form C. 2118.

WAR DIARY
or
INTELLIGENCE SUMMARY.
(Erase heading not required.)

Instructions regarding War Diaries and Intelligence Summaries are contained in F. S. Regs., Part II. and the Staff Manual respectively. Title pages will be prepared in manuscript.

Place	Date	Hour	Summary of Events and Information	Remarks and references to Appendices
	Sept 5th	12.56 p.m.	230th Brigade reported that one company of 10th Buffs had taken MIDINETTE Trench from D.19.d.8.9. to D.19.d.2.9.	
		1.30 p.m.	231st Brigade reported 10th Battn, K.S.L.I. had occupied posts in D.25.a.5.5. and D.25.a.5.8. enemy machine gun located at D.25.d.9.3. enemy also in occupation of LARRIS Trench.	
		1.27 p.m.	5th Australian Division reported their troops in occupation of BOINGT, and Australian Left pushing on to BUSSU, in touch with 74th Division Right.	
		9.40 a.m.	The Squadron of Australian Light Horse attached 230th Brigade to be relieved by Northumberland Hussars and come into Divisional Reserve, but to be available for Advanced Guard if required. One troop of Northumberland Hussars placed at disposal of B.G.C., 231st Brigade.	
		1.30 p.m.	Wire received from 47th Division reporting that their troops have been seen round SIGNAL COPSE.	
		1.40 p.m.	Contact patrol at 12.30 p.m. reported our troops seen in FAUCON Trench V.22.a. along road to V.27.central in trench to D.3.central - D.9.b. - D.15.central - up to road D.15.0.0. - through D.20.b. and c. and in touch E. of AIZECOURT to BUSSU WOOD - J.7.a. Strong patrols seen to be pushing E. of this line apparently meeting with no opposition.	
		2.25 p.m.	230th Brigade reported that they were in possession of MIDINETTE Trench and pushing on to final objective.	
		3.0 p.m.	2.30 p.m. Air patrol reported, Germans holding trenches from NURLU - D.9.d. - D.15.b. and d. including OAT COPSE - D.21 - SEVE WOODS to D.26.	
		3.50 p.m.	230th Brigade report. Left Battalion pushing on to second objective but report that they are not in touch with Brigade on Left. Right Battalion also pushing on, counterattack appears to have been made from direction of BUSSU. Brigade H.Q. to be moved shortly to D.25.d.	

Army Form C. 2118.

WAR DIARY
or
INTELLIGENCE SUMMARY.
(Erase heading not required.)

Instructions regarding War Diaries and Intelligence Summaries are contained in F. S. Regs., Part II. and the Staff Manual respectively. Title pages will be prepared in manuscript.

Place	Date	Hour	Summary of Events and Information	Remarks and references to Appendices
	Sept 5th	4.36 p.m.	230th Brigade report. At 3.50 p.m. Suffolks reported to be in J.1.b.8.8. to D.25.d.9.4. trying to get touch with Australians.	
		5.0 p.m.	Wire to 230th Brigade saying that Australians some distance in rear of 230th Brigade line, and that therefore 231st Brigade must be relied on to protect the flank.	
		5.0 p.m.	47th Division order received. Intention of 47th Division to push on at 7 p.m. under artillery barrage to line of trench in D.9.b. and d. and D.15.a. to main road at D.15.a.9.2. thence S.W. along main road to Divisional Boundary.	
		5.38 p.m.	Left Brigade of 3rd Australian Division entered BUSSU and are established 300 yards E. of that place.	
		6.0 p.m.	230th Brigade report Suffolks D.27.c.central to J.2.d.central.	
		7.0 p.m.	231st Brigade report 25th R.W.F. established their H.Q. at BUSSU WOOD, J.7.a.9.7. and endeavouring to get in touch with Suffolks on 230th Brigade Right. 25th R.W.F. in touch with Australians 300 yards E. of BUSSU.	
		7.45 p.m.	230th Brigade line as follows :- J.13.central to J.3.b.5.8.; D.27.d.7.3. along contour to D.27.b.5.5. Heavy enemy shelling on MIDINETTE Ridge and Valley, E.30 and D.25 including gas.	
		8.20 p.m.	Divisional Order No 85 issued. Ordering the continuation of advance at 8 a.m. on the 6th instant.	
		9.40 p.m.	Situation wire to Corps giving Divisional Front as follows :- J.13.central - J.8.central - J.3.central - thence along track in J.3.b., D.27.b. and d., D.27.b. and c., D.21.b. and c., D.20.b.8.4., on Divisional Boundary. In touch with Australians at BUSSU, but not in touch with 47th Division on left Division Boundary, who are some way behind.	App. IX.

Army Form C. 2118.

WAR DIARY
or
INTELLIGENCE SUMMARY.
(Erase heading not required.)

Instructions regarding War Diaries and Intelligence Summaries are contained in F. S. Regs. Part II. and the Staff Manual respectively. Title pages will be prepared in manuscript.

Place	Date	Hour	Summary of Events and Information	Remarks and references to Appendices
	Sept 5th	10.50 p.m.	Artillery arrangements with reference to Divisional Order No. 85. Wire sent out to 230th, 231st Brigade and C.R.A. conveying congratulations of Corps Commander to the Attacking Brigades and the artillery covering them on the excellent work done by them during the day.	App. X.
	Sept 6th	8.0 a.m.	Wire received from 230th Brigade that they had occupied for the night the line of trench D.8.central - D.3.central - D.27.d. and b. - D.21.c. to Divisional Boundary.	
		9.35 a.m.	Wire from 230th Brigade that Buffs reported at 8.45 a.m. that they had reached first objective line D.28.c.8.5. to D.22.c.3.9., and that Suffolks at 9.28 were advancing 800 yards E. of TEMPLEUX Trenches. Corps informed, also flank Divisions, and all concerned within Division.	
		9.40 a.m.	Order No. 316 from Corps received, - defining policy of heavy pressure on enemy and giving Boundary lines and objectives for various bounds to be made by the III Corps. Northern Boundary line of Division altered from E. and W. line through D.22.a.0.4. to D.22.c.0.4.	
		10.55 a.m.	47th Division reported that they were in possession of whole Trench system in D.10 and D.16. and advancing East.	
		11.20 a.m.	Warning Order issued for 231st Brigade to pass through 230th Brigade and resume the advance tomorrow 7th instant.	App. XI.
		11.35 a.m.	230th Brigade report their Left Battalion on line D.30.c.8.5. to D.24.a.8.0. In touch with Battalion on Right, but no trace of 47th Division on Left. This repeated to Corps, 47th Division and all concerned.	
		1.40 p.m.	74th Divisional Order No 86 issued ordering 231st Brigade to pass through 230th Brigade and carry on attack on morning of 7th instant, also that 229th Brigade Group would move during the afternoon to vicinity of AIZECOURT.	
		3.10 p.m.	Two front line Companies of Buffs reported that final objective was reached. This message was sent by pigeon and arrived at 5.23 p.m., their line was K.3.a.0.9., E.26.central, E.20.d.central.	App. XII.

Army Form C. 2118.

WAR DIARY
or
INTELLIGENCE SUMMARY.
(Erase heading not required.)

Instructions regarding War Diaries and Intelligence Summaries are contained in F. S. Regs., Part II. and the Staff Manual respectively. Title pages will be prepared in manuscript.

Place	Date	Hour	Summary of Events and Information	Remarks and references to Appendices
	Sept 6th	3.35 p.m.	Wire from 230th Brigade confirming phone message that at 2.50 p.m. troops of Left Battalion had been observed E. of LONGAVESNES nearing Blue line. B.G.C., 230th Brigade did not propose to advance further till Divisions on both flanks were up in line with him.	
		6.0 p.m.	230th Brigade reported finally that both Battalions were on their objectives, and that line was:- K.29.central - K.3.central - K.3.a.0.9. - E.26.central, E.20.d., in touch with Brigades on Right and Left. This was reported to Corps and all concerned at 8.10 p.m.	
		6.0 p.m.	230th Operation Order No 63 received giving instructions regarding 231st Brigade resuming the attack and dispositions of 230th Brigade subsequent to relief by 231st Brigade, battalions going to following areas :- Suffolks to K.2., Buffs to E.20.c. and E.26.a., Sussex to D.29. Squadron of Northumberland Hussars to be transferred to 231st Brigade. ~~at 10.30 p.m.~~	
		10.30 p.m.	Intention of 3rd Australian Divisions to advance from 500 yards E. of Red line (see map issued with III Corps O.O. No 316) at 3.30 a.m. morning 7th instant.	
		10.50 pm.	231st Brigade orders received for resumption of advance, 24th Welsh attacking on Right of the line, and 10th K.S.L.I. on Left. 25th Bn. R.W.F. in Brigade Reserve. One Squadron Northumberland Hussars to watch Northern flank. Brigade Headquarters to be at D.28.c.8.4.	
	Sept 7th	5.30 a.m.	Quiet night spent. Troops of 231st Brigade in position ready to pass through 230th Brigade line. 58th Division now on left of the Division having relieved 47th Division during the night.	
		9.40 a.m.	Report received from 231st Brigade that at 8.45 a.m. line ran about 400 yards from VILLERS FAUCON and that troops were working round flanks. Slight Machine gun fire from village was being dealt with by artillery.	
		10.15 a.m.	Priority wire from 231st Brigade reporting that at 9.25 a.m. left Battalion had entered VILLERS FAUCON from both flanks. This was reported to Corps and all concerned.	

Army Form C. 2118.

WAR DIARY
or
INTELLIGENCE SUMMARY.
(Erase heading not required.)

Instructions regarding War Diaries and Intelligence Summaries are contained in F. S. Regs., Part II. and the Staff Manual respectively. Title pages will be prepared in manuscript.

Place	Date	Hour	Summary of Events and Information	Remarks and references to Appendices
	Sept 7th	11.55 a.m.	58th Division reported that their infantry who had been held up at SALCOURT WOOD had passed it and were advancing towards CAPRON COPSE.	
		11.30 a.m.	231st Brigade reported that their Right Battalion had reached Railway line K.5.c. and b. Left Battalion had entered VILLERS FAUCON and their patrols were approaching STE EMILIE.	
		12.15 p.m.	229th Brigade ordered to move to LONGAVESNES during the afternoon to take over duty of Support Brigade on arrival. 230th Brigade on relief to come into Divisional Reserve.	
		2.22 p.m.	58th Division reported that their Right Battalion on line running N. and S. through E.17.cent at 1.45 p.m.	
		2.45 p.m.	231st Brigade reported that patrols of Left Battalion entered STE EMILIE but were forced to withdraw owing to our own heavies shelling the village.	
		3.45 p.m.	231st Brigade Order received. Left Battalion is to conform with advance of 175th Brigade and to swing up their left to trench line F.19.b.3.4. - F.19.c.7.6. - F.19.d.1.0. No advance to be made beyond that line during the night. Battalion to consolidate position and patrol front actively. Patrols of Northumberland Hussars to gain touch with enemy.	App. XIII.
		5.30 p.m.	Order sent out giving New Northern Divisional Boundary as East and West grid line separating E.7 and E.13. Readjustment to take place on morning of Sept 8th by Advanced Guard Brigade passing through that portion 58th Divisional Front South of New Divisional Boundary. Details to be arranged between Brigadiers concerned. The command of the new Sector of the Divisional Front passed to G.O.C., 74th Division at the time the Advanced Guard Brigade passes through the line.	
		5.45 p.m.	231st Brigade reported that they were established on Blue Line.	
		6.45 p.m.	231st Brigade reported that Line of Left Battalion as follows :- E.23.b.9.4. - E.24.a.4.4. - E.24.cent - F.19.c.0.0. - F.25.a.5.0. No further advance possible till 58th Division comes up on left.	

Army Form C. 2118.

WAR DIARY
or
INTELLIGENCE SUMMARY.
(Erase heading not required.)

Instructions regarding War Diaries and Intelligence Summaries are contained in F. S. Regs., Part II. and the Staff Manual respectively. Title pages will be prepared in manuscript.

Place	Date	Hour	Summary of Events and Information	Remarks and references to Appendices
	Sept 7th	9.41 p.m.	229th Brigade reported the move completed and the Brigade Group in area East of LONGAVESNES at 7.30 p.m.	2.
	Sept 8th	12.10 a.m.	231st Brigade informed that 3rd Australian Division on Right do not intend to make any general advance during the day, but will send out patrols to help our advance. The 229th Brigade in Support may be called on to supply such assistance as is necessary to form a defensive flank to the South.	
		5.0 a.m.	Situation. Quiet night. Enemy aircraft active bombing behind the line.	
		7.30 a.m.	Command of new Sector of Divisional Front passed to G.O.C., 74th Division.	
		8.55 a.m.	Left Company of Left Battalion of Advanced Guard Brigade reported to be advancing at 8.15 a.m. simultaneously with troop of 174th Brigade.	
		9.20 a.m.	Advanced Guard Brigade report their left on railway at F.13.a.3.9. 174 Brigade not up in line. Our artillery firing short in neighbourhood.	App. XIV.
		9.50 a.m.	Forecast of moves sent out to 3 Brigades, C.R.A. and 'Q'. 229th Brigade will go through 231st Brigade on morning of 9th instant, or relieve it on night of 8th inst according to the situation. 231st Brigade will become Support Brigade. The 229th Brigade will be supported by 2 Coys of machine guns. Divisional H.Q. will move to J.11.c.central on 9th inst.	
		10.45 a.m.	Advanced Guard Brigade report that line of Right Battalion runs as follows :- L.1.b.3.0. to 100 yards E. of BOULEAUX WOOD in F.25.b. thence to about F.19.d.central when in touch with Left Battalion.	

Army Form C. 2118.

WAR DIARY
or
INTELLIGENCE SUMMARY.
(Erase heading not required.)

Instructions regarding War Diaries and Intelligence Summaries are contained in F. S. Regs., Part II. and the Staff Manual respectively. Title pages will be prepared in manuscript.

Place	Date	Hour	Summary of Events and Information	Remarks and references to Appendices
	Sept. 8th.	11.25 a.m.	Owing to Div. to North of 58th. Div being much behind, it is intention of 58th. Div. Commander not to push on further than high ground East of EPEHY thence through F 26-F 8b and d -F 90. 231 Brigade ordered if practicable to secure high ground in F 25 - F 26a. Eastern Edge of RONSSOY and of BASSE BOULOGNE thence N.W. to join 58th.Div about F 9c.	APP. XV.
		5.0 p.m.	231 Brigade report 2 P/W belonging 2nd Battn. 1st Jaeger Regt. captured F 13b 3.5.	
		5.27 p.m.	Wire received from 58th.Div stating that 175 Brigade report at 4.10 p.m. that they have not been relieved nor have troops of 74th.Div passed through them South of new Divisional Boundary E and W gridLine through F 8c 9.9.	APP. XVI.
		6.10 p.m.	Definite order sent to 231 Brigade to take over responsibility for line to Divisional Boundary on North.	APP. XVII.
		6.15 p.m.	Order sent out for the relief of Advanceded Guard Brigade by 229th. Brigade night 8/9th.Sept. One Company L.G.M.G. Battn. to be attached to Advanced Guard Brigade. Squadron Northumberland Hussars and 44th. Battery R.F.A. to be transferred to 229th.Brigade. 231 Brigade to become Support Brigade, located about LONGAVESNES.	
		8.20 p.m.	Orders sent out that there will be no general advance on 9th.inst. Line to be straightened and consolidated and touch with flanks secured.	
		10.25 p.m.	Australian intention to make a general advance during the night to line R 1 Central to L 7 Central.	
		10.20 p.m.	58th.Div report 9th.Londons in touch with 25th.R.W.F. on left ef of 231 Brigade in E 18b 5.3. At 6.45 p.m. 174 Brigade line reported to be W 29d 6.0 - along trench W 29d 6.0 - along trench E 5b and d - East side of sunken road E 11b - along trench E 11d to boundary line.	
	Sept. 9th.	5.15 a.m.	Situation Wire. Quiet night, nothing to report.	

Army Form C. 2118.

WAR DIARY
or
INTELLIGENCE SUMMARY.
(Erase heading not required.)

Instructions regarding War Diaries and Intelligence Summaries are contained in F. S. Regs., Part II. and the Staff Manual respectively. Title pages will be prepared in manuscript.

Place	Date	Hour	Summary of Events and Information	Remarks and references to Appendices
	Sept. 9th.	7.50 a.m.	10th.Australian Brigade (Left of 3rd.Australian Division) report all their battalions on their objective, and patrols sent out.	APP XVIII
		8.55 a.m.	231 Brigade report that relief of two Battalions 231 Brigade by 229 Brigade completed.	
		9.40 a.m.	58th.Div Report that during the night four Lewis Gun Posts were pushed forward in F 7a and 0.	
		10.30 a.m.	In view of Australian occupation of new line through L 7, L 13, L 19 without opposition, the 229 Brigade ordered to push forward strong patrols, and if practicable make good the following line in Co/operation with 58th. Div - Spur F 26a - RONSSOY - BASSE BOULOGNE- thence N.W. to F 9c.	
		11.40 a.m.	Advanced posts of 58th.Div in F 7a driven in by counter attack.	
		11.59 a.m.	229 Brigade report relief of 231 Brigade completed.	
		12.00 noon	34 Enemy Aircraft reported over 229 Brigade lines at 8 a.m.	
		1.02 p.m.	Patrols of 229 Brigade report enemy holding BOULEAUX WOOD F 25b with Machine Guns. Enemy also located on Ridge F 20 a 5.6.	
		1.05 p.m.	Patrols of 229 Brigade report 3rd. Australian Division have a post at L 7a 6.8. 229 Brigade have established a post at L 7a 5.8 and are in touch with the 3rd.Australian Division.	
		3.00 p.m.	Div. Order No.87 issued ordering 229 Brigade to make good tonight the Spurs in F 26a. F 20 Central - F 19b in order to enable them to advance in conjunction with the 58th.Division on 10th.inst. if their attack on EPEHY was successful.	
		8.30 p.m.	229 Brigade reported that the Devons had established a post in Trench F 26a 3.2.	

Army Form C. 2118.

WAR DIARY
or
INTELLIGENCE SUMMARY.
(Erase heading not required.)

Instructions regarding War Diaries and Intelligence Summaries are contained in F. S. Regs., Part II. and the Staff Manual respectively. Title pages will be prepared in manuscript.

Place	Date	Hour	Summary of Events and Information	Remarks and references to Appendices
	Sept. 9th.	10.55 p.m.	229 Brigade reported that at 6.40 p.m. Patrols were sent out from Left Battalion to make good trench in F 20b - F 14d - F 13d,0 and a. These patrols reported at 10.30 that trench in F 20b 10.4 to F 14c 9.4 very strongly held.	
	Sept. 10th.	5.00 a.m.	No definite information received from 229 Brigade except that a post had been established at F 26a 3.8.	
		10.15 a.m.	Right Battalion succeed in working along Southern Spur as far as Sunken Road in F 20 a and b. Enemy shelled this area heavily also our posts at F 26 a & 3.2 which had to withdraw. During the morning the two advanced Battalions were heavily counter attacked and at 1 p.m. had withdrawn to line L la Central - F 25 Central - F 19 Central - F 13 Central.	
		1.30 p.m.	Order was issued to 229 Brigade to hold the above line and that no further advance would be attempted.	
		1.30 p.m.	Div. Order No.88 was issued ordering 230th.Brigade to relieve 229th.Brigade who would come into Divisional Reserve. 231 Brigade to remain in support.	APP. XX
		5.00 p.m.	No change in the situation.	
	Sept. 11th.	5.00 a.m.	Situation unchanged.	
		12.40 p.m.	230th.Brigade report that a patrol of the 16th. Sussex proceeded at dawn and found BOULEAUX WOOD (F 23b) to F 26c 2.4 and F 26a 2.1 unoccupied by the enemy except for a few snipers in N.E. corner of the Wood. No M.G. Fire was encountered.	
		5.00 p.m.	Situation unchanged. Left Brigade reports front line intermittently shelled by 77mm guns. Trenches West of RONSOY in F 20 b and d reported strongly held by M.G.	

Army Form C. 2118.

WAR DIARY
or
INTELLIGENCE SUMMARY.
(Erase heading not required.)

Instructions regarding War Diaries and Intelligence Summaries are contained in F. S. Regs., Part II. and the Staff Manual respectively. Title pages will be prepared in manuscript.

Place	Date	Hour	Summary of Events and Information	Remarks and references to Appendices
	Sept. 11th.	9.30 p.m.	In accordance with Orders from Corps Instructions were sent that 231 Brigade would be disposed so as to be able to man the main line of resistance at short notice. Two Battalions to be in rear of sector which they may have to hold. Main line of Resistance being K 9 Central - K 3 - E 26 Central - E 20 b and d - E 15 a and b -. 229th. Brigade to be withdrawn to area about TEMPLEUX- LA-FOSSE or trench system J 6 - D 29 - D 23. No units to be located in LONGAVESNES.	APP. XXI
		9.30 p.m.	Warning Order telegraphed to XXII Corps Cyclists Coy to rejoin their Battalion at COMBLES on the 12th.	APP. XXII
	Sept. 12th.		Situation remained unchanged during the day. Patrolling was carried out, Machine Gun fire was experienced, but no enemy patrols were encountered. Defence Instructions No.1 - Covering action to be taken by the Advanced Guard & Support Brigade and Reserve Brigade, supplimenting Appendix XXI above, issued.	APP. XXIII
		6.00 p.m.	Right Battalion report they were establish Lewis Gun post at F 26a - (BOULEAUX WOOD) to-night.	
	Sept. 13th.	5.00 a.m.	Situation unchanged. Quiet night in the line.	
		8.20 a.m.	Sussex - the Right Battalion report Lewis Gun post (referred to above) at F 26a - had to withdraw under cover of a Bombing Party owing to gun jamming during an attack by the enemy during night.	
		3.25 p.m.	Warning Order. 231st.Brigade will relieve 230th. in the line as far South as F 19 d 0.2 on night 14/15th.	
		11.00 a.m.	A Conference was held at Divisional Headquarters at 11 o'clock - Present B.Gs.C.229,230 and 231 Brigades, C.R.A., C.R.E., G.S.O (1) and O.C. 74th. Machine Gun Battalion.	APP. XXIV.
		9.00 p.m.	Considerable Enemy Air Bombing Activity from about 9 p.m. to 12 midnight. Two enemy planes were brought down by our own planes. One wounded Artificer N.C.O. who decended in a parachute from one of these planes was captured by the 16th.Sussex.	

Army Form C. 2118.

WAR DIARY
or
INTELLIGENCE SUMMARY.
(Erase heading not required.)

Instructions regarding War Diaries and Intelligence Summaries are contained in F. S. Regs., Part II. and the Staff Manual respectively. Title pages will be prepared in manuscript.

Place	Date	Hour	Summary of Events and Information	Remarks and references to Appendices
	Sept. 14th.	5.00 a.m.	Situation unchanged, quiet night in the line except for slight enemy artillery activity.	ag
		9.30 a.m.	Conference at Divisional Headquarters at 9.30 a.m. - Present B.Gs.C. 229,230, and 231 Brigades, C.R.A., C.R.E., G.S.O.(1) and O.C. 74th. Machine Gun Battalion.	
		8.00 a.m.	Divisional Order No.89 concerning movement of 231st. Brigade into the line issued.	APP. XXV
	Sept. 15th.	5.00 a.m.	Quiet night - nothing to report.	
		4.30 p.m.	Divisional Order No. 90 issued.	APP. XXVI. ag
		7.20 p.m.	Reference Divisional Order No.90 - 53rd. Brigade will relieve 231st. Brigade in line on night 16/17th. as far South as F 19 c 9.4 and 231st. Brigade will relieve 230th. Brigade in the line as far South as F 25 Central.	APP. XXVII.
	Sept. 16th.	5.00 a.m.	Quiet night - Enemy Artillery active against SPUR QUARRY.	
		3.10 p.m.	Orders issued in accordance with instructions from see III Corps that all troops of 18th. Div Coming into Divisional Area forward of line North and South through E 8 Central would come under tactical command of G.O.C. 74th. Division until 10 p.m. on 17th. inst. and that Battalion of 18th. Division relieving the Left Battalion of the Division would come under the orders of B.G.C. 231st. Brigade till 10 p.m. on 17th. inst.	ag.
	Sept. 17th.	12.30 a.m.	Telephone message received from III Corps that F.O.O. reported VERY Lights were being put up by enemy further East than usual. Accordingly 230th. and 231st. Brigades were ordered to send out patrols to keep in touch with the enemy in case a withdrawal was taking place. No change in enemy dispositions was found by patrols. During the night enemy bombing aeroplanes were active especially in the vicinity of LONGAVESNES where a small amount of damage was done by their bombs.	ou
J.11.c.4.9.		5.0 a.m.	Except for heavy gas shelling of SPUR and FAUSTINE QUARRIES, the night was quiet.	ag.

Army Form C. 2118.

WAR DIARY
or
INTELLIGENCE SUMMARY.
(Erase heading not required.)

Instructions regarding War Diaries and Intelligence
Summaries are contained in F. S. Regs., Part II.
and the Staff Manual respectively. Title pages
will be prepared in manuscript.

Place	Date	Hour	Summary of Events and Information	Remarks and references to Appendices
	Sept 17th	1.0 p.m.	Final order issued stating that Zero hour would be 5.20 a.m. on 18th inst.	a.l.
		5.0 p.m.	Situation unchanged. Right Battalion report an aeroplane with British marking dropped 4 bombs in L.1.a.8.8.	
		5.35 p.m.	Owing to casualties suffered by 12th S.L.I. owing to gas, one Company of 14th Royal Highlrs ordered to join 12th S.L.I. at once.	APP. XXVII.
		5.50 p.m.	Orders issued that one Battery 44th Brigade, R.F.A. and one battery 230th Brigade R.F.A. will be prepared to cover infantry patrol on BLUE LINE.	
		10.30 p.m.	229th Brigade H.Q. opened at FAUSTINE QUARRY.	
	Sept 18th	5.15 a.m.	Situation during the night quiet nothing to report.	
		5.20 a.m.	Zero hour attack started according to plan in the midst of heavy rain and mist. Visual Station unable to see anything.	
		7.0 a.m.	230th Brigade report timed 6.5 a.m. enemy shelling heavy East Of Railway (E.30). All lines to battalions cut, visibility very bad.	
		7.20 a.m.	Telegram timed 7.2 a.m. from 230th Brigade reports no news, lines cut. still Shrapnel fire apparently on our old front line. Heavy shelling of railway continues.	
		7.40 a.m.	Divisional Artillery received wire from 117th Brigade timed 7.35 a.m. "F.O.O. reports first "objective taken. Infantry appear well ahead of consolidation point. Visibility very bad".	a.l.
		7.55 a.m.	Message from 1st Australian Division stating that. "Left Brigade report attack going well. "Troops well passed TEMPLEUX and British troops up with them on left. 7.38 a.m." ends.	

Army Form C. 2118.

WAR DIARY
or
INTELLIGENCE SUMMARY.
(Erase heading not required.)

Instructions regarding War Diaries and Intelligence Summaries are contained in F. S. Regs. Part II. and the Staff Manual respectively. Title pages will be prepared in manuscript.

Place	Date	Hour	Summary of Events and Information	Remarks and references to Appendices
	Sept 18th	8.15 a.m.	Wire from 230th Brigade that mopping up companies through TEMPLEUX. Front line 200 yards off first objective at 6.50 a.m. 50 P/W of 2nd Guard Division, FRANZ Regt reported captured. Reported to Corps and flank Divisions by wire.	
		8.30 a.m.	Nothing further received from 231st Brigade (line down).	
		9.40 a.m.	Definite information received that Right Brigade had reached their first objective, and taken 71 P/W of 2nd Guard Division and 96 I.R. of 38th Division. Reported to Corps, flank Divisions and 229th Brigade. No definite information of Left Brigade.	
		9.40 a.m.	230th Brigade reported that they were moving Brigade Headquarters to F.25.d.6.8. at 9.1 a.m.	
		10.0 a.m.	I.O. reported 1 officer and 20 O.Rs captured in L.2.c. belonging 9th and 11th Coys, 95 I.R. and first M.G.Coy, 94th I.R. (normal).	
		10.15 a.m.	F.O.O. of Left Group reported timed 9.15 a.m. and 9.30 a.m. our infantry approaching second objective and seen crossing ridge in F.29. Enemy barrage on RONSSOY and Valley in F.22.a. and c. Enemy artillery reported firing at short range from N.E. Telephoned to Corps.	
		10.30 a.m.	100 P/W have passed through Divisional Cage.	
		10.40 a.m.	Liaison Officer with 231st Brigade at 9.15 a.m. reported that our infantry were approaching the second objective and that the first objective is being consolidated. Right Battalion of 18th Division is on first objective, but Left Battalion held up in RONSSOY. Telephoned to Corps.	
		10.52 a.m.	44th Brigade R.F.A. does not think infantry have reached 2nd objective but are making good progress. Batteries have got direct observation. Mobile Battery (230th Brigade, R.F.A.) is going forward.	

Army Form C. 2118.

WAR DIARY
or
INTELLIGENCE SUMMARY.
(Erase heading not required.)

Instructions regarding War Diaries and Intelligence Summaries are contained in F.S. Regs., Part II. and the Staff Manual respectively. Title pages will be prepared in manuscript.

Place	Date	Hour	Summary of Events and Information	Remarks and references to Appendices
	Sept 16th	11.10 a.m.	F.O.O. reported 231 Brigade Troops seen on second objective at 10.55 a.m. and moving about freely there. Success signals seen on 18th Division front. Wired to Corps and Flank Divs.	APP. XXVIII.
		12.0 noon	As situation of 18th Division was obscure, half a company, Machine Gun Battalion is placed under orders of 231st Brigade to protect Left flank.	
		12.40 p.m.	231st Brigade report timed 11 a.m. that our infantry are on RED Line. Wired to Corps and flank Divisions.	
		12.40 p.m.	F.O.O. reported from HUSSAR POST that our infantry were East of RED Line at 12.35 p.m.	
		1.40 p.m.	Message No I.O.5 received from Intelligence Officer giving apparent Enemy Order of Battle opposite this Division states that about 500 P/W have passed through Cage. Message repeated to Corps and flank Divisions.	
		2.30 p.m.	230th Brigade reports their troops are reported 1100 yards East of RED Line and are advancing towards BLUE line.) Wired to Corps, 1st Australian Division and 231 Brigade.	
		3.15 p.m.	Left Brigade reported by R.A. not on RED line but in switch and along wire in F.23.c. and a. In touch with 18th Division at F.23.a.5.3. RED line now being attacked by 231 Brigade under artillery bombardment.) Wired to Corps and flank Divs. Buffs reported at 2 p.m. in or nearly in BLUE line.	
		3.35 p.m.	231 Brigade ordered to attack that portion of RED line which has not been occupied at 5 p.m. under an artillery barrage in conjunction with 18th Division who are attacking at the same time.	
		4.15 p.m.	Report from 230 Brigade that their Right Battalion has 2 Coys on RED line and that their Left battalion has not yet reached it being held up by machine guns on their left. Wired to Corps and flank Divisions to cancel report previously sent them that we held RED line and were in or nearly in the BLUE line.	

Army Form C. 2118.

WAR DIARY
or
INTELLIGENCE SUMMARY.
(Erase heading not required.)

Instructions regarding War Diaries and Intelligence Summaries are contained in F. S. Regs., Part II. and the Staff Manual respectively. Title pages will be prepared in manuscript.

Place	Date	Hour	Summary of Events and Information	Remarks and references to Appendices
	Sept. 18th.	5.0 p.m.	Information received from 231 Brigade that Right Battalion have definitely occupied RED line. Left Battalion believed also to have done so, but this not certain. Corps informed that Right Battalion has reached RED Line.	APP. XXIX.
		6.5 p.m.	Telephone message received that our Infantry were seen at 5.45 p.m. crossing Ridge in F 23 b and d behind our barrage.	
		7.0 p.m.	Infantry on RED Line on whole Divisional Front. We are in touch with the Australians, but no information yet about touch with 18th.Division. 550 P/W have passed through Divisional Cage and 108 wounded through A.D.S. Numerous others are still being employed on Road making and carrying wounded. Wired to Corps and Flank Divisions and 229th. Brigade.	APP. XXX.
		7.20 p.m.	Wire sent to Brigades and R.A. ordering the consolidation of the RED Line and no advance on to the BLUE Line tonight, also ordering Heavy Artillery Fire on BLUE line and counter preparation tomorrow at 5 a.m. Corps and Flank Divisions informed.	APP. XXXI.
		7.45 p.m.	18th Division not certain of their line, therefore 231 Brigade must be prepared to form a defensive flank.	
		7.45 p.m.	Orders issued to 229 Brigade to be prepared to man our former front line with 14th Royal Highlrs and that 'A' Coy, Lifs Guards, M.G.C. would come under orders of B.G.C. 229 Brigade.	
		8.50 p.m.	Message from 230th.Brigade that S.O.S. Signal had been sent up on their Left front, and that barrage had been put down by our artillery from F.24.c.3.0. to F.30.a.3.5. also that Right Battalion, 231 Brigade reported that they were being counter-attacked and were holding it.	
		9.0 p.m.	Telephone message from B.G.G.S., III Corps that aeroplane, just landed, reported our troops on general line A.23.d.5.0. - A.26.central - QUENNET COPSE (A.19.d.) thence to CAT COPSE.	
		9.10 p.m.	Phone message from Corps to say that Heavy Artillery O.P. reports S.O.S. Signal on our front at 8.40 p.m.	

Army Form C. 2118.

WAR DIARY
or
INTELLIGENCE SUMMARY.
(Erase heading not required.)

Instructions regarding War Diaries and Intelligence Summaries are contained in F. S. Regs., Part II. and the Staff Manual respectively. Title pages will be prepared in manuscript.

Place	Date	Hour	Summary of Events and Information	Remarks and references to Appendices
	Sept. 18.	10.30 p.m.	Information received that 18th Divisional line now runs F.22.b.6.0. - COLEEN POST - LEMPIRE CENTRAL.	APP. XXXII.
		10.30 p.m.	Orders issued that owing to the 18th Division being considerably behind us a new S.O.S. line will be arranged. 230th Brigade will exploit trenches in A.25 on 19th and C.R.A. will arrange for heavies to fire on trenches in front of 231st Brigade during the night.	
		11.55 p.m.	Orders issued to 231st Brigade that 18th Division are attacking at 11 a.m. in the morning in order to reach the RED line, when 231st Brigade will conform by bringing up their Left flank.	
	19th	6.0 a.m.	No reports received from either Brigades in the line.	
		7.50 a.m.	Order sent out that Battalions of 229th Brigade at present attached to other Brigades would revert to command of 229th Brigade and rejoin Brigade tonight.	
		10.0 a.m.	18 officers and just over 700 P/W through Divisional Cage. In addition 110 P/W O.R. evacuated wounded through Field Ambulance.	
		8.0 a.m.	Both Brigades report quiet night.	
		1.15 p.m.	Telephone message from 1st Australian Division to say that Right of 230th Brigade had withdrawn from ZOGDA Trench to RIFLE PIT SOUTH, leaving Left flank of Australian Division exposed, and asking that they should be instructed if possible to return to it.	
		5.35 p.m.	Evening Situation report sent to Corps etc. that a party of enemy attacked BENJAMIN POST at 1.30 p.m. but were easily driven off by rifle and Lewis Gun fire. Considerable movement seen in trench in G.2.a. and in QUENNEMONT PIT LANE and East of it. Yesterday's captures were 18 officers and 866 O.R. This includes 110 wounded P/W who passed through A.D.S.	
		8.30 p.m.	Corps telephoned to ask for G.O.C's Intentions regarding operations on 20th instz Reply sent that there would be no action beyond patrols on the lines indicated by Corps Commander to G.O.C. in the morning (19th). During the night 230th Brigade reoccupied ZOGDA TRENCH.	

Army Form C. 2118.

WAR DIARY
or
INTELLIGENCE SUMMARY.
(Erase heading not required.)

Instructions regarding War Diaries and Intelligence Summaries are contained in F. S. Regs., Part II. and the Staff Manual respectively. Title pages will be prepared in manuscript.

Place	Date	Hour	Summary of Events and Information	Remarks and references to Appendices
	20th	5.20 a.m.	Quiet night on the Divisional Front.	
		9.0 p.m.	18 Division have reached 'X', 'Y' and 'Z' COPSE.	
		10.45 a.m.	Warning order issued to Brigades, C.R.A. etc. that the BLUE BLUE line would be attacked by 230th and 231st Brigades under an artillery barrage tomorrow 21st inst.	APP. XXXIII.
		12.30 p.m.	The following enemy material captured on 18th inst reported by Brigades :- Ten guns 77 mm guns, three 4.2" Howitzers, five Trench Mortars and about 45 machine guns; also a certain amount of ammunition with the guns and a quantities of S.A.A. Wired to Corps.	
		1.45 p.m.	Wire received from 231st Brigade giving line as follows :- Right Battalion line F.23.d.8.0. to F.23.d.9.9. held by two companies in Support on line F.29.a.95.70. to F.23.c.6.4. Left Battalion hold line F.23.d.1.5. to F.23.c.5.8. with one company; another company F.23.c.5.8. to F.22.b.9.0., with two companies in Support in HUSSAR ROAD F.22.d. and F.23.c. Reserve Battalion on GREEN LINE, (TOINE TRENCH).	
		4.0. p.m.	Wire sent out giving the Infantry forming up line for attack on morning of Sept 21st. Four tanks to be attached to 231st Brigade for the attack. Probable ZERO HOUR at 5.40 a.m. Barrage arrangements laid down.	APP. XXXIV.
		6.0 p.m.	Divisional Order No 91 issued. 230th on Right and 231st Brigade on Left to attack on morning of 21st Sept. Objectives QUENNEMONT FARM, QUENNET COPSE, and GUILLEMONT FARM. 229th Brigade with one Battalion (8th Londons) of 58th Division attached will be in Divisional Reserve in GREEN LINE.	APP. XXXV.
		6.0 p.m.	Special instructions sent to 230th Brigade with reference to Div. Order No. 91. On reaching QUENNEMONT FARM a defensive flank to be formed through A.25. back to RED LINE about MALAKOFF FARM.	APP. XXXVI.

Army Form C. 2118.

WAR DIARY
or
INTELLIGENCE SUMMARY.
(Erase heading not required.)

Instructions regarding War Diaries and Intelligence Summaries are contained in F. S. Regs., Part II. and the Staff Manual respectively. Title pages will be prepared in manuscript.

Place	Date	Hour	Summary of Events and Information	Remarks and references to Appendices
	Sept 21st	6.0 a.m.	Quiet night. Slight shelling of forward areas. Enemy aeroplanes bombed TEMPLEUX le GUERARD.	
		6.55 a.m.	Phone message from 230th Brigade. "No news yet. Visibility bad owing to smoke of shells. Wires broken".	
		7.5 a.m.	R.A. report. "At 6.42 a.m. Our Infantry seen going over first crest. Enemy barrage very heavy".	
		7.10 a.m.	R.A. report. "6.45 a.m.". F.O.O. reports CAT POST in our hands".	
		7.15 a.m.	231st Brigade report capture of CAT POST at 6.45 a.m.	
		7.30 a.m.	230th Brigade seeing success signals on their front. (verbal).	
		7.50 a.m.	Wire from 230th Brigade timed 7.30 a.m. confirming report that 4 Green lights were observed on their front, indicating that BLUE line had been reached. Unable to say on what part of their front.	
		8.0 a.m.	Over 100 P/W observed coming down West of HUSSAR Road.	
		8.25 a.m.	Verbal report from 231st Brigade that 25th R.W.F. are believed to be on their final objective.	
		8.21 a.m.	117th Brigade, R.F.A. reported that 25th R.W.F. have taken their first objective and nearly reached second objective. 200 to 300 prisoners reported to be coming down.	
		8.22 a.m.	44th Brigade, R.F.A. reported that 230th Brigade were on their objective.	
		9.25 a.m.	Message from 25th R.W.F. timed 6.25 a.m. reported that 2 Tanks were broken down about F.24.c. and 2 others knocked out near BULL POST.	
		9.30 a.m.	4 officers and 94 O.R. captured by 230th Brigade about QUENNET COPSE belonged to 56th and 60th Regts of 121st Division.	

Army Form C. 2118.

WAR DIARY
or
INTELLIGENCE SUMMARY.
(Erase heading not required.)

Instructions regarding War Diaries and Intelligence Summaries are contained in F. S. Regs. Part II. and the Staff Manual respectively. Title pages will be prepared in manuscript.

Place	Date	Hour	Summary of Events and Information	Remarks and references to Appendices
	21st contd	10.0 a.m.	25th R.W.F. reached final objective at 6.50 a.m. At least 4 machine guns and 50 P/W captured.	
		10.30 a.m.	Verbal report from 18th Division that 24th WELSH are on their objective.	
		11.30 a.m.	Message sent to Brigades, Corps and Flank Divisions. "Runner reports our troops in GILLEMONT FARM and enemy still in OAT POST and being dealt with. Air report at 11 a.m., GILLEMONT FARM being shelled by enemy, and QUENNEMONT and PIT LANE TRENCHES empty."	
		11.40 a.m.	Wire from 230th Brigade stating that one Company Suffolks ordered to reinforce Sussex at QUENNET COPSE. The Battalion of 229th Brigade at disposal B.G.C., 230th Brigade to be moved forward to occupy RIFLEMAN POST, HUSSAR POST, ARTAXERXES POST and Cross Roads F.29.b.9.9.	
		12.45 p.m.	Report sent to Corps and Flank Divisions that Right Battalion, 230th Brigade driven out of QUENNEMONT FARM and are very reduced in numbers. Support Battalion of Right Brigade sent up to hold line of ZOO Trench. - Left Brigade definitely reported on its objective.	
		1.10 p.m.	Report from C.R.A. and 231st Brigade that enemy is still holding the Quadrilateral in F.18.c. and POT LANE. 117th Brigade shelling this and 10th K.S.L.I. going to attack it. Request by B.G.C., 231st Brigade that another Battalion of 229th Brigade should be put at his disposal.	APP XXXVII.
		1.20 p.m.	229th Brigade ordered to send forward one Battalion at once to occupy BELLICOURT Road from F.29.b.9.9. exclusive to Divisional Boundary. Battalion coming under orders of B.G.C., 231st Brigade on arrival. The remaining Battalion in Brigade Reserve (229th) to occupy GREEN LINE.	
		1.30 p.m.	Verbal report from 1st Australian Division that troops of 230th Brigade are now back in F.30 c. and that left	
		1.50 p.m.	Wire sent to Corps and Flank Divs that 230th Brigade has been driven back to RED LINE. Situation of Right Battn, Left Brigade not clear but Left Battn still believed to be holding GILLEMONT FARM.	
		2.0 p.m.	231st Brigade report out of touch with 54th Brigade, 18th Divn on their Left who have withdrawn from TOMBOIS FARM and EGG POST. 25th R.W.F. reported to have withdrawn to sunken road crossing trenches running through F.23.b. and d. and F.24.a. Enemy artillery increasing.	

Army Form C. 2118.

WAR DIARY
or
INTELLIGENCE SUMMARY.
(Erase heading not required.)

Instructions regarding War Diaries and Intelligence Summaries are contained in F. S. Regs., Part II. and the Staff Manual respectively. Title pages will be prepared in manuscript.

Place	Date	Hour	Summary of Events and Information	Remarks and references to Appendices
	21st contd	2.35 p.m.	Further situation sent to Corps and all concerned reporting withdrawal of 25th R.W.F. to sunken road described above.	
		5.25 p.m.	Situation wire sent to Corps and Flank Divs as follows :- Right Bde are reorganizing from A.25 d.O.0. along sunken road to F.29.b.9.9. with 3 Battns in line and one Battn about TEMPLEUX Switch. About 150 of 25th R.W.F. and 24th Welsh Regt are being reorganized about RIFLEMAN POST and moving to BENJAMIN POST. 10th K.S.L.I. hold RED LINE as far as CAT POST exclusive. One Battalion holding BELLICOURT Road from F.29.b.9.9. exclusive to Divisional Boundary. 229th Brigade holding GREEN LINE with 12th Somersets and 8th Bn, London Regt. Elements of two leading Battalions of Left Brigade were surrounded on three sides during counter attack and had to fight their way back. P/W so far reported 144.	
		6.10 p.m.	Order sent by wire to 231st Brigade reptd other Brigades, Flank Divisions and Corps. The 231st Brigade to attack CAT POST - DUNCAN POST Quadrilateral at 10.30 p.m. in close co-operation with Right Brigade, 18th Division. Intense bombardment to be arranged from 10 p.m. to 10.30 p.m. at which hour bombardment will lift and post will be rushed. RED LINE to be consolidated.	APP XXXVIII.
		6.55 p.m.	Amendment to above Order sent out. The attack will take place at 12.15 a.m. Bombardment will be from 12 midnight to 12.15 a.m.	APP XXXIX
		7.0 p.m.	229 Brigade informed that the Pioneer Battalion had been ordered to move forthwith to occupy Old Front Line L.1.a. - F.25.central - F.19.central, and would come under orders of B.G.C., 229th Brigade on arrival.	
		11.0 p.m.	18th Division counter-attacked and turned out of DOLEFUL POST and trench West of it.	
	Sept 22	2.10 a.m.	18th Divn reported that they had captured DUNCAN POST taking about 50 prisoners.	
		2.25 a.m.	10th K.S.L.I. reported to have occupied Southern portion of CAT POST Quadrilateral with practically no casualties. In touch with 18th Division.	

WAR DIARY
or
INTELLIGENCE SUMMARY.
(Erase heading not required.)

Army Form C. 2118.

Place	Date	Hour	Summary of Events and Information	Remarks and references to Appendices
	22nd contd	3.30 a.m.	Corps informed that Quadrilateral occupied.	
		3.35 a.m.	18th Div. reported to have retaken DOLEFUL POST.	
		5.10 a.m.	Corps informed that Quadrilateral occupied and in touch with 18th Divn.	
		5.55 a.m.	231st Brigade reported that 10th K.S.L.I. occupied the whole of DUNCAN POST – CAT POST Quadrilateral at 4 a.m., and was consolidating. About 50 prisoners sent down. Several machine guns captured and a considerable number of Germans killed. K.S.L.I. in touch with Bedfords on left and 25th R.W.F. on Right.	
		10.0 a.m.	Warning Order issued that the Division will be relieved in the line on night 24th/25th.	APP XL.
		1.15 p.m.	Order No 92 issued that 229 Brigade will relieve 230 Brigade in the line tonight. One Battn 239th Brigade to come under orders of 229th Brigade, remainder of 230th Brigade to be in GREEN LINE from South Divisional Boundary to TOINE POST exclusive.	APP XLI.
		5.30 p.m.	Situation report. Both Brigades disconnected to their Battalions but according to their F.O.O.s there is nothing to report. Estimated captures by K.S.L.I. in CAT POST Quadrilateral were last night were 200P/W, 30 M.Gs, and about 100 enemy dead were counted.	
		5.45 p.m.	Verbal order has been received that 18th Div. has been ordered to take over RED LINE to CAT POST inclusive. This was confirmed at 7.5 p.m. when orders were issued that K.S.L.I. would be relieved by 18th Div. as far South as CAT POST inclusive. On being relieved the K.S.L.I. are to be in Support to 229th Brigade and the area to be occupied by them is to be decided upon by B.Gs.C. 229th and 231st Brigades. The two machine guns in CAT POST will remain there and come under orders of 18th Divn.	
	23rd	2.20 a.m.	Relief by 229th Brigade completed.	
		5.20 a.m.	Quiet night. Slight shelling of Front line and HOSSAR ROAD.	

Army Form C. 2118.

WAR DIARY
or
INTELLIGENCE SUMMARY.

(Erase heading not required.)

Instructions regarding War Diaries and Intelligence Summaries are contained in F. S. Regs., Part II. and the Staff Manual respectively. Title pages will be prepared in manuscript.

Place	Date	Hour	Summary of Events and Information	Remarks and references to Appendices
	23rd contd	8.0 a.m.	231st Brigade reported that relief of 10th K.S.L.I. in CAT POST by 18th Div. was completed by 4 a.m.	
		11.0 a.m.	229th Brigade ordered to meet advance party of the Battalion of the 27th American Division and to show them the line preparatory to relief by that Division on night 24th/25th.	
		1.30 p.m.	Div. Order No 93 issued giving details of Relief of the Division by 1st Battn, 106th American Infantry Regt on night 24th/25th Sept.	APP XLII.
	24th.	5.45 a.m.	Situation wire to Corps. Situation unchanged. Enemy artillery very active throughout the night on forward areas. About 30 Yellow Cross Shells on F.29.b.	APP. XLIII.
		10.50 a.m.	Orders for move of Transport by road to new area.	
		11.45 a.m.	Ref. Div. Order 93. Pioneer Battn ordered to withdraw to CLIFFE POST forthwith. 239 Bde less one Battn and 231st Brigade to commence to withdraw to bivouac area at 7.30 p.m.	ay
		4.0 p.m.	Warning Order issued that 230th and 231st Brigade Groups may entrain at PERONNE, in which case they will bivouac in neighbourhood of TEMPLEUX LA FOSSE.	
		6.40 p.m.	Orders sent out confirming Warning Orders issued at 4 p.m. today.	
	25th		Relief of 229th Brigade in Front line by 1st Battn and one Coy 2nd Battn, 106th American Infy Regt was completed at 6 a.m. During the morning the 229th Brigade Group entrained at TINCOURT and the 230th and 231st Brigade Groups marched to PERONNE where they entrained. The three Brigade Groups detrained at VILLERS BRETONNEUX and were billeted in the following areas :- 229th Brigade Group, CORBIE Area - 230th Brigade Group FOUILLY - 231st Brigade Group VILLERS BRETONNEUX. D.H.Q. closed at BOIS DE BUISE at 10 a.m. and opened at FOUILLY CHATEAU at the same hour.	ay

Army Form C. 2118

WAR DIARY
or
INTELLIGENCE SUMMARY
(Erase heading not required.)

Instructions regarding War Diaries and Intelligence Summaries are contained in F.S. Regs., Part II. and the Staff Manual respectively. Title Pages will be prepared in manuscript.

Place	Date	Hour	Summary of Events and Information	Remarks and references to Appendices
	25th contd	8.0 p.m.	Divisional Order No 94 issued. The Division will move by train to Fifth Army Area on the 27th coming under order of G.O.C., XIII Corps on arrival.	APP. XLIV.
	27th		During the morning the Division commenced to entrain at CORBIE, HEILLY and MERICOURT L'ABBE Stations for move to Fifth Army Area in accordance with Divisional Order No 94. Divl H.Q. was closed at FOUILLY CHATEAU at 10 a.m. and reopened in new Area at NORRENT FONTES at 2 p.m. During the day a warning order was issued to the effect that the Division would shortly relieve the 19th Divn in the line.	APP. XLV.
	28th		The Division arrived in New area during the day, all trains after the first three at each station being about 11 hours late. The Brigade Groups were accomodated in the new area as shown in Divisional Order No 94.	
		5.30 p.m.	Divisional Order No 95 issued giving details for relief of 19th Division in the line commencing night Oct 1st/2nd.	APP. XLVI.
NORRENT FONTES	Sept 29	10 p.m.	Divisional Order No 96 issued, giving objectives and method of advance in event of enemy withdrawal.	APP. XLVII.
"	30		Advance parties proceeded to 19th Division.	

NARRATIVE OF OPERATIONS CARRIED OUT BY 74TH

(YEOMANRY) DIVISION 2-9-18 to 24-9-18.

On September 1st the Division received orders from the III Corps that the attack against the enemy's rearguards would be continued the following morning, and would be pressed with the utmost vigour. The 229th Infantry Brigade was accordingly detailed to carry out this attack. The 230th Infantry Brigade was to support the attack and was ordered to be prepared to form a defensive flank with one Battalion on the South of the 229th Brigade should their advance exceed that made by the Division on their Right. The 231st Infantry Brigade was in Divisional Reserve. The 2nd Australian Division was attacking on the Right, and the 47th British Division on the Left of this Division respectively.

The objectives of the attack were the Spurs West and South-west of NURLU approximately a line D.2.d.3.8. - D.3.central - D.3.d. central - thence due South to D.9.b.5.0. - D.9.d.5.0. The village of MOISLAINS was to be avoided in the actual attack, but the 229th Brigade was to be responsible for mopping it up. In addition one Infantry Brigade of the 47th Division on our left, moving South of MOISLAINS, was to follow the 229th Brigade and form a defensive flank facing North along the Divisional Boundary from MONASTIR Trench to the ridge in D.2.a. and b. The objectives of the 2nd Australian Division and the 47th Division were - MIDINETTES Trench to and MONASTIR Trench respectively.

At 5.30 a.m. therefore on September 2nd the attack was launched. Considerable difficulty had been found in reaching the infantry forming up line on the greater part of the front of attack, as the enemy had pushed out a line of machine gun posts during the night and was in occupation of BROUSSA Trench. This was the first occasion on which he had occupied this trench, and his action was unexpected. These elements of the enemy which were inside the barrage starting line had to be cleared before the barrage could be closely followed, with the result that the advancing infantry lost close touch with the barrage from the start, and owing to difficulties of the ground and the considerable amount of enemy wire, were unable to regain their proper position behind it.

Shortly after this the Right of the leading battalion came under heavy enfilade fire from the direction of HAUT ALLAINES, and instinctively swinging towards this opposition cleared the village and captured numerous prisoners. After this the Battalion again faced towards its proper objective and the advance was resumed. Meanwhile the battalion on the left which had come up into line according to plan, was counter-attacked from the South Western outskirts of MOISLAINS. Although this counter attack was very promptly dealt with by a section of machine guns which had been detailed to deal with any contingency of this sort which might arise, the Battalion suffered considerable casualties both in the counter attack and also from the continuous and heavy enfilade fire directed upon them from machine guns and riflemen in MOISLAINS itself after the counter attack had been repulsed.

After our troops had succeeded in crossing the Canal and in some cases reaching the line through D.14, the enemy who had reinforced his rearguards with troops of the Alpine Corps counter attacked in considerable strength and forced our line back to the CANAL du NORD. As this was found to be a distinctly unfavourable position, our front was subsequently withdrawn to the original starting line running North and South, West of MOISLAINS. During this retirement troops of the Brigade of the 47th Division which were to have passed South of MOISLAINS became intermingled with the men of the 229th Brigade and consequently when the line was re-established west of MOISLAINS there was considerable confusion and troops of the 47th Division were holding ground South of their Southern Boundary.

On/

On the Right of the 230th Brigade which, in accordance with orders had pushed forward a Battalion early in the morning in order to maintain touch between the attacking Brigade and the Left of the Australians had occupied a line running from C.5.b. (in touch with Australian Division) through C.29.c. to SCUTARI Trench in C.28.c. where it was in touch with elements of 229th Brigade. Both Brigades then reorganized and disposed their troops in depth. The 231st Brigade while remaining in Divisional Reserve moved to the high ground on the line B.24, B.18.

Next ~~the~~ day the line was advanced to C.28.d., ANSPACH Trench, MOISLAINS Trench as far as the Divisional Boundary and troops of the 47th Division who were out of their proper position were relieved. The line was held as an Outpost Line and every effort was made to economise troops with a view to a further advance.

On the 3rd instant the Battalion of the 230th Brigade which had been holding the line between the Australians and the 229th Brigade was withdrawn, and the 230th Brigade concentrated in support. The remainder of that day and of the 4th instant was spent in patrolling the neighbourhood of MOISLAINS and the Canal South of it. All patrols reported the ground on their immediate front to be held by the enemy, machine gun fire being experienced from MOISLAINS in every case. Early in the morning of the 4th instant our line was further advanced to the Canal bank at C.18.b.4.9. where touch was gained with the 47th Division, thence the line ran to the SLAG HEAP in C.24.central and C.30.central where touch was gained with the Australian Division on our Right.

On the night of the 4th/5th the 229th Brigade was relieved by the 230th Brigade and the 47th Division and was withdrawn into Divisional Reserve in the area about one mile North of CLERY. On the same night the 231st Brigade took over the Right Sector of the Divisional front relieving the Australian Division as far South as I.6.d.5.7., and the following preparations were made in the event of a sudden retirement on the part of the enemy. The 230th Brigade was detailed to be the Advanced Guard Brigade to the Division and the following troops were attached :- One Squadron Cavalry, one Brigade R.F.A., One section Field Company, R.E., together with one section of the Tunnelling Company.

It is not certain how many prisoners were captured during these operations as a considerable number were handed over during operations to assist the stretcher bearers. Captures are estimated at 100, 7 guns and several Machine Guns were also taken.

****

At 9.45 a.m. on the 5th September, the 47th Division reported that their patrols had made considerable progress and had reached the line D.9.a.0.6. - Quarry in D.15.a. - CAT COPSE. Orders were immediately issued for the 230th Brigade to push on as Advanced Guard to the Division, and for 231st Brigade, while coming into support to form a defensive flank along the Southern Divisional Boundary according as the 230th Brigade advanced. In the first instance this defensive flank was to be formed along the spur in J.8.a. and b., J.7.b. and c.

By 11 a.m. troops of the 230th Brigade had reached MIDINETTES Trench in D.19.d. and by 1 p.m. AIZECOURT-LE-HAUT was occupied. The next objective given to the Advanced Guard Brigade was the line J.4.central, D.28.central, D.22.c. and a., and orders were issued for the advance on this line to be resumed at once. The 230th Brigade by the evening of the 5th instant had occupied the line J.13.central, J.8.central, J.3.central, thence along track J.3.b. to D.27.b. and d., D.21.c., D.20.b. to Divisional Boundary. They were in touch on the Right with the Australians at/

at BUSSU, but not in touch with the troops of the 47th Division on their left, who were reported to be some distance behind. Orders were issued for the resumption of the advance.

Early in the morning of the 6th instant the Brigade had occupied TEMPLEUX Trench and elements of their troops were already some 800 yards East of this objective. By 11.35 a.m. the Left Battalion of the Advanced Guard Brigade had reached the line D.30.c. 8.5. to D.24.a.8.0. where they were in touch on their Right, but not with the Division on their Left who had not yet come up in line. At 2.50 p.m. the Left Battalion of this Brigade was observed to be East of LONGAVESNES and by 4 p.m. the whole of the Advanced Guard Brigade was established on the line of its final objective, that is the high ground in K.3.central, through E.26.central to E.20.d. and b. During this advance the resistance of the enemy, though on the whole considerably less formidable than was experienced by the 229th Brigade was in some places determined. Slight casualties were incurred, some 20 to 30 prisoners were taken, with several machine guns. The total distance covered by the 230th Brigade was just over 8,000 yards within a period of approximately 28 hours.

At this point the 231st Brigade was ordered to pass through the 230th Brigade on their existing line on the following day and resume the pressure against the enemy's rearguard. At 8 a.m. the following morning the troops attached to the 230th Brigade were transferred to the command of the 231st Brigade, and the 230th Brigade was ordered to come into Support and to continue to form the defensive flank on the Southern Divisional Boundary according as the advance progressed. During the whole of this latter advance the 229th Brigade remained in Divisional Reserve.

The objective of the 231st Brigade was the line of trenches and the barbed wire running North and South through F.25.central, F.19.central. The Northern Divisional Boundary remained unchanged. The line of the Southern Divisional Boundary was as follows :- East and West line through K.7.central to K.11.a.0.0. thence the line of the COLOGNE River to F.27.c.0.0. thence due East. The 3rd Australian Division was continuing the attack on the Right having relieved the 2nd Australian Division in the line. The 58th Division were attacking on the Left having relieved the 47th Division.

By 9.40 a.m. on the morning of the 7th our line was reported to be about 400 yards West of VILLERS FAUCON, and the troops were working round both flanks of the village. There was a slight amount of Machine Gun fire from the village itself, and this was being dealt with by the artillery. Shortly afterwards the Left Battalion of the Advance Guard Brigade entered VILLERS FAUCON, and at 11.30 a.m. the Right Battalion was reported on the line of railway through K.5.central.

Orders were issued at 12 noon for the 229th Brigade to move to the LONGAVESNES Area during the evening, and to take over the duties of the Support Brigade on arrival. On relief 230th Brigade were to withdraw into Divisional Reserve.

At 2.45 p.m. the 231st Brigade reported that their patrols had reached STE-EMILIE. By 4 p.m. in the afternoon the Advance Guard Brigade was established on its objective. Between VILLERS FAUCON the Railway and this objective the resistance of the enemy had stiffened considerably, and it became obvious that he intended to make a fight for every foot of ground in rear of his present line.

On the evening of the 7th an order was received from the Corps changing the Southern Divisional Boundary to an East and West line separating Squares F.7. and 13. Orders were accordingly issued for the 231st Brigade to extend their left to take over the additional portion of the line. The readjustment was to take place on the morning of September 8th by the Advance Guard Brigade passing/

passing through that portion of the 58th Divisional front which lay South of the new Southern Divisional Boundary. The Advance Guard Brigade was to resume the advance with a view to establishing themselves on the final objective given by the Corps, that is to say, the line of trenches passing through F.29.central, F.24.a.0.0., F.17.d. and b., thence Northward. Owing to the Division on our left having had very stiff fighting West of EPEHY on the previous day, their line was somewhat in rear of our line and ran from E.12.c.0.0. along line of trench to E.11.b.3.0. thence Northward. This rendered any advance on the part of our Left Battalion over the ground recently occupied by troops of the Left Division a matter of considerable difficulty. Very heavy machine gun fire was met with from the start from the high ground S.E. of EPEHY, and also from the Southern outskirts of the village itself. At the same time on the Centre and on the Right of our front, the advance which had been pressed against very considerable opposition was reported to have reached the line of trenches running through F.26.c. and b., F.20.d. and b., F.14.d. and c., but had afterwards been heavily counter-attacked and forced to retire to their original line. The Australian Corps on our Right did not advance that day. At 6.15 p.m. the 229th Brigade was ordered to relieve the 231st Brigade in the line, attached troops were to be transferred and on relief the 231st Brigade was to become Support Brigade located about LONGAVESNES.

On the morning of the 9th instant, the 10th Australian Brigade who had been slightly in rear of our Right, advanced to and finally established themselves on the line of trenches running through L.13. and L.7.

To co-operate with an attack which was being made by the 58th Division on the village of EPEHY and PEIZIERES, and on the high ground in F.8. and F.2.c. the 229th Brigade were instructed to make good the Horse Shoe Trench running through F.14.c. and d., F.20.b. and d. and F.26.a. on the night of the 9th/10th with a view to establishing themselves on the high ground about RONSSOY on the morning of the 10th should the attack of the 58th Division prove successful. During the night the Brigade succeeded in establishing a post about F.26.a.5.3., and 2 Battalions succeeded in working round as far as the apex of the Horse Shoe. Owing to strong resistance on the part of the enemy, however, the attack of the 58th Division was unsuccessful. These 2 battalions were therefore very much in the air, and after being subjected to heavy machine gun fire from the high ground about F.8. and RONSSOY, they were counter-attacked and compelled to withdraw to the original line.

It was now evident that the enemy considered the retention of the EPEHY - RONSSOY Ridge and the high ground South-west of RONSSOY a matter of the greatest importance, and that he intended to expend a considerable portion of his resources in defending it. It became necessary to abandon the idea of an Advance Guard action, and in its place to organize an attack of sufficient magnitude to enable the enemy to be driven from this strong position.

****

It was decided that the attack which was to take place on the 18th September, was to be carried out on a two Brigade front. The 230th Brigade was to be the Right Attacking Brigade and the 231st the Left Attacking Brigade. One Battalion of the 229th Brigade was attached to each of the Attacking Brigades, the battalions coming under their orders on the evening of 'Y' day, the 17th. Each attacking Brigade also had the following troops attached. Half troop Northumberland Hussars for inter-communication, One section R.E., one machine gun Company less 2 sections, detachment of Tunnelling Company with knowledge of Forward Area.

The/

The Right Divisional Boundary was an East and West line through L.1.d.0.3. as far as L.3.c.0.3. thence to F.29.c.0.0. thence due East. Northern Divisional Boundary East and West line as far as F.19.d.0.4. thence F.20.b.8.0. thence due East to F.23.a.0.0. thence to F.18.c.0.0. thence due East. The inter-Brigade Boundary East and West line as far as F.25.central thence F.28.b.0.3. thence F.29.b.8.8. (Cross Roads inclusive to Northern Brigade) thence due East.

Three objectives were given to the Division. The first objective Old British Trenches running through L.4.central, F.28.central, F.22.central. Second objective A.25.d.0.0. thence along Old British line of Observation through F.30.a.0.0., F.23.d.8.0., CAT POST F.18.c.0.0. Northwards. The line of exploitation was also given as follows:- Line of trenches through G.2.central, A.26.d. and b., A.20.c., A.19.b., and Northwards. The 1st Australian Division was attacking on the Right, and the 18th Division on the Left. The objectives of both Divisions were continuations to the South and North respectively of the objectives given to 74th Division.

About 350 casualties from gas occurred on the night of the 16th among the troops intended to attack on September 18th and the units were much depleted in numbers.

On the morning of the 17th inst. one company of the 14th Royal Highlanders was ordered to join 12th Somerset L.I. and to remain with it during the forthcoming attack owing to the number of gas casualties this battalion had suffered.

At 0520 on September 18th, the attack was launched in the midst of heavy mist and rain under a creeping Artillery barrage and a barrage of Machine Guns. Both Brigades had spent a quiet night, and the Infantry formed up without hindrance on the part of the enemy. By 0650 the 230th Infantry Brigade were within 200 yards of their first objective and 50 prisoners were reported captured. Shortly afterwards definite information was received that these Brigades had reached its first objective and had taken 71 prisoners of the 2nd Guard Division and the 36th Division. The 231st Brigade reached their first objective at about 0650 with numerous prisoners, and both Brigades were reported advancing on the second objective. Both flank Divisions were also reported to have been successful.

The 230th Brigade continuing the advance captured the second objective well up to time. The 231st Brigade were forced to advance more slowly in order to keep pace with the Division on their left which was experiencing considerable opposition in front of the first objective. As the situation on the left of the Division was not clear half a Company of Machine Gun Battalion were placed under the orders of the 231st Brigade and were ordered to protect their left flank from any counter-attack which the enemy might direct upon them with a view to widening the gap which already existed between them and the Right of the 18th Division. Throughout the day the 18th Division were unable to make any appreciable advance beyond this first objective, and consequently the line of the 231st Brigade was refused from about F.23.d.8.4. to the Divisional Boundary in F.23.a.2.1. where touch was established. The 1st Australian Division on the Right had meanwhile reached their second objective and had pushed patrols out in conjunction with 230th Brigade towards the line of exploitation. It was not however found expedient to make any determined attack against the final objective and patrols were therefore withdrawn and the line consolidated in preparation for a further advance to be made later.

This attack which was very successful came as a surprise to the enemy who stated that the barrage put down by our artillery was excellent and gave him little opportunity of putting up a determined resistance.

On the 19th orders were issued that Battalions of the 229th Brigade which had been attached to 230th and 231st Brigades respectively/

respectively were to rejoin the 229th Infantry Brigade in reserve, the whole Brigade being prepared to move to occupy the line of trenches on the old First Objective.

The number of prisoners captured during the operations were :- 18 officers and 873 other ranks., 10 77mm Guns, 3 4.2in. Hows., 5 Trench Mortars and numerous Machine Guns, about 60 were also captured together with a considerable amount of Gun ammunition and large quantities of S.A.A.

In view of the fact that the enemy resistance appeared to be weak and the opportunity of an attack on the HINDENBURG LINE favourable, it was decided to continue the advance with a view to establishing the line on the line of exploitation as given for the previous attack. The 230th and 231st Brigades were ordered to continue the attack on the Right and Left respectively. The Australian Division who had established patrols in front of the second objective of the previous attack were not advancing in conjunction on our right, but were pushing forward their Left flank to keep in touch with any advance made by the 230th Brigade. The Right Boundary of the Division was A.25.d.0.0., A.20.c.8.1., Northern Boundary F.23.c.3.3., A.7.d.8.8., Dividing line between Brigades was F.29.b.7.3., F.29.b.9.9., along the bottom of CLAYMORE VALLEY - A.14.c.0.2. The objectives of the attack were QUENNEMONT FARM, QUENNET COPSE and GILLEMONT FARM, the 18th Division co-operating on the Left was attacking THE KNOLL and FLEECEALL POST.

21th

The attack started at 0540 under a creeping barrage and our infantry were seen to be advancing towards their objective under a fairly heavy counter barrage which was put down by the enemy. At 0645 the 231st Brigade reported the capture of CAT POST in F.24.a.0.8., and that the battalion which had captured this was advancing towards the final objective in accordance with the plan of attack. By 0800 the 230th Brigade after very stiff fighting and under considerable Machine Gun fire from the HINDENBURG LINE occupied QUENNEMONT FARM and QUENNET COPSE and shortly afterwards reported that they reached their objective with the exception of a small portion on the left towards which their troops were unable to advance owing to the intensity of Machine Gun fire.

Shortly after having reached their objectives this Brigade was heavily counter-attacked by superior enemy forces from the direction of the HINDENBURG LINE and owing to the excessive casualties incurred during the advance and after the objective had been reached were forced gradually to withdraw to their original starting line where they were re-organized.

Meanwhile on the 231st Brigade front the 25th R.W.F. succeeded in capturing the QUADRILATERAL and swung Eastwards on to their second objective where they were reported to be in position by 7.30 a.m. The 24th Welsh Regiment, however, losing direction in the heavy fog and the smoke of the enemy's barrage on the QUADRILATERAL, followed the 25th R.W.F. in an Easterly direction instead of making for GILLEMONT FARM. At the same time owing to the 18th Division not being up on our left the enemy were able to dribble men back into the QUADRILATERAL through the sunken road in F.18.d., and the 10th K.S.L.I. coming up to mop up and consolidate this position were met by heavy resistance from the enemy machine gunners and riflemen. From the position the enemy was able to shoot into the rear of the 25th R.W.F. and 24th Welsh Regt, and their position in the BLUE LINE in A.19.a., which was also counter-attacked by the enemy from an Easterly direction, was rendered untenable and these troops were withdrawn to RIFLEMAN POST. Repeated attempts by the 10th K.S.L.I. to bomb their way into the QUADRILATERAL during the day were unsuccessful and in the evening the 10th K.S.L.I. with one section 231st L.T.M.B., held the RED LINE from BENJAMIN POST to BULL POST inclusive.

Very/

Very heavy casualties were incurred during the advance and retirement, and it was considered quite impossible to attempt another attack with the existing forces at the disposal of the Brigadiers. The Brigades were therefore re-organized on the original starting points and orders were given for further consolidation.

Meanwhile the enemy, who was still holding out in the MILL LANE Quadrilateral, had proved of considerable trouble to our troops, and it was decided to eject him from this position in conjunction with an attack by the 18th Division on DUNCAN POST and DOLEFUL POST. The attack was timed to take place at 0015 on the 22nd. After a quarter of an hour's intense bombardment by Field Artillery 10th K.S.L.I. attacked and captured the POST in question taking 200 prisoners and about 30 Machine Guns. Over 150 enemy dead were counted in this vicinity next morning. After this operation both Brigades were relieved in the line by the 229th Brigade with one battalion of 230th Brigade attached, and were withdrawn into reserve positions. The 229th Brigade was ordered to carry on with the consolidation of the line held and to put up wire.

On the night of the 24th/25th instant the Division was relieved in the line by the 27th American Division and proceeded to reserve in the CORBIE area.

The following is a list of the casualties incurred by the Division during the period 2nd September to 28th September, 1918.

Killed.		Wounded.		Missing.	
Off.	O.R.	OFF.	O.R.	Off.	O.R.
34	436	143	2,712	8	188.

Major-General,
Commanding 74th (Yeomanry) Division.

SECRET.

74th DIVISION ORDER No. 82.

1st September 1918.

1. 74th Division will attack to-morrow in co-operation with 2nd Aust.Div. on right and 47th Division on Left. Right boundary C.26.Central - C.29.Central - D.19.Central - D.9.d.5.0. - grid line between D.10 and D.16. Left boundary grid line between C.10 and C.16 - Northern edge of MOISLAINS D.4.a.0.9.
Objective - the spurs West and South-west of NURLU approximately a line D.2.d.3.8. - D.3.Central - D.3.d.Central - thence due South to D.9.b.5.0. - D.9.d.5.0.

2. 229th Brigade will attack supported by 230th Brigade.

3. Zero will be at 5-30 a.m. at which hour troops will form up on starting line. Starting line C.29.Central - C.18.b.7.5.- C.10.d.7.0.

4. Barrage will come down 200 yards East of starting line at zero and will dwell there for 15 minutes. It will then advance at the rate of 100 yards per 5 minutes. Barrage will cease when it has reached approximately line of trench junction in D.8.c. thereafter infantry will be supported by two mobile bdes of 74th Div.Arty.

5. One company Pioneers will be attached to 229th Bde to improve crossings for Artillery over River TORTILLE and Canal du NORD South of MOISLAINS.

6. 229th Brigade will avoid MOISLAINS but will be responsible for mopping it up.

7. Objective of 47th Division MONASTIR Trench as far South as Div. boundary. In addition one Bde, 47th Division moving South of MOISLAINS will follow 229th Bde and will form defensive flank facing North along Div. boundary from MONASTIR Trench to ridge in D.2.a. & b.

8. 230th Brigade will follow Brigade of 47th Div. and will be in support. In event of 2nd Aust.Div. beong behind 229th Brigade, 230th Brigade will be prepared to form defensive flank along road as far as D.9.d.5.0. It will also be prepared to support 229th Brigade.

9. All success will be exploited to utmost and if situation is favourable advance will be pushed beyond final objective.

10. H.Q., 230th Brigade will join H.Q., 229th Brigade tonight. 230th Brigade will advance from present position in such time as to be able to move forward in close support of 229th Brigade.

11. 231st Brigade will reach valley S. of BOUCHAVESNES by 6-30 a.m. H.Q. to B.26.b.9.0.

12. Objectives of 2nd Aust.Div. MIDINETTE Trench.

Signed. A.C.TEMPERLEY.

Lieut.Colonel.
General Staff.
74th (Yeomanry) Division.

Issued at 8-40 p.m.

Copies to:- 229 Bde,   C.R.E,   Div.Train.   2nd Aust.Div.
            230 "   Signals,   III Corps.   Q
            231 "   M.G.Bn.   58 Div-   47 Div-
            C.R.A.   A.D.M.S.

"A" Form
MESSAGES AND SIGNALS.

Army Form C.2121
(In pads of 100)

This message is on a/c of: *appendice*

TO:
- 229 Bde — CRA
- 230 Bde — M.G.B.
- 231 Bde — O.

Sender's Number.	Day of Month.	In reply to Number.	AAA
G.853.	2		

230 Inf. Bde will hold line between 2nd Aus Div. and SCUTARI Trench AAA Thence 229 Bde will hold Northwards along old line to point where 47 Div is holding AAA Boundary between 229 and 230 Bdes will be agreed upon mutually and reported to Div. H.Q. AAA Bdes will reorganise as soon as possible and get their machine guns in depth AAA 231 Bde will be in Divisional Reserve and will occupy high ground with M.G. Coy on line B.24, B.18. AAA 231 Bde will be prepared to move to fresh bivouac about B.22.b.0.0 and B.23.a. this evening.

From: 74 Div.
Place:
Time: 5 P.m.

(Z) Sd H.S. Sharp Capt

"A" Form
MESSAGES AND SIGNALS.

Army Form C. 2121
(In pads of 100)

This message is on a/c of: appendix III

TO	229 Bde	CRA	3 Corps	11 Aus. Inf. Bde
	230 -- --	MGR	2 Aust. Div	
	231 -- --	Q	47 Div	

Sender's Number	Day of Month	In reply to Number	AAA
G.858	2		

Reference G.853 AAA 229 and 230 Bdes will advance their line at dusk to approximately C.28.d. - ANSPACH Trench - MOISLAINS trench as far as Divisional boundary AAA 47 Div will be relieved in C.17.b. & d. AAA line will be held as an outpost line and troops will be economised as much as possible particularly in valley in C.28. AAA 230 Bde will not employ more than a battalion North of Canal AAA Completion of relief to be reported AAA Divl Northern boundary is grid line between C.11 & C.17. AAA Acknowledge AAA Addd all concerned rept 3 Corps 2nd Aust. Div. 47 Div & 11 Aust Inf Bde.

From: 74 Div
Place:
Time: 7.40 am

(Z) Sd A Galloway Capt.

"A" Form
MESSAGES AND SIGNALS.

Army Form C. 2121
(In pads of 100)

This message is on a/c of: Appendix

TO	229 Bde	CRA
	230 Bde	2nd Aust. Div
	231 Bde	3 Corps

Sender's Number.	Day of Month.	In reply to Number.	AAA
G.878	3		

229 Bde in co-operation with Left Bde 2nd Aust. Div. will advance the line to approximately C.30.Central – C.24.Central hence back to the old line about C.17 Central. AAA When line is established 230 Bde will remain in support AAA Method of advancing will be by patrols which will establish small posts. The line will then be made good AAA 229 Bde to acknowledge AAA Added 229, 230, 231 Bdes rep'd CRA, 2 Aust Div, 3 Corps.

From: H.A.
Place:
Time: 10.20 a.m.

(Z) Sd. A C Temperley
Lt Col.

SECRET.

74th DIVISION ORDER No.83.

3rd September 1918.

1.   Indications enemy is withdrawing.

2.   In case of advance Advanced Guard Brigade will be formed as under;-

    230th Infantry Brigade.
    1 Sqdn. Northumberland Hussars.
    117th Bde, R.F.A.
    1 Section, R.M.R.E.
    1 Section, 253 Tunnelling Company.

3.   Right Divisional Boundary, C.29.Central - C.30.Central thence Eastward.
    Left Divisional Boundary, grid line Eastward between C.11 and C.17.

4.   ACKNOWLEDGE.

Signed. A.C.TEMPERLEY.

Lieut.Colonel.
General Staff.
74th (Yeomanry) Division.

Issued at 10-40 a.m.

Copies to:- 229th Bde.   C.R.A.   'Q'   Div.Train.
           230th "   C.R.E.   M.G.Bn. Sqdn,N.H.
           231st "   Signals. A.D.M.S. 2 Aus.Div.
      III Corps.   47 Division.

SECRET.

74th DIVISION ORDER NO 84.

4th September 1918.

1. 74th Division will side-slip southwards to-night.
Right boundary East and West grid line through I.12.central.
Left boundary East and West grid line through C.23.a.0.4.

2. 231st Brigade will relieve 2nd Australian Division in Right Sector. 230th Brigade will relieve 229th Brigade in Left Sector, dividing line between Brigades East and West grid line through C.30.c.0.4.
    141st Brigade will relieve 229th Brigade as far South as Divisional boundary.
    All details will be arranged direct between B.Gs C. concerned.

3. Command of new Divisional front will pass to 74th Division at midnight.

4. On relief, 229th Brigade and 'B' Coy, M.G.Bn. will be withdrawn to Divisional Reserve about B.23.d. and B.30. Brigade H.Q. to B.26.b.9.0.
    Details of M.G. Coy reliefs will be arranged by O.C. M.G.Bn.

5. On completion of relief, Divisional Reserve will be 229th Brigade, 2 Coys M.G.Bn., 1 Squadron Northumberland Hussars, No 2 Coy. Cyclists.

6. ACKNOWLEDGE.

                               (Signed) A.C.TEMPERLEY.
                                       Lieut Colonel.
                                General Staff.
                             74th (Yeomanry) Division.

Issued at 11.30 a.m.

Copies to :-   229th Brigade.   A.D.M.S.
               230th Brigade.   Train.
               231st Brigade.   3rd Corps.
               C.R.A.   47 Div.
               C.R.E.   2nd Aust Div.
               'Q'   'B' Sqdn N.Hussars.
               Signal Coy.   Cyclist Coy.
               M.G.Battn.

For day of month 5
read
    day of month 4
See G.S. Diary.

"A" Form
MESSAGES AND SIGNALS.

Army Form C. 2121 (In pads of 100)

Prefix....Code....m.	Words.	Charge.	This message is on a/c of:	
Office of Origin and Service Instructions	Sent			Recd. at....m.
Priority	At....m.		*appendix* Service.	Date VII
3 Bdes.	To.			From.
Lt Col. GS.	By.		(Signature of "Franking Officer.")	By.

TO	9 Bde	C.R.A.		
	230 Bde	M.G.Bn.	'Q'	
	231 Bde			

Sender's Number.	Day of Month.	In reply to Number.	
* G 950	5		AAA

Reference Div Order No 83 aaa Further strong indications to-day of enemy withdrawal aaa 47 Div sending forward advanced forward bde at dawn to-morrow aaa In event of enemy trenches opposite Divisional front being found unoccupied advanced guard bde will push forward with greatest boldness and be prepared to exploit success in accordance with Div Order 83 ~~addressed 3 bdes C.R.A. M.G.Bn. 'Q'~~

From 74 Div
Place
Time 11.25 p.m.

The above may be forwarded as now corrected. (Z)
(Sd.) A.C. Temperley.
Censor. Signature of Addresser or person authorised to telegraph in his name
Lt Col. GS.

"A" Form
MESSAGES AND SIGNALS.

Army Form C.
(In pads of 100)

Prefix ..... Code ..... m. Words. Charge.

Office of Origin and Service Instructions:

Urgent operation
Priority.
(Sd) A.C.T.
Lt. Col. G.S.

Sent At ..... m. To ..... By .....

This message is on a/c of:

Appendix VIII

Recd. at ..... m.
Service. Date.
From .....
By .....

TO
229 Bde	C.R.A.	M.G.Bn.	3rd Corps.
230 Bde	C.R.E.	A.D.M.S.	47 Div
231 Bde	Signals.	'Q'	5 Aus Div

| Sender's Number. | Day of Month. | In reply to Number. | |
| *G 975 | 5 | | AAA |

230 Bde had reached MIDINETTE Trench at
10.15 a.m. and was pushing on to PERONNE
- NURLU Road aaa Thence an immediate advance
will be made to the next objective which
will be J.4.central - D.28.central - D.22.c.
& a. aaa 231 Bde will form a defensive flank
along ridge in J.7.c. & b. - J.8.a. & b.
aaa No advance will be made beyond objective
except by patrols until touch has been
established with 47 Div and position made
good aaa Reserve coy machine gun battn will
come under orders of 230 Bde to consolidate
objective Usual addresses repeated Corps
flank div

From 74 Div
Place
Time 12.40 p.m.

The above may be forwarded as now corrected.
(Sd) A.C.Temperley.
Censor. Signature of Addressor or person authorised to telegraph. Lt.Col. GS.

* This line should be erased if not required.

Headquarters
7H/10 Div.

BM2/28

In continuation of this
Office B.16.2.28 of the 16th inst,
herewith War Diary of 15th Suffolk's
for month of September.

D C Gilroy
Capt
for Lt. Col.
Comdg 230 Inf. Bde.

19/10/18

SECRET.
* * * * * * *

74th DIVISION ORDER NO 85.

5th September 1918.

1.   The advance will be resumed to-morrow at 8. a.m. by the Advanced Guard Brigade.

2.   231st Brigade will continue to form a defensive flank to South as required.
        First Objective will be TINCOURT WOOD - D.30.central - D.24.a.8.2.
        Second objective K.9.central - K.3.central - E.26.central - E.20.d.central.
        In event of the Brigade not reaching the final objective to-day, TEMPLEUX TRENCH will be the first objective.
        C.R.A. will arrange the barrage for the first objective.

3.   Main cable route ALLAINES - AIZECOURT - DRIENCOURT - LONGAVÆSNES.

4.   The next Divisional H.Q. will be at I.10.b.central.

5.   ACKNOWLEDGE.

                                (Signed) A.C.TEMPERLEY.
                                        Lieut Colonel.
                                    General Staff.
                                74th (Yeomanry) Division.

Copies to :-   229th Inf. Bde.   M.G.Battn.
                230th Inf. Bde.   A.D.M.S.
                231st Inf. Bde.   Div. Train.
                C.R.A.   3rd Corps.
                C.R.E.   47th Division.
                'Q'   3rd Australian Division.
                Signals.

"A" Form
MESSAGES AND SIGNALS.

Army Form C.2121
(In pads of 100)

Prefix	Code	m.	Words.	Charge.

Office of Origin and Service Instructions

Urgent operation
Priority to
230 & 231 Bdes.
(Sd) A.C.T

This message is on a/c of:
Appendix

Recd. at .... m.
Date ....
From ....
By ....

TO	230 Bde	47 Div		
	231 Bde	3 Aus Div		
	C.R.A.			

Sender's Number	Day of Month	In reply to Number	AAA
G 3	5		

Reference Div Order 85 AAA Heavy artillery
will bombard TEMPLEUX and GURLU Wood
trenches within Div. boundaries from 7.45 a.m.
to 8. a.m. AAA At 8. a.m. heavy artillery
will lift on to TEMPLEUX Defences Field Arty
will bombard objective from 8. a.m. to
8.10 a.m. under cover of which infantry will
advance AAA At 8.10 a.m. Field Artillery will
lift off objective and search ground beyond as
Advance to next objective will be covered
by mobile sections of 117 Bde R.F.A. and
by 290 and 291 Bdes R.F.A. which will move
forward after bombardment of 1st objective
AAA Addsd 230 231 Bdes C.R.A. reptd 47
Div 3 Aus Div

From 74 Div
Place
Time 10.50 p.m.

The above may be forwarded as now corrected.
(Z)(Sd) A.C. TEMPERLEY. Lt. Col.
GS.

"A" Form
MESSAGES AND SIGNALS.

Army Form C. 2121
(in pads of 100.)

TO	230 Bde.
	231 Bde.

Sender's Number.	Day of Month.	In reply to Number.	AAA
* G 27	6		

Forecast of reliefs tonight aaa 231 Bde will pass through 230 Bde during night and continue advance tomorrow AAA Orders later AAA Added 230. 231 Bdes septd 70'

From: N H Dw

SECRET.
****

74th DIVISION ORDER NO 86.
====================================

6th September 1918.

1. 231st Brigade will relieve 230th Brigade as Advanced Guard Brigade to-night and will continue advance to-morrow morning.

2. 230th Brigade will become Support Brigade and will take over duty of covering Southern flank of Advanced Guard Brigade as required.

3. Troops attached to 230th Brigade will be transferred to 231st Brigade, less 'A' Coy M.G.Battn which will revert to Divisional Reserve.

4. 229th Brigade and M.G. Coy will move this afternoon to area in vicinity of AIZECOURT.
   Cyclist coy will cease to be attached to 229th Brigade and will remain in Divisional Reserve in present position.

5. Completion of moves and reliefs to be reported by wire.

6. Road allotted to Division AIZECOURT-le-HAUT - DRIENCOURT - LONGAVESNES - VILLERS FAUCON - TEMPLEUX le GUERARD - HARGICOURT.

7. Map showing new Divisional boundaries and objectives being sent to those concerned.

(Signed) A.C.TEMPERLEY.
Lieut Colonel.
General Staff.
74th (Yeomanry) Division.

Issued at 1.40 p.m.

Copies to :-
229th Inf. Bde.	M.G.Battn.
230th Inf. Bde.	A.D.M.S.
231st Inf. Bde.	Div. Train.
C.R.A.	3rd Corps.
C.R.E.	47 Division.
'Q'	3rd Australian Division.
Signals.	58th Division.

"A" Form
MESSAGES AND SIGNALS.

Army Form C. 2121 (In pads of 100)

Prefix .... Code .... m. | Words. | Charge.

Office of Origin and Service Instructions

Urgent operation Sent
Priority to At............m.
231 Bde. To..........
(Sd.) E.S.Girdwood. M.G.

This message is on a/c of:
appendice .... Service.
(Signature of "Franking Officer.")

Rec'd at .... m.
XIII
From..........
By............

TO			
3rd Corps	229 Bde	C.R.A.	Train.
58 Div	230 Bde	C.R.E.	A.D.M.S.
3 Aus Div	231 Bde	M.G.B.N.	Q¹ Signals.

| Sender's Number. | Day of Month. | In reply to Number. | AAA |
| * G 94 | 7 | | |

Northern Div boundary is changed to an east and West line through grid separating E.7. and E.13. aaa On morning of Sept 8th front will be readjusted in accordance with above by advanced guard bde advancing through that portion of 58 Div front south of new div boundary aaa Details to be arranged direct between Brigadiers aaa Hour of advance to-morrow will be notified later aaa Road allotted to div is as follows aaa CLERY - MONT ST QUENTIN - ST DENIS - D.20. - TEMPLEUX LA FOSSE - J.4. - LONGAVESNES - VILLERS FAUCON - RONSSOY - F.16.c.9.0. aaa added 231 Bde reptd all concerned

From 74 Div
Place
Time 5.30 p.m.

The above may be forwarded as now corrected.
Censor.

(Sd.) M.S.Sharp. Capt. for
Lieut Col. G.S.
Signature of Addresser

```
229 Bde.
230 Bde.      'Q'
231 Bde.      C.R.A.


G.117.        8th.


Forecast of moves AAA 229 Bde will go through
231 Bde to-morrow morning or relieve it
to-night according to situation AAA 231 Bde
will become support bde AAA 229 Bde will be
supported by 2. M.G. Coys aaa Div H.Q. to
J.11.c.central to-morrow.   Addressed 3 Bdes
repeated C.R.A.  'Q'.




74 Div.

9.50 a.m.                    (Sd) A.C. TEMPERLEY.
                                  Lieut Col. G.S.
```

"A" Form
MESSAGES AND SIGNALS.

Army Form C. 2121 (In pads of 100)

Urgent operation Priority to 231 Bde (Sd) A.C.T.

This message is on a/c of: XV

TO	231 Bde	C.R.A.
	229 Bde	58 Div

Sender's Number.	Day of Month.	In reply to Number.	
G 120	8		AAA

Div North of 58 Div is much behind aaa G.O.C. 58 Div does not consider he can do more than make good high ground East of EPEHY thence through F.2.c - F.8.b. & d. - F.9.c. aaa You will if practicable secure high ground in F.25. - F.26.a. eastern edge of RONSSOY and of BASSE BOULOGNE thence North west to 58 Div about F.9.c. addsd 231 Bde reptd 229 Bde C.R.A. 58 Div.

From **74 Div**
Place
Time **11.25 a.m.**

(Sd) **A.C.TEMPERLEY.**
LIEUT.COL. G.S.

Urgent operation Priority. (Sd) A.C.T.

231 Bde.   58 Div.

G.138.   8.

58 Div reports that 175 Bde has not been relieved
south of new Divnl boundary nor have any troops
of 74 Div passed through them aaa 58 Div has been
asked to withdraw their bde at once and you will
immediately take over responsibility as far North
as Div Boundary which is East and West line between
Sqs F.7. and F.13. aaa Troops of 175 Bde are in
CAPRON COPSE line aaa Bde H.Q. at D.17.d.1.2. Ack
aaa addsd 231 Bde reptd 58 Div.

74 Div.

6.10. p.m.   (Sgd) A.GALLOWAY.
                                              Capt.

XVII

Priority to
229 Bde and 231 Bde.
(Sgd) A.C.T.

229 Bde.	C.R.A.	Train.	'Q'
230 Bde.	C.R.E.	A.D.M.S.	3 Corps.
231 Bde.	M.G.Bn.	Signals.	58 Div.
			3 Aus Div.

G.139.   8th.

229 Bde will relieve 231 Bde in the line to-night aaa M.G.Coys will remain attached to present Bdes aaa One coy Life Guards M.G.Bn. will be attached 229 Bde aaa Sqdrn and 44th Bde R.F.A. will be transferred to 229 Bde aaa On completion of relief 231 Bde will become support bde and will be located about LONGAVESNES aaa Completion of relief will be reported to this office by wire aaa Ack aaa Usual addresses.

74 Div.

6.15 p.m.

(Sgd) A.GALLOWAY.
CAPT.

War Diary

SECRET.
* * * * * * *

XVIII

74th DIVISION ORDER NO 87.

9th September 1918.

1. The 58th Division is attacking PEIZIERE and EPEHY at 5.15 a.m. to-morrow under creeping barrage.

2. The 229th Brigade will make good to-night the spurs in F.26.a. - F.20.central - F.19.b.
   The Right Battalion of the 58th Division, prior to zero, is pushing forward a line of posts through F.7.c. - F.7.b. - F.1.d.
   The 229th Brigade will throw forward their left before zero to join this line on the Divisional boundary about F.7.c.4.0.
   The left of 229th Brigade and the Right Battalion of the 173rd Brigade will then advance to the line F.20.b. - F.14. central with a liaison post at KNOLL POST in F.8.d.6.0.
   The exact time for this advance will depend upon the success at EPEHY and cannot be fixed, but it will not be before 6.5. a.m.

3. B.G.C. 229th Infantry Brigade will arrange all details for co-operation in this attack with B.G.C. 173rd Brigade.

4. The bombardment to cover this advance will be arranged with O.C. 44th Bde, R.F.A.
   On reaching the objective, patrols will be pushed forward and success will be exploited towards RONSSOY - BASSE BOULOGNE.

5. The 229th Brigade will have a call on one battalion of The 231st Brigade if required.

6. ACKNOWLEDGE.

(Signed) A.C.TEMPERLEY.
Lieut Colonel.
General Staff.
74th (Yeomanry) Division.

Issued at 8.p.m.

Copies to :-

229th Inf. Bde.	'Q' Branch.
230th Inf. Bde.	3rd Corps.
231st Inf. Bde.	58th Division.
C.R.A.	3rd Australian Division.
C.R.E.	A.D.M.S.
Signals.	Train.
M.G.Battn.	

SECRET.
******

74th DIVISION ORDER NO 88.
=============================

10th September 1918.

1. The 230th Brigade will relieve the 229th Brigade in the line to-night.
    The 229th Brigade will withdraw to Divisional Reserve.

2. The 231st Brigade will become the Support Brigade and will be prepared to hold the line K.3.c. & a. - E.26.central - E.20.d. - E.14.c. as the line of Resistance.
    This line is already manned by one company of the Life Guards M.G.Battn.

3. The troops now attached to the 229th Brigade will be transferred to the 230th Brigade except 2 M.G.Coys which will be withdrawn to Divisional Reserve.

4. O.C. M.G.Battn will detail 2 M.G.companies to be attached to the 230th Brigade, and he will arrange all details of their relief.

5. Completion of relief will be wired to Divisional H.Q.

6. ACKNOWLEDGE.

                                    (Signed) A.C.TEMPERLEY.
                                         Lieut Colonel.
                                         General Staff.
                                    74th (Yeomanry) Division.

Issued at 1. p.m.

Copies to :-   229th Inf. Bde.   A.D.M.S.
               230th Inf. Bde.   Signals.
               231st Inf. Bde.   'Q'
               C.R.A.   Train.
               C.R.E.   3rd Corps.
               M.G.Battn.   58th Division.
                                    3rd Australian Division.

"A" Form.
MESSAGES AND SIGNALS.

Army Form C. 2121.
(In pads of 100.)

To:
- 229 Bde.
- 230 —
- 231 —
- CRA

Appendix XXI

Sender's Number: Gabo
Day of Month: 11

231 Bde will be disposed so as to be able to man main line of resistance at short notice aaa for this purpose two Battalions will be disposed in rear of sectors which they may have to hold with third Battalion in Brigade Reserve aaa 229 Bde will be withdrawn to area about TEMPLEUX LA FOSSE or in trench system J.6 - D.29. - D.23 aaa Short defence instructions being issued tomorrow

"A" Form.
MESSAGES AND SIGNALS.

Army Form C. 2121.
(In pads of 100.)

aaa moves will take place tomorrow in small parties aaa That of 24 Welsh will take place after dusk aaa no units will be located in LONGAVESNES aaa Main line of resistance K.9.cent - K.3 - E.26.cent - E.20.b. and d - E.15.a. and c - aaa Dispositions on completion of moves will be reported to this office aaa Added 229 and 231 Bdes repeated 230 Bde and CRA.

From: 74 Div.

(Sgd) J H Naylor Lt.

"A" Form.
MESSAGES AND SIGNALS.

Army Form C. 2121.
(In pads of 100.)

TO: No 2 Coy. N.Z.C.C.
"Q"
Signals.

XXII

Sender's Number.	Day of Month.	In reply to Number.	AAA
G264	12		

You will proceed as soon as possible after receipt of this order to rejoin your BN at B.d.3.g. Sheet 62c AAA Orderlies returned herewith aaa Added N.Z.C.C. reptd Q & Signals

From: 74 Div
Place:
Time: 9.15 am

(Sgd) A Galloway Capt.

SECRET.   Copy No. 13

DEFENCE INSTRUCTIONS No.1.

App. XXIII

1. During a temporary pause in the offensive operations the Division is responsible for holding the Front Line, the main line of Resistance and the Intermediate line. In rear of those lines is a Corps line which will be held by a Reserve Division.
   All of these lines are shown on the attached map.

2. The Divisional Sector will be organised as under:-

   (a) An Advanced Guard (or Outpost) Brigade.

   This Brigade (to which 2 M.G.Coys are attached) will hold the Front line and will be organised in depth. Its role will be to hold the outpost zone and to counter-attack to regain any part of the front line which has been lost.
   In the event of an attack by the enemy on a large scale and of the Outpost Brigade being unable to maintain its position, it will fall back fighting, disputing every yard of ground, upon the main line of Resistance.
   In the event of an attack from the direction of EPEHY the the Outpost Brigade will be prepared to man the CAPRON COPSE Line.

   (b) A Support Brigade.

   This Brigade will be located West of the main line of Resistance, with 2 battalions roughly in rear of the Sectors they may be called upon to man and one battalion in Bde Reserve. 2 M.G.Coys are attached to this Brigade, one of which is already occupying the main line of Resistance.

   (c) A Reserve Brigade.

   This Brigade is located in the trench system in J.6, D.29, D.23. One M.G.Coy is attached to this Brigade and is located in the Intermediate line. It will be prepared to-
   (i) Man the Intermediate line.
   (ii) Counter-attack to regain any portion of the main line of Resistance temporarily occupied by the enemy.
   (iii) Reinforce the Outpost Brigade in the CAPRON COPSE Line.

3. In addition to the Reserve Brigade the following troops are also in Divisional Reserve:-
   Pioneer Battalion.
   3 Field Companies, R.E.
   1 M.G. Company.
   1 Sqdn, Northumberland Hussars.
   All troops in Divisional Reserve will be ready to move at 2 hours notice.

4. One Brigade, R.F.A. is under the direct orders of the Advanced Guard Brigade. The B.G.C. has also a call upon 3 other Brigades, R.F.A. if required, these Brigades are under the orders of the C.R.A.

5. Reconnaissances of the lines to be occupied in case of emergency will be carried out at once.

6. Shelter for troops is of the utmost importance and every effort must be made to provide it.

                                                Lieut.Colonel,
                                                General Staff.
12th September 1918.   74th (Yeomanry) Division.

P.T.O.

DISTRIBUTION.

Copy No		
1.	229th Infantry Brigade.
2.	230th Infantry Brigade.
3.	231st Infantry Brigade.
4.	C.R.A.
5.	C.R.E.
6.	'Q'
7.	A.D.M.S.
8.	M.G.Battn.
9.	Signal Coy.
10.	III Corps.
11.	58th Division.
12.	1st Australian Division.
13 - 14.	War Diary.
15.	File.

SHEET 62c

EDITION 1

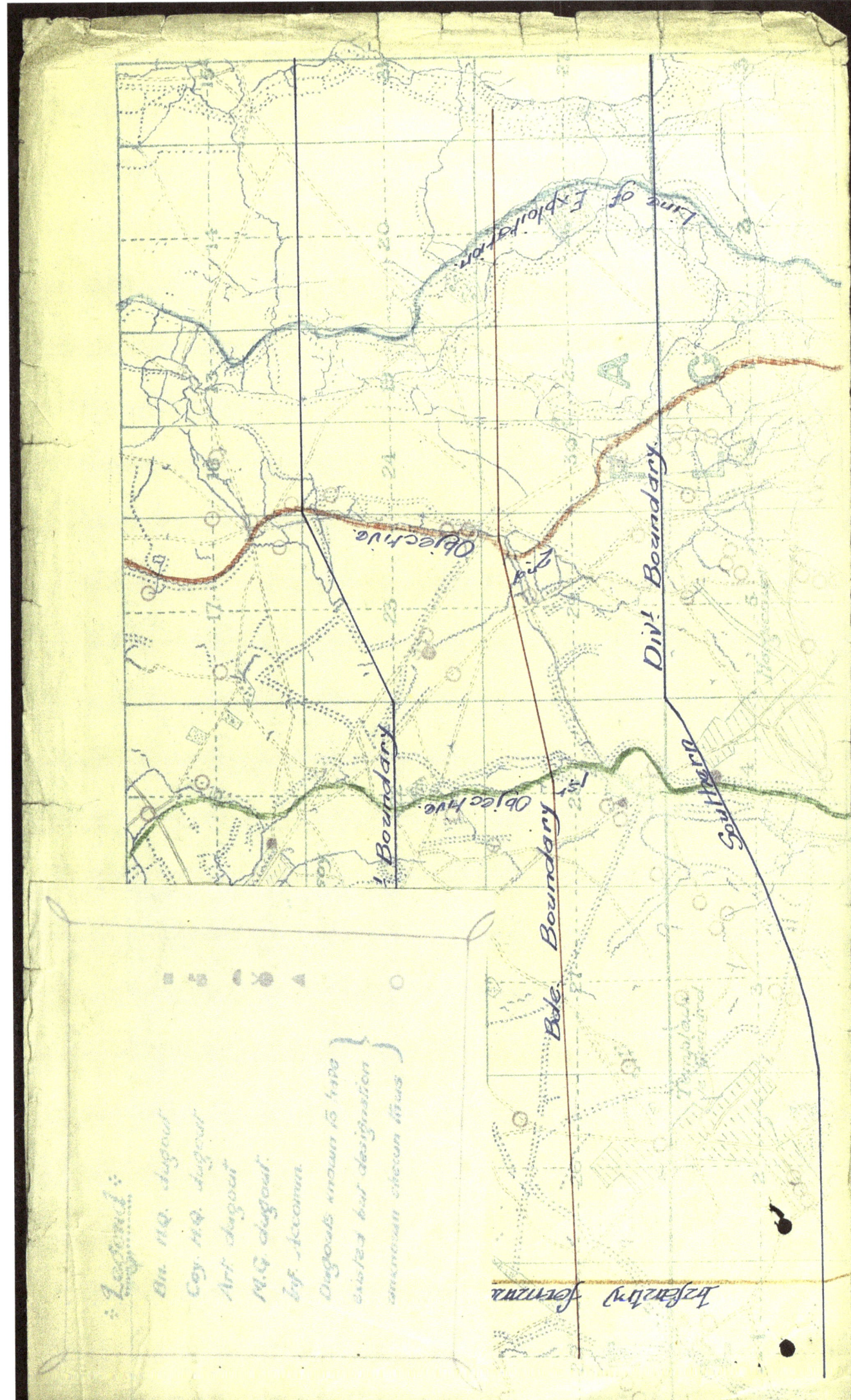

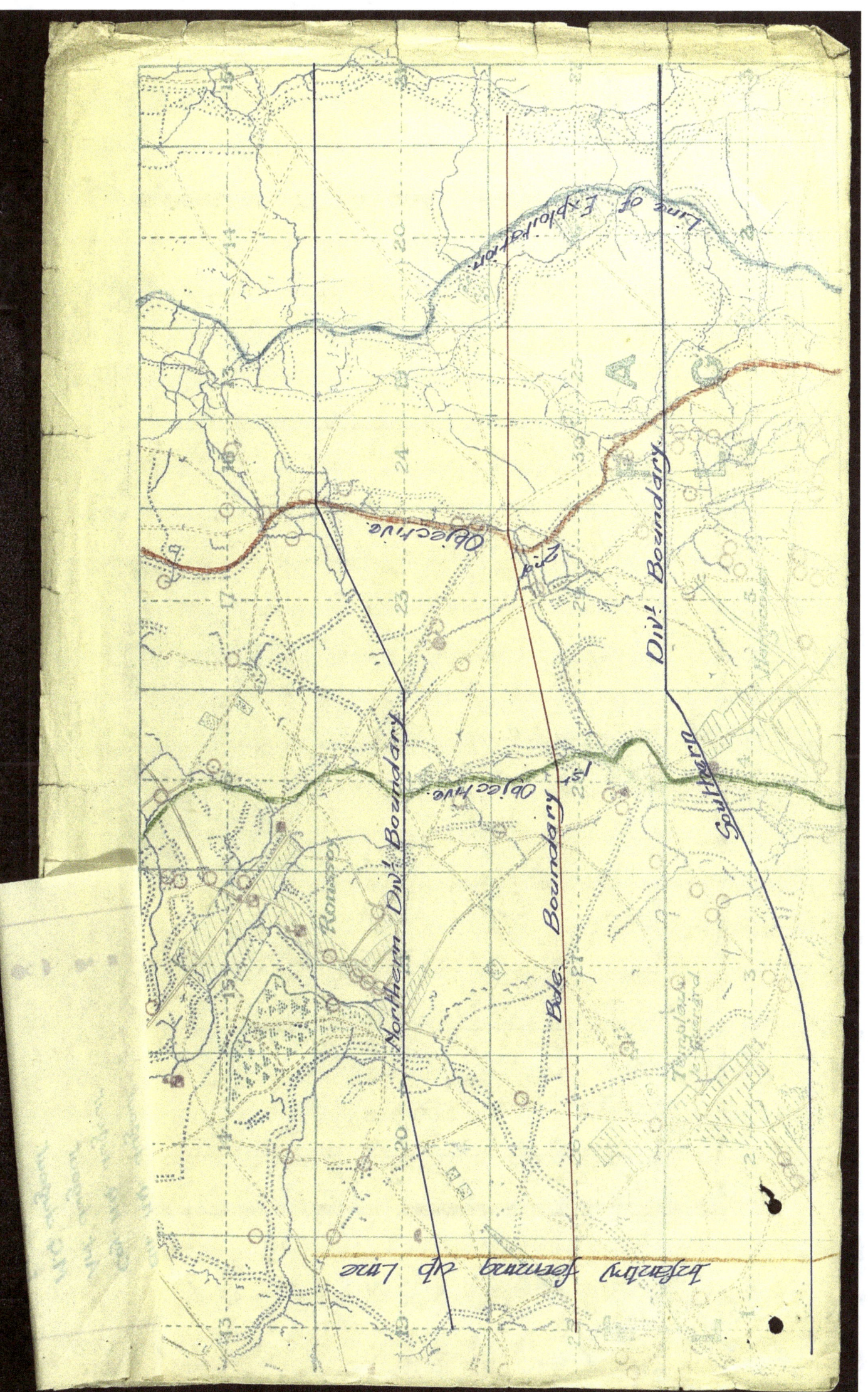

"A" Form
MESSAGES AND SIGNALS.

Army Form C. 2121 (in pads of 100).

This message is on a/c of App XXIV Service

Copy.

TO: 231 Bde "Q"
230 Bde
CRA

Sender's Number	Day of Month	In reply to Number	AAA
G.294	13		

231 Bde will relieve 230 Bde in the line as far South as F.19.d.0.2 on night 14/15th aaa Further orders later aaa Added 231 230 Bdes reptd CRA Q

From 74th Divn
Place
Time 3.25 pm

(Sgd) A Galloway Capt.

App XXV

SECRET.
******

Copy No. 17

74th DIVISION ORDER NO 89.

14th September 1918.

1. On the night 14th/15th instant 231st Brigade will relieve 230th Brigade in the line as far South as F.19.d.0.2.

2. All details of relief will be arranged direct between B.G.C's concerned.

3. Pending a redistribution of Machine Gun Companies throughout the Division, M.G's covering the respective sector will be grouped temporarily, each under the command of the senior M.G. officer.

4. On completion of relief, the artillery covering the front will be disposed as follows :-

   86th Bde and 117th Bde R.F.A. covering Left Brigade Sectors
   44th Bde and 104th Bde R.F.A.   " Right Brigade Sector.

5. Completion of Infantry reliefs will be reported by wire to this office.

6. Dispositions of Brigades will be reported on completion of relief.

7. ACKNOWLEDGE.

ACTemperley.

Lieut Colonel
General Staff.
74th (Yeomanry) Division.

Issued at ...8 am...

Copies to :-
No 1.	'G'	No 12.	A.D.M.S.
2 -4.	'Q'	13.	Div. Train.
5.	C.R.A.	14.	3rd Corps.
6.	C.R.E.	15.	58th Division.
7.	O.C. Signal Coy.	16.	1st Aust. Div.
8.	O.C. M.G. Battn.	17 -18.	War Diary.
9.	229th Inf. Bde.	19.	File.
10.	230th Inf. Bde.		
11.	231st Inf. Bde.		

"A" Form.
MESSAGES AND SIGNALS.

Army Form C. 2121.
(In pads of 100.)

TO:
- 230 Bde.
- 231 Bde.
- MGBn.

Sender's Number.	Day of Month.	In reply to Number.	A A A
G308	14		

Para 3 Div Order 89 is cancelled aaa Each brigade will be covered by one MG Coy distributed in depth aaa Details will be arranged direct between Bgadiers and OC MGBn.

From 74 Div

"A" Form.
MESSAGES AND SIGNALS.

Army Form C. 2121.
(In pads of 100.)

TO: 230 Bde.
231 Bde.

Sender's Number: G 318
Day of Month: 14
AAA

Reference Div Order No 89 Bde boundary will be on East and West line through J.19d.0.2. AAA One battn in each Bde will be located in rear of main line of Resistance and will be responsible for manning it in case of emergency.

From: 74 Div
Place:
Time: 5 pm

MM Parry Major

"A" Form.
MESSAGES AND SIGNALS.

Army Form C. 2121.
(In pads of 100.)
No. of Message................

Pref......**A**....Code............m	Words.	Charge.	This message is on a/c of :	Recd. at ....m.
Office of Origin and Service Instructions.	Sent			Date.................
	At................m.		............................Service.	From ....
	To..................			
	By.................	(Signature of "Franking Officer.")	By....................

TO	229 Bde	CRA	D,	
	230 Bde	CRE	Signals	
	231 Bde	MGBn	ADMS	

Sender's Number.	Day of Month.	In reply to Number.	**A A A**
G 324	14		

Ref SG 65/1 AAA Amend para 2
as follows AAA Left Div
boundary F.19 central - F.23 central -
F.18 a & b thence eastward MILL LANE
trench exclusive to 4th Div
aaa Brigade boundary E.29 central
- F.25 central - F.27 a.g.1 - F.28.b.35.35.
F.29.b.90.85 - F.26.b.80.85 aaa
Acknowledge aaa Added all
reprints of SG 65/1

From: 4H Div
Place:
Time: 6 p.m.

The above may be forwarded as now corrected. (Z) (Sd) AC Temperley

Censor.   Signature of Addressor or person authorised to telegraph in his name.

"A" Form.
MESSAGES AND SIGNALS.

Army Form C. 2121.
(In pads of 100.)

TO	229 Bde.	CRA.	G
	230 Bde.	CRE.	Signals
	231 Bde.	MGBn.	ADMS

Sender's Number.	Day of Month.	In reply to Number.	A A A
G 337	14		

Ref this office G324 again 3rd co-ordinate of Left Div boundary should read J.18.c.0.4. and not J.18.c.40. and last co-ordinate of Brigade boundary should read A.26.b.00.85 and not J.26.b.00.85

From: 7th Div
Time: 10-40 pm

(Sd) A Galloway Capt GS

S E C R E T.
* * * * * *

Copy No...... 12

17th September 1918.

AMENDMENT TO 74th DIVISION ORDER NO 90.
----

1.   Reference para 4.   M.G.Coy attached 229th Brigade will remain at LONGAVESNES.

2.   Reference para 18. 230th Brigade H.Q. will be at E.28.b.0.2.

M M Pang-Jones Major
for

Lieut Colonel.
General Staff.
74th (Yeomanry) Division.

Issued at...... 10 a.m.

Copies to all recipients of 74th Division Order No 90.

S E C R E T. Copy No. 18

17th September 1918.

Reference Divisional Order No 90, para 1.

Zero hour will be 5·20 a.m. 18th inst.

ACKNOWLEDGE.

A C Temperley

Lieut Colonel.
General Staff.
74th (Yeomanry) Division.

Issued at. 1·10 a.m.

Copies to all recipients of 74th Division Order No 90.

S E C R E T.

Copy No. 19

17th September 1918.

Reference Divisional Order No 90, para 1.

Zero hour will be 5.20 am 18th inst.

ACKNOWLEDGE.

AC Temperley

Lieut Colonel.
General Staff.
74th (Yeomanry) Division.

Issued at 1.10p

Copies to all recipients of 74th Division Order No 90.

S E C R E T.

With reference to para 1 of 74th Division Order No 90. "Z" Day will be the 18th September.

The hour of zero will be notified at 1 p.m. on "Y" Day.

ACKNOWLEDGE.

signature

Lieut Colonel.
General Staff.
16th September 1918. 74th (Yeomanry) Division.

Copies to :-
    "Q"
    C.R.A.
    C.R.E.
    O.C. Signal Coy.
    O.C. M.G.Battn.
    229th Infantry Brigade.
    230th Infantry Brigade.
    231st Infantry Brigade.
    A.D.M.S.
    Div. Train.

SECRET.

App. XXVI

Copy No. 18

74th DIVISION ORDER No.90.

15th Sept 1918.

1. The IIIrd Corps is continuing the attack in conjunction with Corps and Armies on either flank, with a view to securing a position affording good observation of the HINDENBURG Line.
   The 1st Australian Division will be on our right and the 18th Division will be on our left.
   Z day and zero hour will be notified later.

2. There will be three objectives.

   First objective ... ... GREEN LINE.
   Second objective ... ... RED LINE.
   LINE of EXPLOITATION. ... ... BLUE LINE.

   The objectives and Divisional and Brigade Boundaries are shown on the attached map. TOINE POST will be inclusive to Right Brigade on 1st Objective and BENJAMIN POST inclusive to Left Brigade on 2nd Objective. The map also shows the dugouts previously existing in the area to be attacked.

3. The 38th Division, with 96th, 95th and 94th Inf.Regts from right to left, is believed to be holding the enemy line from TEMPLEUX le GUERARD to RONSSOY.

4. DISTRIBUTION OF TROOPS.
   230th Brigade will be the right attacking Brigade, 231st Brigade will be the left attacking Brigade,. To each Brigade one battalion of 229th Brigade will be attached, 16th Devon Regt to 231st Brigade, 12th Somerset L.I. to 230th Brigade. These battalions will come under the orders of the attacking Brigades on Y day.
   To each attacking Brigade will also be attached,-
   ½ Troop Northumberland Hussars for intercommunication.
   1 Section R.E.
   1 Machine Gun Coy (less 2 Sections).
   Detachment Tunnelling Coy with knowledge of the forward area.
   Assembly area allotted to attacking Brigades is East of a North and South line through E.28.Central.
   230th and 231st Brigades will take over their attacking fronts on X/Y night.
   229th Brigade (less 2 Battns), to which one M.G.Company will be attached, will be in Divisional Reserve. It will be located about FAUSTINE Quarry in K.5.c. on Y/Z night.

5. METHOD OF ATTACK.
   Both Brigades will attack the 1st Objective with 2 Battns and will "leap frog" two Battalions through for the attack upon the 2nd Objective.
   230th Brigade will on Y/Z night, move its right battalion South of the COLOGNE River and will be allotted ground by the 1st Australian Division as far South as L.8.a.0.0. 230th Brigade will attack TEMPLEUX le GUERARD and the Quarries East of it with the battalion South of the COLOGNE River moving in a N.E. direction in close co-operation with the left of the 1st Australian Division which will attack BOLSOVER SWITCH in L.4.c. simultaneously with the 230th Brigade attack upon the Quarries in L.3.a. and b. The Left battalion, 230th Brigade will attack TEMPLEUX and the QUARRIES from the N.W. Special parties will be detailed for the mopping up of TEMPLEUX le GUERARD and the QUARRIES.
   The general line of advance of the 231st Brigade will be in an E.N.E. direction along the spur in F.26.a and B - F.20.d thence in an Easterly direction to the 1st Objective.

/The advance

The advance of both Brigades from the 1st to the 2nd Objectives will be along the high ground in a E.N.E. direction. 230th Brigade keeping touch with 1st Australian Brigade on the Divisional Boundary.

Objectives gained will be consolidated and the defence organised in depth. In view of the probability of the enemy having registered the existing trench systems, troops should, when possible, dig in on lines some 300 yards in advance of the old systems.

Special mopping up parties will be detailed sufficiently large for the objectives captured to be thoroughly searched. Special attention is to be paid to the routes to be followed by troops passing through to take the second Objective, so as to avoid these troops getting delayed by uncompleted mopping up of localities.

Each platoon will fire a GREEN Very light on reaching the GREEN Line and a RED Very light on reaching the RED Line. Special watch will be kept by F.O.O.s for these "success" signals and they will be immediately reported.

The barrage will come down at zero on the North and South grid line between F.19 and F.20. The infantry forming up line will be 200 yards West of this line and will be taped prior to zero.

The infantry forming up line of the 1st Australian Division runs from the Divisional Boundary at L.1.d.7.0. thence through about L.4.d.0.0.

6. **LINE OF EXPLOITATION.**

When the RED Line has been taken and consolidation is proceeding, every effort will be made to establish posts in the BLUE Line, and especially to secure MALAKOFF Wood spur and QUENNEMONT FARM.

Certain batteries will move forward, so soon as the RED Line has been secured, and will be prepared to cover posts established in the BLUE Line: the S.O.S. barrage for the Divisional front will be arranged to cover that line. (See next para)

7. **ARTILLERY.**

230th Inf. Brigade will be covered by a group formed of 44th and 104th F.A.Brigades under Lt.Col.C.C.ROBERTSON, D.S.O. who will send a liaison officer not below the rank of Captain to 230th Brigade H.Q.

231st Inf. Brigade will be covered by a Group formed of 86th and 117th F.A.Brigades under Lt.Col.W.KINNEAR, D.S.O., whose H.Q. will be beside that of 231st Inf.Brigade.

The attack will be carried out under the protection of
(a) a creeping Field Artillery barrage.
(b) Heavy Artillery back barrage.
(c) Machine Gun barrage.

There will be no preliminary bombardment on Z day. The lifts of the barrage (which will always be 100 yards) will be at the following times:-

First lift (from barrage start line) 0+3
Second Lift 0+5
Third lift 0+8

and so on in three minute lifts till the eleventh lift at 0+32.

The twelfth and all subsequent lifts of the barrage will be at the rate of 100 yards in 4 minutes, i.e.,-

Twelfth lift 0+36
Thirteenth lift 0+40

and so on.

There will be a halt on the GREEN Line of over an hour, and the barrage will commence to creep from the GREEN Line at zero + 3 hours and 10 minutes, and continue at the rate of 100 yards in four minutes to the RED Line. The barrage will thicken up three minutes before the advance to warn the troops of the lift.

/On lifting off

On lifting off the 2nd Objective the barrage will remain as a protective barrage for 15 minutes and will then die away.

The S.O.S. barrage will be arranged in the first instance to cover the RED Line but will be moved forward to cover the BLUE Line should the exploitation prove successful.

8. MACHINE GUNS.

(a) Barrage to cover advance from Starting Line to line N. and S. through F.27.Central will be carried out by 2 Companies 2nd Life Guards M.G.Battalion. On completion 1 Company will remain in or about old Front line as garrison. Remaining company will be withdrawn to Divisional Reserve.

(b) Barrage for advance from 1st Objective (GREEN Line) to 2nd Objective (RED Line) will be carried out by two sections A Coy, D Coy, and two sections C Coy, 74th M.G.Bn. On completion two sections A Coy and two sections C Coy will undertake consolidation West of and including 1st Objective. D Coy will remain on or about 1st Objective, but will be disposed in depth. All these guns will be prepared to put down S.O.S. barrage in front of 2nd Objective in emergency.

(c) Advance from line N. and S. through F.27.Central to the 1st Objective will be covered by direct overhead fire of two sections of each of A and C Companies allotted to 230th and 231st Brigades respectively. These Sections, under the orders of B.G.s.C, will also be responsible for the consolidation of ground between 1st and 2nd Objectives.

(d) After "Stand to" on Z+1 day, unless otherwise ordered, D Coy will revert to Divisional Reserve and whole of A Coy and whole of C Coy to 230th and 231st Inf.Brigades respectively.

(e) B Coy, 74th M.G.Bn during operations will be in Divisional Reserve and ready to move forward at short notice.

(f) The Machine Gun barrage will move 250 yards in front of the 18 pdr barrage and will lift 250 yards at a time.

9. SIGNAL COMMUNICATIONS.

(a) Brigade Forward Stations will be established for 230th Brigade about the Quarries East of TEMPLEUX le GUERARD, for 231st Brigade about CLIFFE POST in F.20.d. Personnel for these Forward Stations will be provided in accordance with SS.191. Divisional Signal Company will take over lines up to the Forward Stations as soon as Brigade H.Q. is established there.

(b) Visual.

A central Visual Station will be established on K.3.Central. It will be connected by wire with Divisional H.Q. This visual station will be for the use of all formations. The Call will be V.S.

(c) Power Buzzers.

Each attacking Brigade will be provided with two complete loopsets. This will provide communication for 2 battalion H.Q., one Report Centre and one Brigade H.Q. Messages can be sent in clear when fighting is in progress at the discretion of C.O.s.

(d) Wireless.

Wireless sets will be established at Brigade H.Q. and should move forward when Brigade H.Q. moves to the Forward Station.

(e) Pigeons.

Pigeons will be provided for use of Brigade and Battalion H.Q.

10. ROYAL ENGINEERS.

The Field Coys, R.E. (less 2 Sections) and Pioneer Battn. will be under the orders of the C.R.E.

The C.R.E. will arrange for,-

(a) parties to assist the R.A. to clear wire and prepare crossings over trenches.
(b) special parties to reconnoitre for and develop water.
(c) improvement of forward roads in the Divisional area.

A forward R.E. dump is being formed from which Infantry Brigades can obtain material for consolidation. The C.R.E. will notify Inf. Brigades of the contents of the dump and its location.

- 4 -

11. LIAISON.
Liaison will be made by special patrols under an officer with flank divisions at the following places:-

(a) by 230th Brigade.
in BOLSOVER Switch about L.3.d.9.8.
on the RONSSOY - HARGICOURT Road L.4.b.4.5.
MALAKOFF Farm in F.30.
A.26.d.5.0.

(b) by 231st Brigade.
at Wood F.22.d.0.8.
in CAT POST F.24.a.2.9.
at A.14.c.1.0.

12. SECRECY.
The necessity for secrecy is to be impressed on all concerned. Reconnaissance should be reduced to a minimum. Listening sets are probably already installed in the HINDENBURG Line and no reference on the telephone East of Divisional H.Q. must be made to moves or to the operations.

13. CAPTURED GUNS.
In the event of the capture of hostile guns, information should be sent to the nearest Inf.Bde H.Q. for transmission to the artillery, giving exact location of guns, nature of gun and whether ammunition is at hand. This information should be passed on to the C.R.A., who will arrange to send up personnel to man the guns. Spare parts, sights, etc must not be removed as souvenirs from captured guns.

14. ROADS.
Roads are allotted to this Division as under:-

VILLERS FAUCON - TEMPLEUX - RONSSOY.-
VILLERS FAUCON - St.EMILIE - RONSSOY - F.30.a.
(to be used by 18th Division if required)

15. AEROPLANES.
(a) A contact aeroplane will fly over the Corps Front at:-

Zero + 2 hours and 15 minutes.
Zero + 5 hours.
Zero + 7 hours.

and subsequently as ordered.
Troops will be specially warned to be on the look-out for these planes and to indicate their position by means of flares, rifles in rows and waving of helmets. Red flares only will be used.
Brigade and battalion H.Q. will display their ground signal sheets and strips when our aeroplanes are flying over the Divisional Front.
(b) Aeroplanes are being supplied to machine gun and bomb hostile batteries and columns of troops and transport on roads in rear of the BLUE Line.
(c) A counter-attack plane will be up continuously from daylight onwards with the sole mission of detecting the approach of enemy counter-attacks. The aeroplane will fly in the direction of the enemy dropping a WHITE Parachute flare as near to the counter-attacking troops as possible.

16. S.O.S. SIGNAL.
The IIIrd Corps and Australian Corps S.O.S. Signal is,-

RED over RED over RED.

17. TIME.

An officer will visit Inf.Bde H.Q. about 1 p.m. and
6-30 p.m. on Y day to synchronize watches.   Synchronization
must not be carried out by telephone East of Divisional H.Q.

18. HEADQUARTERS.

    74th Div. H.Q.   in its present position.
    230th Bde H.Q.   SPUR QUARRY (E.29.d)
    231st Bde H.Q.   E.23.b.7.2.
    229th Bde H.Q.   FAUSTINE QUARRY (K.5.c)

19. ACKNOWLEDGE.

ACTemperley

Lieut.Colonel,
General Staff,
74th (Yeomanry) Division.

Issued at. 4-30 pm.

Copies to:-
No.		No.	
1.	'G.O.C.	13.	A.D.M.S.
2.	'G'	14.	Div. Train
3-5.	'Q'	15.	IIIrd Corps.
6.	C.R.A.	16.	1st Australian Division.
7.	C.R.E.	18.	13th Division.
8.	Signal Coy.	18-19.	War Diary.
9.	M.G.Battn.	20.	File.
10.	229th Inf.Bde.	21-26.	Spare.
11.	230th " "		
12.	231st " "		

"A" Form.
MESSAGES AND SIGNALS.

Army Form C. 2121.
(In pads of 100.)

Office of Origin and Service Instructions:
Priority to 230 & 231 Bdes
(Sd) A Galloway
Capt GS

TO:
229 Bde CRA
230 —"—
231 —"—

Sender's Number: G.417
Day of Month: 17

Addenda to Div Order no 90 AAA para 6 Infantry patrols pushing forward to BLUE line will be covered by battery H/K Bde RFA in Right Sector and battery 230 Bde RFA in left sector AAA F.O.O's will be in HUSSAR POST and BENJAMIN POST respectively will inform infantry when batteries are ready AAA para 15(a) platoon commanders will be responsible for lighting at least one flare per platoon

From: 74 Div
Time: 5.50 pm

"A" Form.
MESSAGES AND SIGNALS.

Army Form C. 2121.
(In pads of 100.)

TO	229 Bde	CRA	Signals
	230 Bde	CRE	ADMS
	231 Bde	D	18 Div

Sender's Number.	Day of Month.	In reply to Number.	A A A
G 351	15.		

Reference Div Order 90 aaa 53rd Bde will relieve 231 Bde in the line on night Sept 16th/17th as far South as T.19.c.9.4 aaa 231 Bde will relieve 230 Bde in line as far South as T.25 central aaa All arrangements direct between Brigadiers concerned addsd 230 231 Bdes reptd CRA CRE D Signals ADMS & 18 Div & M.G.Bn.

From 74 Div
Time 7.20pm

(Sd) A C Temperley

SECRET

SG.65/13

Headquarters.
   229th Infantry Brigade.
   230th Infantry Brigade.
   231st Infantry Brigade.
O.C. 74th Bn. M.G.C.

Herewith barrage maps distributed as under :-

229th Brigade.	6.
230th Brigade.	22.
231st Brigade.	22.
M.G.Battn.	5.
	55.

5 to each of 4 Bns.

Maps for detached Battns of 229th Brigade are included in the allotment of Brigades to which they are attached.

[signature]
Lieut Colonel.
General Staff.
16th Sept. 1918.   74th (Yeomanry) Division.

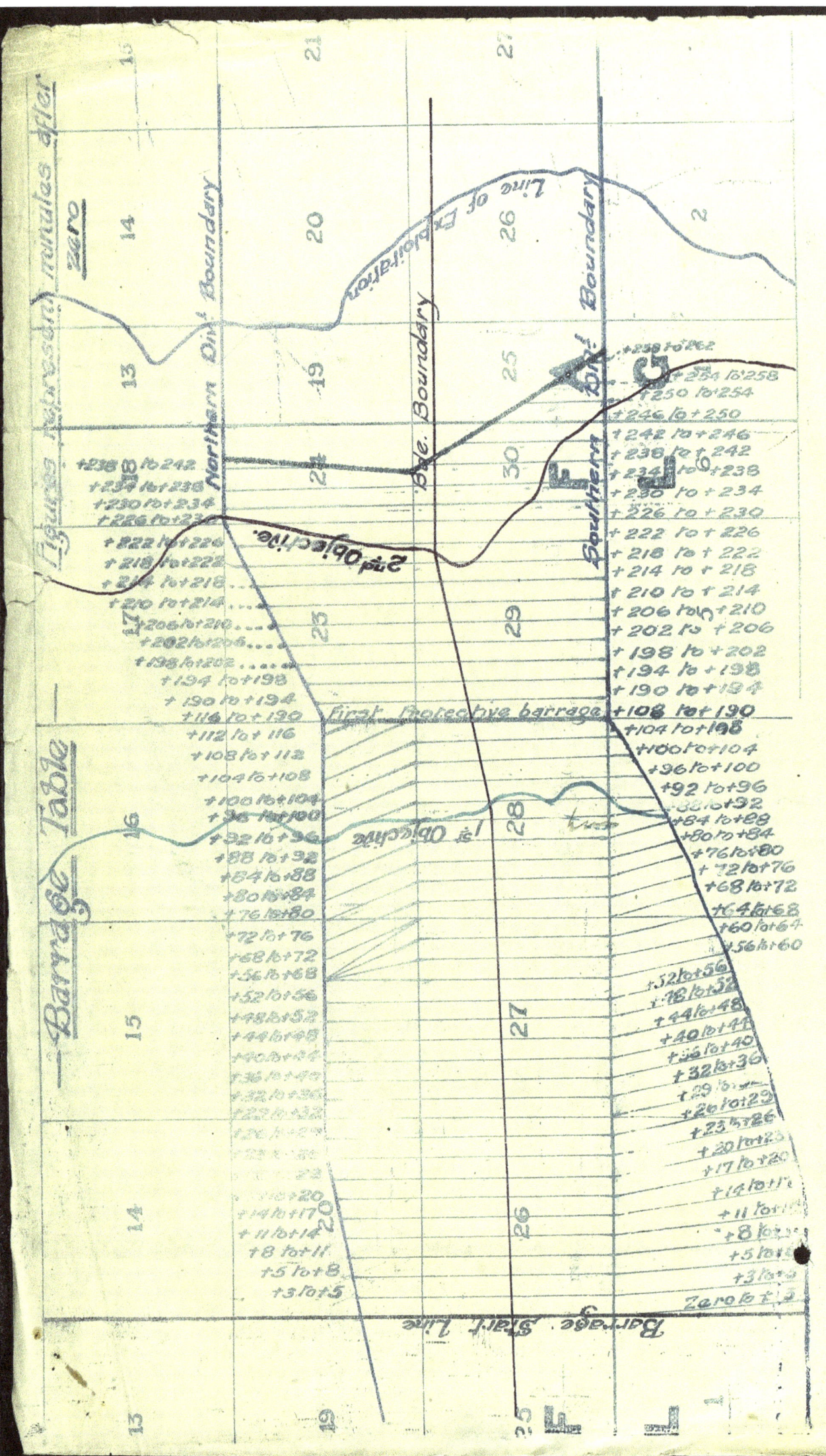

SECRET.
****

74TH DIVISION ORDER NO 91.

20th September 1918.

1. The Division will attack the BLUE Line to-morrow.
The objectives are QUENNEMONT FARM, QUENNET COPSE, and GILLEMONT FARM.
The boundaries are as given in Warning Order.
The objectives of the 18th Division are THE KNOLL and FLEECEALL POST.
1st Australian Division is attacking the spur in G.2.a.

2. The 230th Brigade will attack on the right and the 231st Brigade on the left.

3. 4 Tanks will be attached to the 231st Brigade to assist in the capture of DUNCAN POST, CAT POST, and GILLEMONT FARM.
The 231st Brigade will issue orders direct to O.C. 'B' Coy Tanks.

4. The 229th Brigade, to which one battalion of the 58th Division will be attached, will hold the GREEN Line with two battalions, and will be in occupation of it by 5. a.m.

5. Arrangements for barrage and forming up line will be as given in G.506.

6. "A" and "C" Companies, Machine Gun Battn, will be attached to 230th and 231st Brigades respectively.
O.C. Machine Gun Battn is arranging for the advance of both Brigades to be covered by Machine Guns, and for the consolidation of the Divisional Sector in depth from the Infantry forming up line Westward.
Two companies of Machine Gun Battn will be in Divisional Reserve.

7. Contact planes will fly at 1½ and 3 hours after zero.
Troops will be specially warned to indicate their positions by flares, rows of rifles, and waving of helmets.

8. Zero hour will be at 5.40 a.m.

9. ACKNOWLEDGE.

(Sgd) A.C. TEMPERLEY.
Lieut Colonel.
General Staff.
74th (Yeomanry) Division.

Issued at 6.p.m.

Copies to :- 229th Inf. Bde.   Machine Gun Battn.
              230th Inf. Bde.   A.D.M.S.
              231st Inf. Bde.   Div. Train.
              C.R.A.   "B" Coy, 2nd Tank Battn.
              C.R.E.   3rd Corps.
              'Q' Branch.   18th Division.
              Signals.   1st Australian Division.

"A" Form.
MESSAGES AND SIGNALS.

Army Form C. 2121.
(In pads of 100.)

Urgent Operation Priority to 231 Bde.

TO	230 Bde	C.R.A.
	231 Bde	18 Div
	229 Bde	3 Corps.

Sender's Number.	Day of Month.	In reply to Number.	AAA
G. 556	21		

To clear up situation in CAT POST - DUNCAN POST quadrilateral 231 Bde will arrange to attack position at 10.30 p.m. tonight in close co-operation with Right Bde 18 Div aaa intense bombardment of quadrilateral will be arranged by C.R.A. from 10 p.m. to 10.30 p.m. aaa at 10.30 p.m. bombardment will lift and posts will be rushed aaa RED Line will be consolidated after capture aaa troops will be withdrawn to safe distance during bombardment aaa 231 Bde to acknowledge aaa Addsd 231 Bde C.R.A. reptd 230 and 229 Bdes 18 Div and 3 Corps.

From 74 Div
Place
Time 6.10 p.m.

(Sd) H.S. SHARP Capt G.S.

"A" Form.
MESSAGES AND SIGNALS.

Army Form C. 2121.
(In pads of 100.)

TO	230 Bde	CRA
	231 Bde	229 Bde
	MGBn	

Sender's Number.	Day of Month.	In reply to Number.	AAA
G 515	20.		

Special instruction to 230 Bde reference Div Order 91 aaa On reaching QUENNEMONT FARM you will form a defensive flank through A.25 back to Red line about MALAKOFF farm aaa The enemy trenches in low ground in A.26 will be kept under MG and artillery fire during the operation aaa During your advance D. Coy 2nd Life Guards will provide the MG fire for this purpose aaa after your objective has

"A" Form.
MESSAGES AND SIGNALS.

Army Form C. 2121.
(In pads of 100.)

TO — 2

been reached you will arrange for machine guns attached to your Bde to engage these trenches aaa 1st Aust Div may advance northwards towards MALAKOFF wood and no fire should be directed south of southern edge of the wood added 230 Bde rptd all concerned

From 7th Div
Time 4pm

(Sd) Ct Hempenly

"A" Form.
MESSAGES AND SIGNALS.

Army Form C. 2121.
(In pads of 100.)

Office of Origin and Service Instructions.
Urgent Operation
Priority 229,
231 Bdes.

TO:
- 229 Bde. C.R.A.
- 230 Bde
- 231 Bde

Sender's Number: G. 547
Day of Month: 21
AAA

229 Bde will send forward one battn immediately to occupy BELLICOURT Road from F.29.b.9.9. exclusive to Divl Boundary aaa Bn on arrival will come under orders of 231 Bde aaa remaining Bn in Bde reserve will occupy GREEN LINE aaa 229 Bde will report when moves complete aaa 229 and 231 Bdes to ack aaa Addsd 229 230 231 Bdes and C.R.A.

From: 74 Div
Time: 1.20 p.m.

(Sd) T.H. NAYLOR, Lt.

"A" Form.
MESSAGES AND SIGNALS.

Army Form C. 2121.
(In pads of 100.)

Prefix........ Code............ m	Words.	Charge.	This message is on a/c of:	Recd. at .... m.
Office of Origin and Service Instructions. Urgent Operation Priority to 231 Bde.	Sent At...........m. To.............. By.............		XXXIX ...Service. (Signature of "Franking Officer.")	Date............ From .... By ....

TO	231 Bde 230 Bde 229 Bde	C.R.A. 18 Div 3 Corps.		
Sender's Number. *G. 558	Day of Month. 21	In reply to Number.	A A A	

Reference G.556 attack will be at 12.15 a.m. aaa Bombardment will be from 12 midnight to 12.15 a.m. aaa Heavies will not take part aaa Addsd 231 Bde to acknowledge reptd all concerned.

From 74 Div.
Place
Time 6.55 p.m.

The above may be forwarded as now corrected.
(Z)
(Sd) A. GALLOWAY Capt G.S.

Censor. Signature of Addressor or person authorised to telegraph in his name.

* This line should be erased if not required.

S E C R E T.

Appendix XL

WARNING ORDER.

22nd September 1918.

74th Division will be relieved in the line on the night September 24th/25th.

Further details later.

[signature]

Lieut Colonel.
General Staff.
Issued at 10.a.m. 74th (Yeomanry) Division.

Copies to :-   "G"
              "Q"
              C.R.A.   A.D.M.S.
              C.R.E.   Div. Train.
              Signal Coy.   War Diary.
              M.G.Battn.   File.
              229th Inf. Bde.
              230th Inf. Bde.
              231st Inf. Bde.

Appendix XLI

SECRET.
* * * * * *

74TH DIVISION ORDER NO 92.

22nd September 1918.

1. The 229th Brigade, to which the Suffolks will be attached, will take over the RED Line as far North as ~~BENJAMIN POST (inclusive)~~. CAT POST (exclusive)
Thence line as far as Divisional boundary will be held by the 231st Brigade.

2. The 230th Brigade, less one battn, will take over the GREEN Line from the Southern Divisional Boundary to TOINE POST (exclusive).
The 8th London Regiment and responsibility for the GREEN Line north of TOINE POST (inclusive) will pass to 18th Division at 8.p.m. to-night.

3. The 74th Machine Guns covering the GREEN Line north of TOINE POST will be relieved by machine guns with the 174th Brigade.

4. The Pioneer Battn and Life Guards Machine Gun Company will be transferred to the 230th Brigade, and the Devons will rejoin the 229th Brigade.

5. O.C. Machine Gun Battn will make the necessary readjustments of Machine Guns.

6. Brigades will be disposed in depth.

7. Command of sectors will pass on completion of relief which will be reported by wire.

8. The Northern Divisional boundary from 8.p.m. will be F.19.c.0.4. - CLIFFE POST (inclusive) - TOINE POST (exclusive) - MILL LANE (inclusive) thence due East.

9. ACKNOWLEDGE.

(Signed) A.C. TEMPERLEY.
Lieut Colonel.
General Staff.
74th (Yeomanry) Division.

Issued at 1.15 p.m.

Copies to :—
229th Inf. Bde.
230th Inf. Bde.
231st Inf. Bde.
C.R.A.
C.R.E.
'Q'
Signals.
M.G.Battn.

A.D.M.S.
Div Train.
3rd Corps.
18th Division.
1st Australian Division.

appendix XLII

SECRET.   Copy No. 21

74th DIVISION ORDER NO 93.

23rd Sept 1918.

1.   The 74th Division and 18th Division are being relieved
        in the line by 53rd Brigade 27th American Division on the
        night September 24th/25th.

2.   The 1st Battalion, 106th American Regt with one coy
        2nd Battn attached will relieve 229th Brigade in the RED Line.
            The coy of the 2nd Battn will take over from BULL POST
        inclusive to the Northern Divisional boundary.

3.   The 174th Brigade, attached to 18th Division, will take
        over to-night the GREEN Line from 230th Brigade as far South
        as the Divisional boundary and will hand over the whole GREEN
        line in the present 18th and 74th Division Sectors to 105th
        American Regt on the night September 24th/25th.
            The 230th Brigade less one battn will withdraw to
        Divisional Reserve and will be prepared to reinforce the
        GREEN Line if required.

4.   Relief of Machine Guns will be arranged direct between
        O.C. Machine Gun Battn and the Machine Gun Officer of the
        27th American Division.
            On completion of relief the Life Guards Machine Gun
        coys will come under the orders of III Corps and will
        subsequently join IX Corps.

5.   (a) Relief of Signals, Field Ambulances and R.E. Units
             will be arranged direct by O.C. Signals, A.D.M.S.
             and C.R.E.
                 Sufficient personnel will be left until the
             night Sept 25th/26th to ensure continuity.

        (b) The following will be left in the line until the
             night Sept 25th/26th.

             229th Brigade   2 Officers per Battn.
                                 2 N.C.Os per company.

             M.G.Battn.   1 Officer per coy.
                                 1 N.C.O. per section.

        The move of personnel mentioned in this para to the new
        area will be arranged by III Corps and Australian Corps,
        under whose orders they will be.

                                                by Brigade Groups
7.   On relief, the Division will concentrate as follows
        less those units already bivouaced West of these areas.

             229th Brigade Group   in K.5.c. & d.   - K.11.a.
             230th Brigade Group   in K.5.a. & b.   E.29.d.
             231st Brigade Group   in E.29.a. b. & c.

8.   The dismounted personnel of the Division will move by
        tactical trains to the CORBIE Area on Sept 25th.
            The first train will probably start from TINCOURT
        about 10. a.m. The route to TINCOURT will be via
        ROISEL.
            Units of Brigade Groups not located in the Brigade
        bivouac areas will march direct to TINCOURT Station.

                                                /9. Orders

9.   Orders for the move of 1st Line Transport will be issued later.

10.   The 74th Divisional Artillery less S.A.A. Section will remain under the orders of the III Corps.

11.   All distances on the march will be as laid down in Divisional March Standing Orders.

12.   Completion of reliefs will be reported by wire to Divisional H.Q.

13.   Command of the Divisional Sector will pass to G.O.C. 27th American Division at 10. a.m. on September 25th.

14.   Divisional H.Q. will close at present position at 10.a.m. on September 25th and open at CORBIE at the same hour.

15.   ACKNOWLEDGE.

[signature]

Lieut Colonel.
General Staff.
74th (Yeomanry) Division.

Issued at.....1.30p...

Copies to:-
```
     No. 1.   'G!B.C.            13.   A.D.M.S.
         2.   'G'                14.   Div.Train.
       3-5.   'Q'                15.   III Corps.
         6.   C.R.A.             16.   1st Aust.Div.
         7.   C.R.E.             17.   18th Division.
         8.   Signal Coy.        18.   27th American Div.
         9.   M.G.Battn.         19.         Aus.Corps.
        10.   229th Inf.Bde   20-21.   War Diary.
        11.   230th   "    "    22.   File.
        12.   231st   "    "
```

Appendix XLIII

SECRET.

Copy No ...31...

ADDENDUM NO 2 TO
74TH DIVISION ORDER NO 93.
====================================

24th September 1918.

1. Horse Transport of Brigade Groups (less certain vehicles) will pass the starting point (Railway Crossing at ROISEL in K.16.a.) on route to CORBIE area tonight as under :-

   229th Infantry Brigade Group.   8 p.m.
   230th Infantry Brigade Group.   9 p.m.
   231st Infantry Brigade Group.   10 p.m.

   Route - BUSSU - ST DENIS - CLERY - MARICOURT - BRAY - CORBIE.

   Transport will be clear of CLERY by 4 a.m. on Septr 25th and will halt in the area A.22, 23, 28 and 29.
   The march will be resumed at 5 p.m. on Septr 25th to final destinations under the orders of Major F.B. HARDY, Divisional Train.

2. Brigade Groups will be under the command of Os.C. affiliated Companies of Div. Train. Major F.B. HARDY, A.S.C. will be in command of all the transport and will issue orders for the second stage of the march.

3. Transport of Units attached to Brigade Groups not bivouaced in Brigade Areas may join grouped transport under Brigade arrangements en route but before joining column it must be halted short of road junctions.
   Divisional H.Q. will march with 229th Brigade Group, and will join it at BUSSU.
   The A.P.M. will arrange for Traffic control at the Starting Point.
   Brigade Starting Points will be fixed in Brigade Areas and heads of Columns will not approach the Starting Point before the time ordered.

4. Cookers, Limbered G.S. Wagons for Machine Guns and Lewis Guns will remain behind in the ROISEL - ST EMILIE Valley till the morning of Septr 25th. These wagons of the 3 Brigades will march to the staging area at 10 a.m. under orders of an officer to be detailed by B.G.C., 229th Infantry Brigade. They will halt there for the night and resume the march to final destinations on the morning of Septr 26th.

5. Guides will be detailed to meet the transport at CORBIE and guide it to Brigade areas.

6. Locations of Brigades will be as under :-

   Divisional H.Q.   CORBIE.
   229th Brigade Group.   CORBIE - LAMEUVILLE.
        Brigade H.Q.   CORBIE.
   230th Brigade Group.   GLISY - BLANGY TRONVILLE - FOULLOY.
        Brigade H.Q.   GLISY
   231st Brigade Group.   VILLERS - BRETONNEUX - HAMELET.
        Brigade H.Q.   VILLERS - BRETONNEUX.

7. Distances will be in accordance with Div. March Standing Orders

8. ACKNOWLEDGE.

Acemperley
Lieut-Colonel,
General Staff,
74th (Yeomanry) Division.

- 2 -

Copies to all recipients of 74th Division Order No. 95
plus one Copy Major HARDY, Divisional Train.
~~one extra copy~~ 229th Infantry Brigade.

SECRET.   Copy No. 71

ADDENDUM TO

74th DIVISION ORDER NO 93.   23rd September 1918.

Brigade Groups will be formed as under:-

229th Infantry Brigade Group.   **230th Infantry Brigade Group.**

    229th Infantry Brigade.   230th Infantry Brigade.
    439th Field Coy R.E.   R.M. Field Coy R.E.
    S.A.A. Section, D.A.C.   Machine Gun Battalion.
    No 2 Coy Div. Train.   No 3 Coy Div. Train.
    229th Field Ambulance.   230th Field Ambulance.

231st Infantry Brigade Group.

    231st Infantry Brigade.
    R.A. Field Coy R.E.
    Pioneer Battalion.
    No 4 Coy Div. Train.
    231st Field Ambulance.

[signature: A.C. Temperley]

                                               Lieut Colonel.
                                               General Staff,
Issued at 8.p.m.   74th (Yeomanry) Division.

Copies to all recipients of 74th Division Order No 93.

Appendix XLIV

S E C R E T.

Copy No...17...

74th DIVISION ORDER NO 94.

25th September 1918.

1. 74th Division is moving by train on September 27th and 28th to Fifth Army area, where it will come under the orders of the G.O.C., XIII Corps.

2. The move will be carried out in accordance with the attached table. Detailed instructions will be issued by the A.A. & Q.M.G.

3. Divisional H.Q. will close at its present position at 10 a.m. and open at ST HILAIRE at 2 p.m. on September 27th.

4. ACKNOWLEDGE.

A C Temperley.

Lieut-Colonel,
General Staff,
74th (Yeomanry) Division.

Issued at 8 p.m.

Copies to:-
No. 1.	G.O.C.	12.	231st Inf.Bde.
2.	'G'.	13.	A.D.M.S.
3-5.	'Q'.	14.	Div.Train.
6.	C.R.A.	15.	XIII Corps.
7.	C.R.E.	16.	War Diary.
8.	Signal Coy.	17.	War Diary.
9.	M.G.Battn.	18.	File.
10.	229th Inf.Bde.	19.	III Corps.
11.	230th Inf.Bde.		

UNIT.	ENTRAINING STATION.	DETRAINING STATION.	NEW BILLETTING AREA.	REMARKS.
229th Brigade Group.	MERICOURT L'ABBE	BERGUETTE.	HAM-EN-ARTOIS.	March to Station by road through I.35.b., I.30.a. and c., cross roads J.21.a.
230th Brigade Group.	HEILLY.	LILLERS.	ECQUEDECQUES - HURIONVILLE - BURBURE.	Machine Gun Battn to western portion of GONNEHEM - BAS RIEUX area.
231st Brigade Group.	CORBIE.	CHOCQUES.	GONNEHEM - BAS RIEUX.	by road through I.29.d. and b.

S E C R E T.
＊＊＊＊＊＊＊＊＊＊

Appendix XLV

WARNING ORDER.

27th September 1918.

1. The 74th Division is relieving 19th Division in the line commencing probably on the night Oct. 2nd/3rd.

2. 19th Division holds roughly the old British front line from S.23.a. to M.30.a. A plan of the present dispositions is being sent to you.

3. There are two Brigades in the line and one in Divisional Reserve. The front is roughly 6,000 yards.

4. Details of relief will be notified later.
    230th and 231st Brigades will be the Right and Left Brigades respectively in the line.

(Sd) A.E. TEMPERLEY,
Lieut-Colonel,
General Staff,
74th (Yeomanry) Division.

Copies to:-
229th Infantry Brigade.
230th Infantry Brigade.
231st Infantry Brigade.
C.R.E.
'Q'.
74th Bn, M.G.C.
A.D.M.S.
74th Div. Train.
74th Div. Signal Coy.

SECRET.   Copy No. 14

WARNING ORDER.

Ref. Map:-   28th Sept., 1918.
    36. 1/40,000

1. 74th Division relieves 19th Division in the line commencing probably on night October 2nd/3rd.

    The 19th Division holds roughly the old British Front Line from S.23.a. to M.30.a., some 8,000 yards.

2. 231st Infantry Brigade will hold the Left Sector of this front with 230th Infantry Brigade on its Right.

    10th K.S.L.I. will be on the Right.
    24th Welsh R. will be on the Left.
    25th R.W.F.   will be in Reserve.

                                    Brigade Major,
                                    231st Infantry Brigade.

Issued at 3/6... D.R.L.S. and Runner.

Copies to:-

No.1 74th Div.	No.6 231st L.T.M.B.	No.11 Sig. Officer.
2 B.G.C.	7 R.A.R.E.	12 War Diary.
3 25th R.W.F.	8 450th A.S.C.	13 War Diary.
4 24th Welsh R.	9 Supply Officer.	14 File.
5 10th K.S.L.I.	10 Staff Capt.	15 Spare.

Appendix XLVI

SECRET.   Copy No. 19

74th DIVISION ORDER NO. 95.

                                                28th September 1918.

1. 74th Division will relieve 19th Division in the line in accordance with the attached Table.

2. Two Brigade Groups will move by Light Railway from BURBURE and CHOCQUES. Times of trains will be notified later.

3. B.G.C., 230th Brigade and O.C., M.G.Battn will arrange for cookers to meet the troops at railhead on Oct. 1st in order to give them a hot meal prior to going into the line.

4. All details of relief will be arranged direct between Brigadiers concerned.

5. O.C., Machine Gun Battn, C.R.E., O.C., Signal Company and A.D.M.S. will arrange all details direct with those concerned.

6. All transport will move by road, distances will be kept in accordance with Divisional March Standing Orders.

7. Completion of all reliefs will be reported by wire to Divisional Headquarters.

8. All troops entering 19th Divisional Area will be under the command of G.O.C., 19th Division until command passes.

9. Command of the Divisional Sector will pass to G.O.C., 74th Division at 10 a.m. on Oct. 3rd, at which hour Div. H.Q. will open at W.30.a.7.8. and close at MORRENT FONTES.

10. ACKNOWLEDGE.

                                        A.C. Sempull
                                        Lieut-Colonel,
                                        General Staff,
                                        74th (Yeomanry) Division.

Issued at... 5.30 p.m.

Copies to:-
Copy No. 1.	G.O.C.	No. 13.	A.D.M.S.
2.	'G'	14.	Div. Train.
3-5.	'Q'.	15.	XIth Corps.
6.	C.R.A.	16.	19th Division.
7.	C.R.E.	17.	55th Division.
8.	Signal Coy.	18-19	War Diary.
9.	M.G. Battn.	20.	File.
10.	229th Inf. Bde.		
11.	230th " "		
12.	231st " "		

RELIEF TABLE.

DATE.	UNIT.	TO RELIEVE.	HOW.	REMARKS.
Sept 30th.	One M.G.Coy.	Left Brigade Sector.	By lorry.	Take over night Oct 1st/2nd.
Oct. 1st.	231st Infantry Brigade Group.	Brigade in Divisional Reserve.	By march route.	advance parties to line by lorries.
Oct 1st/2nd.	230th Infantry Brigade Group.	Right Brigade Sector.	by light railway from CHOCQUES.	Take over night Oct 2nd/3rd.
"	One M.G.Coy.	"	"	
Oct. 2nd.	229th Infantry Brigade Group.	231st Infantry Brigade in Divl Reserve.	by light railway from BURBURE.	
"	One M.G.Coy.	Line of Retention.	by light railway from CHOCQUES.	
"	One M.G.Coy.	Divisional Reserve.	From Div. Reserve	
Oct 2nd/3rd.	231st Infantry Brigade Group.	Left Brigade Sector.		

SECRET.   Copy No. 19

74TH DIVISION ORDER NO. 96.

29th September 1918.

1.   The successful offensives being conducted by the Allied Armies may cause the enemy opposite the front of the Fifth Army to continue his withdrawal to the line of the DOUAI - LILLE Canal and the LILLE defences.

2.   In order to test the strength of the enemy forces opposed to the XI Corps, minor operations are being carried out by 3 Divisions tomorrow morning.

3.   On taking over the front of the 19th Division, it is of great importance that this Division should be prepared to act promptly as soon as indications are obtained that the enemy intends to withdraw, or is in process of retiring.

4.   It is not the intention of the Divisional Commander to force a withdrawal, but he intends to follow up and hasten a withdrawal should it commence, and to cut off isolated posts of the enemy should the opportunity occur. Troops in the front line must act with vigour, and be prepared to go on a pre-arranged plan without waiting for orders.

5.   Each Brigade will have its own Advanced Guard ready detailed which will be directed upon the most important tactical localities during this advance and will not necessarily advance in lines or waves.

6.   In order to gain information of the intentions of the enemy, the following steps will be taken :-
   (a) Patrols will maintain touch with enemy's front line system of defences.
   (b) Raiding parties will kill or capture the garrison of small posts with the object of obtaining information as to the enemy's dispositions.
   (c) In those parts of the line where patrols and raiding parties cannot find any hostile posts, our line will be advanced and promptly held, and defences will be constructed so as to form a jumping off place for the further action of patrols and raiding parties.

7.   Boundaries and the first objectives of the Division are shown on the attached map. The third objective is the line ILLIES - HERLIES - FROMELLES. Further objectives will be issued later.

8.   The road allotted to the Division for traffic and for signal communication is the HALPEGARBE - HERLIES Road running East from S.17.b. Brigade and Div. H.Q. will be located as near this road as is practicable.

9.   ACKNOWLEDGE.

A.C.Temperley.
Lieut-Colonel,
General Staff,
74th (Yeomanry) Division.

Issued at 10.3pm.

For distribution see overleaf.

Copies to:-

Copy No. 1.	G.O.C.	No. 13.	A.D.M.S.
2.	'G'.	14.	Div. Train.
3-5.	'Q'.	15.	XIth Corps.
6.	C.R.A., 19th Div.	16.	19th Division.
7.	C.R.E.	17.	55th Division.
8.	Signal Coy.	18-19.	War Diary.
9.	M.G. Battn.	20.	File.
10.	229th Inf. Bde.		
11.	230th " "		
12.	231st " "		

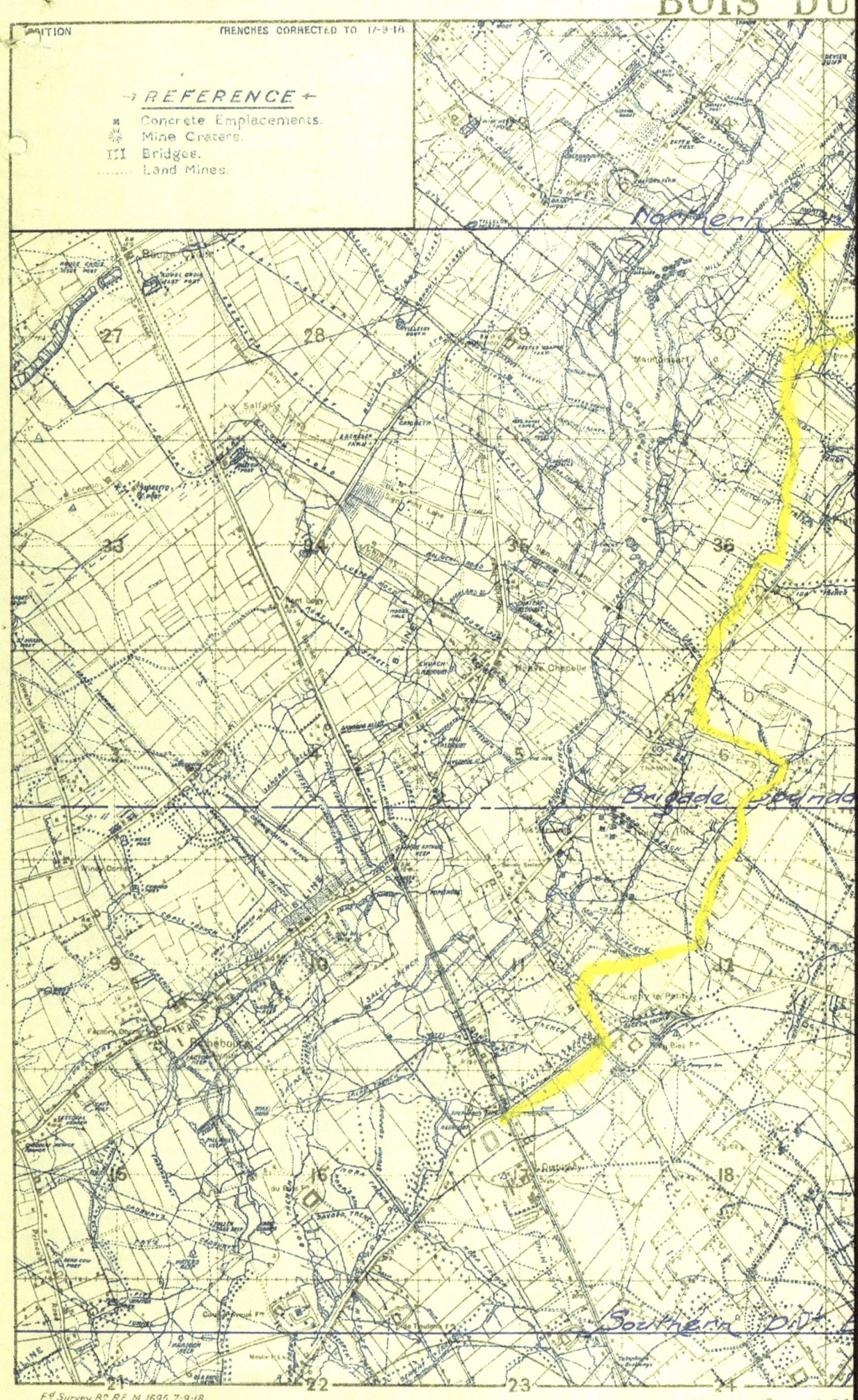

BIEZ

Confidential

War Diary

of

74th (Yeo) Division

General Staff,

From 1st Octr 1918 To 31st Octr 1918.

9/27

Army Form C. 2118.

G.S. 74th Division
October 1918

WAR DIARY
or
INTELLIGENCE SUMMARY.
(Erase heading not required.)

Sheet 36 S.W. 1/40,000.

Place	Date	Hour	Summary of Events and Information	Remarks and references to Appendices
NORRENT FONTES	Oct. 1st.		230th Brigade Group proceeded from CHOCQUES by light railway to take over Right sector of 19th Division. 231st Brigade Group marched to relieve Brigade in Divisional Reserve in 19th Division and completed relief by 1705.	O.C.
	Oct. 2nd.	0100	Relief of 58th Brigade by 230th Brigade completed.	
		1330	229th Brigade moved by light railway and relieved 231st Brigade in Divisional Reserve.	
		1300	Air report timed 1210 that our infantry in HOGRON (U.19) and advancing towards SAINGHIN.	
		1415	Air report timed 1328 that our infantry are in FOURNES and are advancing along the road towards BEAUCAMPS.	
		1500	230th Brigade report at 1340 that their patrols are East of WICRES and the SUGAR FACTORY.	
		1510	Order issued for 229th Brigade to move to occupy 'B' line with its H.Q. at CURZON POST.	
		1600	230th Brigade report that at 1330 their troops could be seen on SUGAR FACTORY - WICRES line and at 1420 patrols were reported at GDE RUE.	APP. I
		1750	Situation sent to Corps and all concerned that Right Battalion 230th Brigade had reached gde RUE and left Battalion were last reported passing through Eastern edge of T.12. 231st Brigade had one Battalion from U.1.c.7.4. - 0.31.d.3.1. to 0.31.a.9.4. and left Battalion echeloned back to Divisional Boundary U.8.b. and d.: not yet in touch with 55th Division. Left Brigade Right Battalion is on line FOURNES - U.32.central. Left battalion was last reported at LES MOTTES Chateau - BAS FLANDRE but has probably advanced since then. In touch with 47th Division.	
		1930	Final Situation report sent to all concerned that Right Brigade is on line BASSERUE	
	Oct. 3rd.	0130	Relief of 56th Brigade by 231st Brigade completed.	
		0600	Line ran along LA BASSEE, AUBERS, FROMELLES line from T.20.a.central to N.21.c.4.0.	
		1250	Right Brigade reported at 1120 on line from T.21.b.1.5. to T.11.c.0.0. thence North to HERULES whence Left Brigade line ran to LE GRAND PRIEZ:- Divisional Boundary in N.23.c.3.0. Patrols reported in WICRES, FOURNES and on road in 0.31.a. Wired to Corps and flank Divisions.	O.C.

Army Form C. 2118.

WAR DIARY
or
INTELLIGENCE SUMMARY.
(Erase heading not required.)

Instructions regarding War Diaries and Intelligence Summaries are contained in F. S. Regs., Part II. and the Staff Manual respectively. Title pages will be prepared in manuscript.

Place	Date	Hour	Summary of Events and Information	Remarks and references to Appendices
	Oct 3rd	(contd) 2040	Orders issued for resumption of advance at 0800 on the 4th instant.	APP. II.
		2200	Reconnaissance ordered for men South of LILLE. O.C. Troop of 'G' Squadron, 1 K.E.H. conducting reconnaissance starting 0730.	
		2359	Order sent out that Platoon of Cyclists will report to 231st Brigade at 0720 on 4th inst in order to establish a chain of relay posts with mounted patrol reconnaissance.	a.
	Oct 4th	0905	Order sent out that 1 troop of K.E.H. would be attached to 230th Brigade and 1 troops to 231st Brigade remainder of Squadron to be moved to vicinity of HERLIES and be in Divisional Reserve.	
		1000	Report from 230th Brigade to say that they reached first objective at 0800. No opposition encountered.	
		1212	Report from 230th Brigade timed 1155 to the effect that they had advanced well east of LATTRE. Experienced no M.G. fire but fairly heavy shelling.	a.
		1355	Report from 231st Brigade timed 1205 - "Right Battalion reached first objective at 1000. Left Battalion also have one Company on first objective but exact location of left Company not known. Enemy holding position in front of 231st Brigade in strength. Considerable opposition and fairly heavy shelling.	
		1600	Line ran East of WAVRIN and LATTRES with Right flank refused to U.22.a., thence along railway to LA HAIE - O.34.b.9.4. - O.28.a.6.4. Resistance stiffened considerably and Division is opposed to a definite outpost position.	
	Oct 5th	0600	Quiet night spent and situation unchanged on Divisional front. All patrols on the front were met by determined resistance and considerable Machine Gun fire.	a.
		1600	Divisional Headquarters closed at present position (W.30.a.7.8.) and opened same hour at S.12.d.8.7.	
		1715	Situation remained unchanged.	
	Oct 6th	0600	Situation remained unchanged. Nothing worthy of note.	
		1925	Warning Order issued that 229th Brigade would relieve 231st Brigade on the night 9th/10th	APP III.

October.

Army Form C. 2118.

WAR DIARY
or
INTELLIGENCE SUMMARY.
(Erase heading not required.)

Instructions regarding War Diaries and Intelligence Summaries are contained in F. S. Regs., Part II. and the Staff Manual respectively. Title pages will be prepared in manuscript.

Place	Date	Hour	Summary of Events and Information	Remarks and references to Appendices
	Oct 7th.	0600	Situation remained unchanged. Night patrols of 230th Brigade made further progress than usual but morning patrols reported enemy still in occupation of posts West of Canal.	APP IV.
		1315	Orders issued that Northern Boundary would be altered tonight and 231st Brigade would take over new area. Inter Brigade Boundary was also altered.	
	8th.	0600	Situation unchanged.	
		1000	Command of Sector held by 55th and 74th Divisions passed to G.O.C., III Corps from G.O.C., XI Corps.	APP. V.
		1100	Instructions received that 1 Officer and 40 O.R. of 'C' Squadron 1st K.E.H. were to report to A.P.M. III Corps at 1200 on 9th inst for traffic control.	
		1400	Relief of 231st Brigade by 229th Brigade cancelled 24 hours.	
		1700	Divisional Order No 98 issued - ordering readjustment of Divisional and Brigade boundaries and also detailing reliefs to take place on night 10th/11th instant.	
		1745	Situation remained unchanged.	
		2200	O.C., 'C' Squadron K.E.H. ordered to send back platoon XI Corps Cyclists Battalion to rejoin their Battalion Headquarters by 1200 on 9th instant. One troop of the Squadron also moving to Headquarters, 55th Division.	
	9th	0530	Situation reported quiet. At 0615 Enemy raided one of our posts between O.35.c.8.8. and O.35.d.5.6. No details available at the time but enemy believed to have entered our line under cover of a heavy mist. 24 men of 10th K.S.L.I. missing. Subsequent to raid enemy put down a heavy barrage on our Front line in the vicinity of the portion raided.	
		0615		
		1330	Lt.Col. A.C. TEMPERLEY, G.S.O.1 proceeded on 10 days leave. Lt.Col. BROAD assumed duties of G.S.O. 1 in his temporary absence.	
		1530	Situation unchanged. Quiet day in the line.	
		2200	Defence Instructions issued.	APP VII.
		2200	Order issued giving alteration in Northern Boundary.	APP VI.
	10th	0515	K.S.L.I. carried out a successful raid on enemy post at LA HAIE, killing 9 of the enemy and taking one P/W belonging to 9th Coy, 3rd Bn, 91 R.I.R., 2nd Gd Reserve Division. About 20 casualties are believed to have been incurred by the enemy altogether. Our casualties were 6 wounded all of whom returned.	

Army Form C. 2118.

WAR DIARY
or
INTELLIGENCE SUMMARY.
(Erase heading not required.)

Instructions regarding War Diaries and Intelligence Summaries are contained in F. S. Regs., Part II. and the Staff Manual respectively. Title pages will be prepared in manuscript.

Place	Date	Hour	Summary of Events and Information	Remarks and references to Appendices
	Oct 10th	0530	During the night nothing unusual occurred. Situation unchanged.	
		1530	Patrols who had been pushed out unable to clear up situation regarding possible enemy retirement; reported the enemy still to be in position on his usual posts. Information concerning enemy retirement was given by 3 Portuguese escaped P/W.	APP. VIII.
		2000	Divisional Order No 99 issued.	
	11th	0530	Situation remained unchanged.	
		1000	A conference was held at Divisional Headquarters at which the various schemes for an advance were put forward. Relief of 231st Brigade by 229th Brigade completed. 231st Brigade in Divisional Reserve.	
	12th		Night patrols of 16th Sussex visited RIEZ CHARLOT and bombed the enemy in hedges there. LA HAIE was found occupied. T.M's very active from E. of LA HAIE. Proposals for barrage for attack on railway line submitted to III Corps.	APP IX.
		1100	Divisional Order No 100 issued. Situation unchanged.	
	13th		Two small raids carried out during the night against enemy posts in vicinity of LA HAIE and HAU DE BRULLE. LA HAIE was found strongly held by M.G's and had to withdraw. Post at HAU DU BRULLE found to have been vacated by the enemy.	
		0510	Enemy raided posts of Right Brigade on railway line. Raid was made under cover of Artillery and T.M. smoke barrage. Raid was repulsed by rifle and M.G. fire and enemy withdrawal harassed by M.G's pushed well forward. Throughout the day owing to expected enemy withdrawal active patrolling was carried out on the whole Divisional Front. Enemy was everywhere in position and heavy M.G. fire was experienced. One of our men was missing in LA HAIE Wood.	
	14th		Active patrolling was continued throughout the day. No change in enemy's dispositions.	

Army Form C. 2118.

WAR DIARY
or
INTELLIGENCE SUMMARY.
(Erase heading not required.)

Instructions regarding War Diaries and Intelligence Summaries are contained in F. S. Regs., Part II. and the Staff Manual respectively. Title pages will be prepared in manuscript.

Place	Date	Hour	Summary of Events and Information	Remarks and references to Appendices
	Oct 15	0500	230th Brigade report that: they raided LA HAIE and found it unoccupied. They then proceeded to occupy the Railway line as far North as the Brigade Boundary.	
		0700	229th Brigade who had pushed out patrols in view of above, wired that they had occupied the line of the railway in their sector and had patrols beyond it.	
		0845	Verbal message from 229th Brigade that patrols of Royal Highlanders had reached SANTES.	
		0900	Verbal report from 230th Brigade that enemy were in BOIS de RIVE Farm and that 230th Brigade were in touch with them and trying to establish a line through O.36.central.	
		0930	Situation wired to Corps that patrols of Left Brigade have found OPTIC TRENCH O.36.b.7.9. unoccupied but fired on from V.1.a.0.1. Right Brigade are on railway along the whole front with patrols well out in front as far as SANTES and LEZ HAUBOURDIN. Held up by M.G's in BRICKFIELD O.24.b. In touch with Division on left.	
		1025	O.C. Troop, K.E.H. ordered to send half troop to each front line Brigade.	
		1125	Right Brigade report that advanced guard battalion are establishing themselves on road LACHERIE to O.36.central with patrols forward. Opposition being experienced from BOIS de RIVE. Corps informed.	
		1220	Left Brigade report that they are on first objective with patrols in P.25.d.	
		1500	Left Brigade report that in order to conform with Division on left the line of their left Company runs O.24.central to O.23.b.9.9. not in touch with 47th Division.	
		1530	Right Brigade report timed 1325 that: they are on first objective.	
		1635	231st Brigade ordered to send one battalion to occupy old outpost line of resistance and to be prepared to move a second battalion to Corps Battle line tonight.	
		1830	Report to Corps that Divisional line runs V.1.c.2.0. (in touch with 55th Division) - V.1.c.4.5. - V.1.a.9.1. - V.1.b.9.2. - V.2.a.4.4. - V.2.a.5.9. - P.31.d.9.2. - P.31.d.9.9. - P.31.b.8. - P.25.d.8.1. - P.25.a.3.0. - O.24.d.9.0. - O.24.central - O.23.b.9.9. - O.23.b.9.3. (in touch with 47th Division).	
		1920	Order issued that Divisional Headquarters will open at FOURNES Chateau at 1000 tomorrow.	
		1930	Orders issued that the outpost line of resistance will be the line of the railway and that the main line of resistance will be the old outpost line of resistance.	

Army Form C. 2118.

WAR DIARY
or
INTELLIGENCE SUMMARY.
(Erase heading not required.)

Instructions regarding War Diaries and Intelligence Summaries are contained in F. S. Regs., Part II and the Staff Manual respectively. Title pages will be prepared in manuscript.

Place	Date	Hour	Summary of Events and Information	Remarks and references to Appendices
	Oct 15th	1930	No further advance was made today. Little opposition apart from numerous isolated M.G. posts was encountered throughout the advance. The enemy appears to be fairly strong on the line of the Canal.	APP. X.
		0010	Order issued giving objectives for next advance.	
	16th	0500	Quiet night except for occasional heavy bursts of shelling in the back areas of 230th Brigade.	
			Patrols of 230th Brigade reached Canal in V.2.d. but withdrew to their original line owing to heavy M.G. fire from east bank of the Canal.	
		1015	229th Brigade reported they had reached line P.25.d.7.5. - P.25.b.2.5. - P.19.central - P.19.a.5.2. - P.13.c.4.9. with patrols in P.20.d. who report factory held by enemy.	
		1600	Orders issued that 231st Brigade would relieve the 230th Brigade on the night 17/18th Oct.	APP. XI.
	17th	1010	229th Brigade report their patrols crossed Canal at P.21.a.0.8. and have reached second objective at P.28.a.5.6. They report bridge at P.21.a.0.8. can only be crossed by infantry in single file.	
		1015	230th Brigade report 0945 that whole of leading Battalion are across Canal and advancing.	
		1030	229th Brigade report 1005 patrols of both Battalions now on second objective. No enemy seen.	
		1115	Corps report 55th Division through WATTIGNIES and TEMPLEMARS.	
		1130	230th Brigade report Left Company of their leading Battalion through EMMERIN.	
		1215	P.O.W. 1st Bty, 23rd Res. F.A.R. reported captured in HAUBOURDIN.	
		1330	Message from 229th Brigade 1215 to say that patrols have reached LOOS Station.	
		1510	230th Brigade report third objective reached and have patrols in ARBRISSEAU and WATTIGNIES.	
		1555	Wire from 230th Brigade that Buffs are pushing on to line of third objective.	
		1600	Further objective given to attacking Brigade - the railway line from X.2.c. to Q.17.b.8.0. Brigade H.Q. ordered to move to following places :-	
		1730	229th Brigade H.Q. LA CROISETTE. - 230th and 231st Brigades to L'ARBRISSEAU. Situation to Corps. No definite news of front line troops but believed to be well on towards the objective.	

Army Form C. 2118.

WAR DIARY
or
INTELLIGENCE SUMMARY.
(Erase heading not required.)

Instructions regarding War Diaries and Intelligence Summaries are contained in F. S. Regs., Part II. and the Staff Manual respectively. Title pages will be prepared in manuscript.

Place	Date	Hour	Summary of Events and Information	Remarks and references to Appendices
	17th	1800	Divisional Order No. 101 issued giving further special objectives to the front Brigade the objectives being the crossings of the River MARCQ.	APP. XII.
		2205	Reference Divisional order 101, special objectives for Right Brigade is LA PLACE (S.1). CIRUSON (M.33), Left Brigade PONT à TRESSIN (M.20.b.). Left Brigade to form defensive flank on line ASCQ - HELLEMMES.	
	18th	0200	231st Brigade report that they have reached final objective for the day and have patrols out on line X.3 - R.26. 230th Brigade withdrawn into reserve in WATTIGNIES - FLEQUIERES area.	
		0330	229th Brigade report Devons reached final objective and have line of picquets on high ground running through R.20.	
		0530	Situation reported to Corps.	
		1200	Information received that our Right Brigade had patrol in SAINGHIN Village at 0930, and that our Left Brigade Advanced Guard had reached line ASCQ - R.23.c. at 0930 and was pushing on to objective. Defensive Flank in position ASCQ - HELLEMMES line. Left Brigade reports not yet in touch with 59th Division on their left.	
		1400	Information from 59th Division that enemy reported in L.13.b, L.26 and L.14.a.4.2. 59th Division dealing with same. 229th Brigade informed.	
WATTIGNIES.		1530	Divisional Headquarters closed at FOURNES CHATEAU and opened same hour at WATTIGNIES CHATEAU.	
		1600	Divisional line at 1300 ran as follows,- X.5.c.9.0. - eastern outskirts of SAINGHIN WOOD. - FORT de la JONCHERE, in touch with 55th Division on right. Thence line ran through M.19.d. and b. with refused flank along railway from M.13.a. to HELLEMMES. Nothing seen of 59th Division on Left.	
		1845	Divisional Order No 102 issued giving orders for the advance on 19th instant to line S.4. central - M.28.central - CHERENG - TRESSIN.	APP. XIII.
		1900	Right Brigade command Western bank of 4A MARCQ, R.6.c. to M.32.a. thence along railway to M.26.central. Eastern bank of LA MARCQ held by enemy M.Gs	
		2335	Order issued that advance will continue at 0900 tomorrow.	
	19th	0800	229th Brigade report crossing of MARCQ at M.20.b.0.5. made good. Bridge in M.20.b.0.5. CHERENG and TRESSIN reported clear of enemy.	

Army Form C. 2118.

WAR DIARY
or
INTELLIGENCE SUMMARY.
(Erase heading not required.)

Instructions regarding War Diaries and Intelligence Summaries are contained in F.S. Regs., Part II. and the Staff Manual respectively. Title pages will be prepared in manuscript.

Place	Date	Hour	Summary of Events and Information	Remarks and references to Appendices
	19th	0945	231st Brigade reports patrols had crossed MARCQ river at 0640 and were pushing on to railway. Leading 2 Companies following up to make good railway. Leading Battalion in touch with 55th Division. MARCQ river ready for bridging.	
		1230	25th R.W.F. on second objective. 10th K.S.L.I. moving to line of railway. 24th Welsh under orders to move to SAINGHIN.	
		1330	230th Infantry Brigade, Support Company M.G. Battalion, 179th Army F.A. Brigade formed into Brigade Group under B.G.C., 230th Brigade. One section Field Coy. R.E. attached.	
		1430	229th Brigade report Devons were on line M.16.a.0.0. South to M.22.a.2.0. to M.28.central at 1500.	
		1515	Aeroplane report our troops seen in BAISIEUX and CAMPHIN at 1500. Troops on Southern Divisional front seen at BOURGHELLES.	
		1816	230th Brigade Headquarters closed at LESQUIN.	
		1833	231st Brigade reports their troops occupied CAMPHIN and K.E.H. patrol reconnoitring cross roads and high ground N.35.D., N.36.c. and T.5.B.	
		2030	Divisional Order No. 103 issued giving objectives for 20th instant and new Divisional Boundary.	APP. XIV.
		2210	231st Brigade report K.E.H. patrols report MARQUAIN - HAUDION - road junction N.36.c. clear of enemy.	
	20th	0600	Situation. Troops had reached their final objective and were on the line HAUDION - N.16 with patrols in front.	APP. XV.
		0900	Instructions issued for the advance on and capture of TOURNAI.	
		1020	Wire from 229th Brigade to say that at 0900 - First objective had been reached, line N.29.d. - N.17.d. - with patrols in MARQUAIN. Mounted patrol reconnoitred enemy in eastern edge MARQUAIN and had 1 killed, 1 wounded and 2 horses killed.	
		1200	Information received from 229th Brigade that enemy hold high ground in O.25, O.19, O.13. both rifle and M.G. fire experienced. Artillery of Advanced Guard dealing with situation.	
		1200	Divisional Headquarters closed at WATTIGNIES and opened at PONT à TRESSIN at 12 noon.	

Army Form C. 2118.

WAR DIARY
or
INTELLIGENCE SUMMARY.
(Erase heading not required.)

Instructions regarding War Diaries and Intelligence Summaries are contained in F. S. Regs., Part II. and the Staff Manual respectively. Title pages will be prepared in manuscript.

Place	Date	Hour	Summary of Events and Information	Remarks and references to Appendices
	20th	1730	Advance Guard Brigade hold line running immediately east of MARQUAIN. The enemy holding high ground West and N.W. of ORCQ has temporarily held up the advance. In touch with the 55th and 57th Divisions on the Right and Left respectively.	
		2130	Divisional Order No 104 issued giving orders for tomorrow's advance and to form a bridgehead East of TOURNAI.	APP. XVI.
	21st	0520	Situation unchanged. Enemy artillery and M.G's active during the night. MARQUAIN and right of line heavily shelled several times during the night. Enemy still hold O.19 and wood in O.13.d. and have several T.Ms and M.Gs in ORCQ.	
		1100	Verbal report from 229th Brigade that a patrol had entered ORCQ and found it occupied by enemy who had several M.Gs in the village.	
		1605	Right of line advanced to line 0.26.c.3.2. - 0.25.c.8.6. - 0.25.a.3.2. Patrol got within 50 yards of post in 0.26.a.2.0. and came under heavy M.G. fire and had to withdraw suffering a few casualties. Enemy artillery shelled MARQUAIN from 1345 to 1440. The guns seemed to be fired at close range and consisted of at least 1 battery 77mms.	
		2230	Divisional Order No 105 issued giving instructions about picqueting of TOURNAI by 231st Brigade.	APP XVII.
	22nd	0320	Situation sent to Corps giving result of previous night's attack. Right Company, S.L.I. held up by M.G. 400 yards from its objective - in touch at 0.27.c.5.3. with Division on right. Gap between left of Company and right of next Company at 0.21.c.7.3. whence line continued, 0.21.a.3.5., 0.21.a.30.95., 0.14.0.50.75 - 0.13.b.5.0. where in touch with Division on left. Considerable M.G. fire experienced along whole front especially from FAUBG de LILLE. T.M. fire also experienced from 0.21.a.8.5. and 0.15.d.3.3.	
		0530	Situation sent to Corps - unchanged except for left of our line which ran from 0.15.c.4.0. - 0.15.a.4.0. - where touch had been established with 57th Division on the left. Considerable M.G. fire experienced throughout the day on the whole Divisional Front.	
		1730		
		2000	Divisional Order No 106 issued that 230th Brigade would relieve 229th Brigade on the night 23rd/24th October.	APP. XVIII

Army Form C. 2118.

WAR DIARY
or
INTELLIGENCE SUMMARY.
(Erase heading not required.)

Instructions regarding War Diaries and Intelligence Summaries are contained in F. S. Regs., Part II. and the Staff Manual respectively. Title pages will be prepared in manuscript.

Place	Date	Hour	Summary of Events and Information	Remarks and references to Appendices
	23rd	0530	Situation unchanged. Considerable M.G. fire throughout the night on whole Divisional Front.	
		2000	Report from 229th Brigade that they attacked the sunken road in O.27.c. - in conjunction with brigade on right at 1645. Attack unsuccessful and our casualties were very heavy, considering the number of troops engaged. 1 Officer and 5 O.R. killed, 2 Officers and 23 O.R. being wounded.	
	24th	0530	Situation unchanged. Same active Machine Gun fire as previously experienced.	
		1730	Situation unchanged. Enemy M.Gs were still active. Intermittent shelling of main road from front line to a mile west of MARQUAIN during the day.	APP. XIX. APP. XX.
		2130	Relief of 229th Brigade by 230th Brigade completed.	
		2230	Divisional Order No 107 issued giving outpost line of resistance and main line of resistance and instructions for manning these lines.	
		2230	Divisional Order No 108 issued giving orders and objectives for future advance.	
	25th	0530	Quiet night. Enemy M.Gs less active during the day. ORCQ and vicinity heavily shelled from 1600-1700.	
	26th	0530	Quiet night.	
		0810	230th Brigade report that patrols were held up by M.G. fire. There appears to be no weakening of enemy front.	
		1730	No change during the day.	
PONT a TRESSIN.	27th	0530	No change in the line. ORCQ slightly shelled at 0530. Nothing to report. No change in enemy's attitude.	
	28th		No change in the line. Considerable E.A. activity throughout the day. Less enemy artillery and A.A. M.G. fire than previously.	
	29th	1500	350 shells (H.E. and Gas) fired on MARQUAIN between 0100 and 0200. Divisional Order No 109 issued giving instructions to Advanced Guard Brigade, TOURNAI Brigade and reserve Brigade, and orders for the military occupation of TOURNAI.	APP. XXI.

Army Form C. 2118.

WAR DIARY
or
INTELLIGENCE SUMMARY.
(Erase heading not required.)

Instructions regarding War Diaries and Intelligence Summaries are contained in F. S. Regs., Part II. and the Staff Manual respectively. Title pages will be prepared in manuscript.

Place	Date	Hour	Summary of Events and Information	Remarks and references to Appendices
	30th	0500	Quiet night - no change.	
		2200.	No change during the day. Considerable decrease in hostile artillery activity. Relief of 230th Brigade by 231st Brigade completed.	
	31st	2200	No change in situation.	
		2200	Divisional Order No 110 issued ordering a minor operation to be undertaken by 231st Brigade on November 2nd at 0515 with artillery bombardment.	APP. XXII.

"C" Form.
MESSAGES AND SIGNALS.

Army Form C 2121
(In books of 100.)

No. of Message _____

Prefix _____ Code _____ Words 31

Charges to Collect

Service Instructions

Received. From _____ By _____

Sent, or sent out. At _____ m. To _____ By _____

Office Stamp.

Handed in at YGD   Office 1855 m. Received

TO 55 DIV

Sender's Number	Day of Month.	In reply to Number	AAA
G8/4	5		

Outpost line of resistance will be BASSEE RUE U8B U2C all PETIT HAYCOURT O26B aaa nps battle line remains ILLIES SERLIES FROMELLES usual addresses

G501

FROM PLACE & TIME 74 Div 1800

* This line should be erased if not required.

3810—W.14832—100,000—2/17—E.P.Co.—(E930.)

"A" Form.
MESSAGES AND SIGNALS.

Army Form C. 2121.
(In pads of 100.)

TO	XI Corps.	229 Bde.	C.R.A.	'Q'.
	47 Div.	230 Bde.	C.R.E.	M.G.Bn.
	55 Div.	231 Bde.	Signals.	

Sender's Number.	Day of Month.	In reply to Number.	AAA
G. 789	3		

229 Bde will move to B line Bde H.Q. to CURZON POST and will be disposed in depth aaa A Coy M.G.Bn is now holding this line aaa M.G.Bn H.Q. and C Coy to S.10.a.central aaa Next objective already given verbally Bdes is BASSE RUE - U.9.a. - PETIT HAUBOURDIN - O.26.b.

Addsd	229 Bde	C.R.A.	'Q'.
	230 Bde.	C.R.E.	M.G.Bn.
	231 Bde.	Signals.	
Reptd.	11 Corps.		
	47 Div.		
	55 Div.		

From: 74 Div.
Place:
Time: 1510

(Sd) H.S. SHARP. for Lt. Col
Capt
G.S.

"A" Form.
MESSAGES AND SIGNALS.

Army Form C. 2121.
(In pads of 100.)

Priority to 3 Brigades.

TO				
229 Bde.	C.R.A.	Signals.	Div. Train.	
230 Bde.	C.R.E.	'Q'.	21 Sq. R.A.F.	
231 Bde.	M.G.Bn.	A.D.M.S.	11 Corps.	
			47 Div.	55 Div.

Sender's Number.	Day of Month.	In reply to Number.	AAA
G. 808	3		

Advance will be resumed tomorrow at 0800 aaa First objective U.22.b. - WAVRIN O.29.central - ERQUINGHEM aaa At 1030 advance will be made to Second Objective line of CANAL to HAUBOURDIN thence Northwards aaa Bridgehead will be established by 230th Brigade at LA PLANCHE des SANTES aaa Officers Patrol of K.E. Horse is reconnoitring to South of LILLE aaa 229 Brigade and one M.G.Coy to be detailed by O.C. M.G.Bn will move to an area West of HERLIES move to be complete by 1100 aaa Corps Battle Line after capture of Second Objective will be approximately SAINGHIN - BEAUCAMPS - RADINGHEM aaa Boundaries as before aaa Acknowledge Usual addresses.

From 74 Div.
Place
Time 2040.

(Sd) H.S. SHARP, Capt.

"A" Form.
MESSAGES AND SIGNALS.

Army Form C. 2121.
(In pads of 100.)

TO	229 Bde.	C.R.A.	Signals.
	230 Bde.	C.R.E.	'Q'.
	231 Bde.	M.G.Bn.	A.DM.S.

Sender's Number.	Day of Month.	In reply to Number.	AAA
G. 896	6		

Warning Order aaa 229 Bde will relieve 231 Bde in line on night Octr 9/10th aaa Addsd all concerned.

From 74 Div.
Place
Time 1925

(Sd) A.C. TEMPERLEY. Lt.Col

G.S.

"A" Form
MESSAGES AND SIGNALS.

Army Form C. 2121 (In pads of 100.)

Prefix ...... Code ...... m.	Words.	Charge.	This message is on a/c of:	Recd. at ...... m
Office of Origin and Service Instructions.	Sent			Date
Priority to 230 and 231 Bdes. (Sd) A.C.T. Lt Col. G.S.	At ...... m. To By		...... Service. (Signature of "Franking Officer.")	From By

TO	229 Bde	C.R.A.	Signals.	47 Div
	230 Bde	C.R.E.	M.G.Bn.	55 Div
	231 Bde	'Q'	11th Corps.	G Sqd KEH.

Sender's Number.	Day of Month.	In reply to Number.	AAA
* G 912	7		

Northern Divisional boundary is altered to line from O.20.c.0.0. to P.11.a.6.3. AAA In consequence 231 Bde will take over to-night from 47 Div as far North as O.22.a.3.3. AAA Inter Brigade boundary is altered to railway junction at U.5.b.7.6. AAA Eastward Bde boundary will be forwarded later AAA Completion of relief by 231 and 230 Bdes will be reported by wire AAA 230 and 231 Bdes to acknowledge Usual addresses

From: 74 Division
Place:
Time: 1325

The above may be forwarded as now corrected. (Z) (Sd) A.C.Temperley. Lt Cols.
Censor. Signature of Addressor or person authorised to telegraph in his name. G.S.

* This line should be erased if not required.

(1539). Wt. W3253/P511. 200,000 Pads. 2/18. H.C.&L., Ltd.

SECRET.
******

Appendix V
Copy No...20...

74TH DIVISION ORDER NO. 98.   8th Octr. 1918.

1.   Divisional Order No. 97 is cancelled.

2.   The Divisional and Brigade Boundaries are being readjusted as follows :-

   South Divisional Boundary.
   grid line between T.11 and T.17 (cross roads at T.11.c. inclusive to 55th Division) - T.12.c.0.0. - U.3.c.0.0. - grid line East between U.3. and U.9.

   North Divisional Boundary.
   O.20.c.0.0. - P.11.a.6.3. -
   P.11.b.8.3. - P.12.d.5.0. - P.14.c.0.8. - thence eastward.
   Inter Brigade Boundary.
   O.31.d.2.4. - O.34.b.9.4. (road junction inclusive to Right Brigade) - P.27.a.0.0. - thence eastward.

3.   On the night October 10th/11th the following reliefs will take place :-
   (a) 230th Infantry Brigade will be relieved in the line as far North as the new Southern Divisional Boundary by 55th Division.
   (b) 230th Infantry Brigade will relieve 231st Infantry Brigade as far North as inter Brigade Boundary.
   (c) 229th Infantry Brigade will relieve 231st Infantry Brigade from new inter Brigade Boundary to Northern Divisional Boundary.
   (d) Details of reliefs of machine guns will be arranged by O.C., Machine Gun Battalion.
   (e) All reliefs will be arranged direct between Brigadiers.
   (f) Completion of relief will be reported by wire to Divisional H.Q.

4.   (a) The Corps Battle line, on completion of this readjustment will be the line MARQUILLIES - East of WICRES - East of FOURNES - BAS FLANDRE.
   Brigades in the line will be disposed in depth on a one Battalion Front. The Battalion in Brigade Reserve and a proportion of the machine guns being located near the Corps Battle line which they will be prepared to occupy.
   (b) The outpost line of resistance will be the general line CHATEAU de la VALLEE CARNOYE Farm - O.26.b.

5.   The artillery will be disposed in depth to give support to any offensive action by the infantry, to maintain harassing fire and to cover the Corps Battle line.

6.   The Brigade in Divisional Reserve will be located West of a North and South line through T.5.central where the most shelter is available for the troops. It will be ready to move at one hours notice.

7.   ACKNOWLEDGE.

ACTemperley

Lieut-Colonel,
General Staff,
74th (Yeomanry) Division.

Issued at...1700...

Copies to :-

No. 1.	G.O.C.	No. 13.	A.D.M.S.
2.	'G'.	14.	Div. Train.
3-5.	'Q'.	15.	IIIrd Corps.
6.	C.R.A., 19th Div.	16.	47th Division.
7.	C.R.E.	17.	55th Division.
8.	Signal Coy.	18.	'C' Sqdn, 1/KEH.
9.	M.G. Battn.	19-20.	War Diary.
10.	229th Inf. Bde.	21.	File.
11.	230th Inf. Bde.		
12.	231st Inf. Bde.		

SECRET.
****

Copy No. 21

74TH DIVISION ORDER NO. 97.

7th October 1918.

1. The 229th Infantry Brigade will relieve 231st Infantry Brigade in the line on the night October 9th/10th.

2. On relief 231st Infantry Brigade will be disposed about the Corps Battle line - SUGAR FACTORY (T.17.d.) - HERLIES - FROMELLES.
   2 Sections Machine Gun Battalion are in action on this line.

3. Sections R.E. will remain attached to their present Brigades.
   Machine Gun Company in the Left Brigade Sector will remain in its present position and come under the orders of the B.G.C., 229th Infantry Brigade on relief.

4. 'B' teams of 229th Brigade will return to the Reception Camp under orders to be issued by the A.A. & Q.M.G.

5. All details of relief will be arranged direct between Brigadiers.

6. Completion of relief will be reported by wire to Div. H.Q.

7. ACKNOWLEDGE.

A.C.Temperley

Lieut-Colonel,
General Staff,
74th (Yeomanry) Division.

Issued at 1400.

Copies to :-

No.		No.	
1.	G.O.C.	13.	A.D.M.S.
2.	'G'.	14.	Div. Train.
3-5.	'Q'.	15.	XIth Corps.
6.	C.R.A., 19th Div.	16.	IIIrd Corps.
7.	C.R.E.	17.	47th Division.
8.	Signal Coy.	18.	55th Division.
9.	M.G. Battn.	19.	'C' Sqdn, 1/K.E.H.
10.	229th Inf.Bde.	20-21.	War Diary.
11.	230th Inf.Bde.	22.	File.
12.	231st Inf.Bde.		

"A" Form
MESSAGES AND SIGNALS.

Army Form C. 2121 (in pads of 100.)

TO	229 Bde	C.R.A.	Signals	M.G.Bn.
	230 Bde	C.R.E.	3 Corps	55 Div
	231 Bde	A.D.M.S.	47 Div	'Q' 21 Sqd RAF.

Sender's Number.	Day of Month.	In reply to Number.	
G 982	9		AAA

Reference Div Order No 98 AAA Northern Div Boundary is altered and will run as follows AAA R.13.central - thence east and west grid line to Q.16.a.6.0. - Q.22.a.5.3. - Q.15.c.6.3. - Q.15.c.4.1. - Q.14.d.5.5. - Q.14.d.3.2. - Q.14.c.2.3. - Q.14.c.2.5. - P.18.d.2.4. - thence along western edge of road to P.11.b.6.2. - P.11.a.8.4. - P.10.c.0.5. - P.13.c.0.6. - O.22.central.- O.20.d.9.1. thence as before AAA 229 Bde will arrange to take over as far as this boundary on night 10th/11th inst Addsd all concerned

From: 74 Div
Place:
Time: 2200

(Sd.) A.GALLOWAY. CAPT.

SECRET.   Copy No......

Appendix VII
16

DEFENCE INSTRUCTION.

A. SYSTEM OF DEFENCE.

1. The Divisional Sector is organized into two systems.
   (a) the outpost system.
   (b) the Battle System or the Corps Battle line.

2. The outpost system is held by two Brigades in line organized in depth. Each sector consists of
   (a) a line of observation consisting of section posts.
   (b) a picquet line consisting of platoon posts.
   (c) an outpost line of resistance.

3. Reserves will be kept in hand by Commanders of all units, from platoons upwards, for the purpose of counter attack.

B. DISTRIBUTION OF TROOPS.

1. <u>In the outpost system.</u>
   Each Brigade Sector is organized on a one battalion front. One battalion is in the outpost line of resistance and one battalion on the Corps Battle line. One Machine Gun Company is attached to each Brigade and is organized in depth.

2. <u>The Corps Battle line.</u>
   On this line is the Reserve Battalion of each Front line Brigade and one Machine Gun Company.

3. In rear of the Corps Battle line is the Divisional Reserve, consisting of
   - 1 Infantry Brigade.
   - 1 Machine Gun Company.
   - 1 Pioneer Battalion.
   - 3 Field Companies.
   - 1 Troop K.E.H.

C. ACTION IN CASE OF ATTACK.

1. <u>In the outpost system.</u>
   The Brigades holding the outpost system will fight on the outpost line of resistance and will employ their Brigade Reserves to regain any portion of this line lost. The Reserve Battalion in the Corps Battle line may be employed as Brigade Reserve less one platoon per Company which will remain as nucleus garrisons until relieved by troops of the Brigade in Divisional Reserve. In the event of the enemy attack being in such strength as to render the retention of the outpost system impossible the Brigades will fall back, fighting rearguard actions upon the Corps Battle line.

2. <u>On the Corps Battle line.</u>
   This is the line for the retention of which the Division will expend the whole of its resources.

3. <u>Divisional Reserve.</u>
   The Divisional Reserve will be prepared
   (a) to counter attack to regain any portion of the Corps Battle line temporarily occupied by the enemy.
   (b) to reinforce the Division on either flank.

                                              Lieut-Colonel,
                                              General Staff,
9th October, 1918.   74th (Yeomanry) Division.

Copies to :-

No. 1.	G.O.C.	12.	231st Inf.Bde.
2.	'G'.	13.	III Corps.
3-5.	'Q'.	14.	55th Division.
6.	C.R.A.	15.	47th Division.
7.	C.R.E.	16-17.	War Diary.
8.	Signal Coy.	18.	File.
9.	M.G.Battn.		
10.	229th Inf.Bde.		
11.	230th Inf.Bde.		

SECRET.

Copy No. 20

74th DIVISION ORDER No.99.

10th October 1918.

1. In order to take prompt advantage of any further withdrawal by the enemy, each Infantry Brigade in the line will arrange so that it can immediately advance covered by a properly constituted Advance Guard.
In addition to the infantry, each Advance Guard will consist of,-
   one 18-pdr Battery to be detailed from affiliated F.A. Brigade.
   one mobile 6" Newton T.M. to be detailed by C.R.A.
   one section M.G. Bn to be detailed from affiliated M.G. Coy.
   one section Field Coy, R.E. to be detailed by C.R.E.
   This section will again come under the orders of the C.R.E. immediately the Field Coys arrive at the CANAL and bridge construction is commenced by them.

2. The advance will be made by the two Infantry Brigades in the line and affiliated troops in a series of bounds. Each objective being made good before the Advance Guard proceeds to the next one.
   The first objective will be the general line V.1.d.0.0. - ROSOIR - SANTES - O.24.Central - LEZ HAUBOURDIN.
   The second objective the line of the CANAL DE LA HAUTE-DEULE from LA PLANCHE DES SANTES to HAUBOURDIN and thence along the stream to BOIS DE L'ABBAYE.

3. Advantage will be taken of any opportunity to establish small bridgeheads East of the CANAL. The Advance Guard Batteries must be prepared to cross the CANAL with any material locally obtainable should it be found necessary to push detachments on further East to the high ground about Q.25.

4. Orders will be issued by the Division for the advance of the Reserve Infantry Brigade and remaining troops of the Division.

5. The C.R.E. will prepare plans for bridging the CANAL for wheeled traffic at LA PLANCHE DES SANTES and at HAUBOURDIN.
   Infantry Bridges will be prepared by the side of the above two bridges and also about P.32.b.7.5., P.27.a.2.6., P.21.c.7.2.

6. Vigorous patrolling will be carried out by day and night along the whole Divisional front to keep in touch with the enemy in order to seize every opportunity of pushing forward immediately the enemy's resistance weakens.

/7.

- 2 -

7. In the event of the enemy retiring East of LILLE, the action of the right Division of the XIth Corps will be as follows.

The 47th Division is to detach a force not exceeding one Infantry Brigade Group to secure the Southern and South-eastern exits of LILLE, and to maintain touch with the 74th Division. The route proposed for this detachment is via LE MARAIS (P.4) - LOOS (P.18) - FAUBOURG DES POSTES (Q.13 & 14) to PORTE DE DOUAI (Q.22.a).

The action of the 55th Division will be similar to that of the 74th Division.

8. Troops will be warned of the necessity for lighting flares or for exhibiting tin discs or white flaps whenever aeroplanes sound their Klaxon horns.

9. ACKNOWLEDGE.

CBrook

Lieut.Colonel,
General Staff,
74th (Yeomanry) Division.

Issued at..20.00..

Copies to:-
- No.1. G.O.C.
- 2. 'G'
- 3-5. 'Q'
- 6. C.R.A.
- 7. C.R.E.
- 8. Signal Coy.
- 9. M.G.Bn.
- 10. 229th Inf.Bde.
- 11. 230th " "
- 12. 231st " "
- 13. A.D.M.S.
- 14. Div.Train.
- 15. III Corps.
- 16. 55th Division.
- 17. 47th Division.
- 18. 'C' Sqdn., K.E.H.
- 19-20. War Diary.
- 21. File.
- 22. 52nd Bde. R.F.A.

SECRET.

Appendix IX

Copy No. 20

74th DIVISION ORDER No. 100.

12th October 1918.

1. The 74th Divisional Artillery will come under the orders of the 74th Division on arrival at BETHUNE and CHOCQUES on the 13th October.

2. 74th Divisional Artillery will be staged in the ESSARS Area on nights 13/14th and 14/15th October. Accommodation will be obtained from Area Commandant, ESSARS.

3. 74th Divisional Artillery will relieve 19th Divisional Artillery, at present covering 74th Divisional front, in the line on the nights 14/15th and 15/16th October. All details of relief will be arranged between C.R.A.s.
   The relief will be completed by 10.00, 16th October. Completion of relief to be reported to 74th Div. H.Q.

4. (a) Headquarters, 19th Divisional Artillery will be billetted in BETHUNE on the night 16/17th October. Billets will be obtained from Area Commandant, BETHUNE.

   (b) 19th Divisional Artillery will be accommodated in the ESSARS Area on the night 16/17th October. Accommodation will be obtained from Area Commandant, ESSARS.

5. There are no restrictions as to routes or times of marching to and from BETHUNE and CHOCQUES.
   Distances to be kept on the march will be as laid down in S.S.724 para. 19.

6. The entrainment of the 19th Divisional Artillery and the detrainment of the 74th Divisional Artillery will be carried out under orders to be issued by III Corps 'Q'.
   Attention is called to G.H.Q., pamphlet No. 45/1 Q.A.1 dated September 1918.

7. ACKNOWLEDGE.

Lieut.Colonel,
General Staff,
74th (Yeomanry) Division.

Issued at..1100....

Copies to:-
- No. 1. G.O.C.
- 2. 'G'
- 3-5. 'Q'
- 6. C.R.A., 18th Div.
- 7. C.R.E.
- 8. Signal Coy.
- 9. M.G.Bn.
- 10. 229th Inf.Bde.
- 11. 230th " "
- 12. 231st " "
- 13. A.D.M.S.
- 14. Div.Train.
- 15. III Corps.
- 16. 55th Division.
- 17. 47th Division.
- 18. C.R.A., 74th Div.
- 19. 52nd Bde, R.G A
- 20-21. War Diary.
- 22. File.

"A" Form
MESSAGES AND SIGNALS.
Army Form C. 2121 (in pads of 100.)

This message is on a/c of:
Appendix X
Service.

TO	229 Bde	C in C R.A.	C.R.A.	21 Sqdn R.A.F.
	230 -	52 Bde R.G.A.	Signals	4 Balloon Sec.
	231 -	3 Corps	Q	
	C.R.A.	57 Div.	55 Div.	47 Div.

Sender's Number.	Day of Month.	In reply to Number.	AAA
G.178	16		

Objective for tomorrow AAA First objective all crossings over HAUTE DEULE Canal AAA Second objective right Bde enemy defences in V.3.c & a EMMERIN to Eastern outskirts AAA left Bde BEAUPRE Chateau and road P.28.a.5.0 P.16.c.9.1 P.16.a.4.4. AAA Third objective approximate line W.1.c.t.a Q.31.d & b. Q.25.d b & a. P.30 b & a P.23.d & b P.17.d & b P.11.d AAA Hour of Start 0600 AAA Added 229 230 Inf Bdes Repd all concerned. ACK.

From 74 Div.
Place
Time 0010

"A" Form.
MESSAGES AND SIGNALS.

Army Form C. 2121.
(In pads of 100.)

This message is on a/c of: Appendix XI

TO: Q. M.G.Bn. CRE. 47 Div.
229 Bde. ADMS. Signal Coy. Sgt K.O.H.
230 Bde. Div Train 3 Corps. 52 Bde R.G.A.
231 Bde. CRA. 55 Div. War Diary File.

Sender's Number.	Day of Month.	In reply to Number.	AAA
G168	16		

231	Bde	will	relieve
230	Bde	in	the
Right	Bde	Section	night
17/18	Oct	AAA	On
relief	230 Bde		will
occupy	billets	and	defences
vacated	by	231	Bde
AAA	Completion	of	relief
will	be	reported	to
Div HQ	AAA	Troops	at
present	attached	to	230
Bde	will	come	under
orders	231	Bde	on
relief	AAA	Usual	addresses

From: 7th Div
Time: 1500

(Z) Sqnn M Parry Jones
Major GS

"C" FORM.
MESSAGES AND SIGNALS.

Army Form C. 2123
(In books of 100.)

Prefix	Code	Words 21	Sent, or sent out. At ... m.	Office Stamp.
Received from	By		To	
Service Instructions			By	

Handed in at .... Office .... m. Received .... m.

TO: 52 Div

Sender's Number.	Day of Month.	In reply to Number.	A A A
G227	17		
Ref	order	101	aaa
special	objective	night	Bde
LAPLACE (S1)		CRUSOE (M33	
cat	Bde	DONT	A
TRESSIN	M20B)	aaa	left
Bde	G	from	defensive
flank	aaa	line	xx
(R16)	HELLENES (R7)		aaa
G226	reply	cancelled	aaa
attack	aaa	addressed to	
all	concerned		

FROM: 74 Div
PLACE & TIME: 2205

SECRET.

Appendix XII

Copy No..... 19

74th DIVISION ORDER No. 101.

17th October 1918

1. The Divisional front will be held to-night as follows:-

OUTPOST LINE OF RESISTANCE. - The Railway line through X.1 and Q.24. Picquets will be pushed out in advance of this line to make good the high ground in R.20.c. and X.3 central.

MAIN LINE OF RESISTANCE. - Approximate line W.3.d. - FACHES - Q.27.b. - Q.21.c.

2. The Outpost line of Resistance will be held by the 231st Infantry Brigade on the right and the 229th Infantry Brigade on the left.

The 230th Brigade after relief by 231st Brigade will be in Divisional Reserve West of the Main line of Resistance about WATTIGNIES.

3. The Support Company M.G.Battalion will occupy the Main Line of Resistance.

The Reserve Company Machine Gun Battalion will move forward to-morrow to BARGUES.

4. The 55th Div will be disposed in depth on the right of the 74th Division.

5. Infantry Brigade H.Qs will be established as follows :-

231st and 230th Infantry Brigades   L'ARBRISSEAU   Q.26.c.
229th Infantry Brigade.   LA CROISETTE.   Q.26.b.

H.Qrs of affiliated Brigades of Artillery will be established close to Headquarters of Infantry Brigades.

6. Telephone communication will be opened between Divisional H.Q. and Brigade H.Q. mentioned in para 5 as soon as possible.
One wireless Station is being sent up to L'ARBRISSEAU.

7. The 229th Infantry Brigade will picquet all roads leading into LILLE until relieved by the 57th Division.
No troops will be allowed to enter LILLE and no civilians will be allowed to come out.

8. Mounted men at disposal of Brigades will be pushed ahead to gain touch with the enemy. These detachments will be shortly reinforced Brigades will in addition form mounted detachments from any available horses.

9. The advance will be continued to-morrow covered by Advanced Guards constituted as in Divisional Order No 99, starting at 0600.

10. To-morrow's objective will be the line of the River MARCQ. The East bank of the river will become the Outpost Line of Resistance, picquets being pushed out further East.

11. Divisional and Brigade Boundaries will be as follows :-

South Boundary   Grid East from   X.1.c.0.0.
North Boundary.   Grid East from   R.13.a.0.0.
Inter Brigade Boundary.   Grid East from   R.25.a.0.0.

12. ACKNOWLEDGE.

Lieut Colonel.
General Staff.
74th (Yeomanry)

Issued at 1800

Copies to :-

No 1.	G.O.C.	13.	A.D.M.S.
2.	'G'	14.	Div Train.
3 -5.	'Q'	15.	III Corps.
6.	C.R.A.	16.	55th Division.
7.	C.R.E.	17.	57th Division.
8.	Signal Coy.	18.	52nd Bde R.G.A.
9.	M.G.Battn.	19.- 20.	War Diary.
10.	229th Inf. Bde.	21.	File.
11.	230th Inf. Bde.		
12.	231st Inf. Bde.		

SECRET. Copy No. 21

Appendix XIII

74th DIVISION ORDER No.102.

18th October 1918.

Ref. Map. Sheets 36 & 37. 1:10,000

INFORMATION.
1. Our troops hold the line X.6 - R.36 - M.26 - M.20 - M.13 - M.14 - ASCQ - HELLEMMES.
   Headquarters are located as follows:-
   Div. H.Q.   WATTIGNIES Chateau (W.1.o.7.3)
   229th Inf.Bde H.Q.   LEZENNES.
   230th   "   "   "   LESQUIN.
   231st   "   "   "   LESQUIN.
   74th M.G.Bn.   WATTIGNIES.

   The left Brigade of the 55th Division is on a line through X.11.
   The 59th Division is not yet reported in touch with 74th Division.
   The enemy is holding the line SIN - M.28 - S.4 with weak rear guards only.

INTENTION.
2. The G.O.C. intends to occupy the line M.4.Central - M.28.Central - CHERENG - TRESSIN - tomorrow in order to deny observation to the enemy over the crossings of the River LA MARCQ.
   The 55th Division will occupy a line through CYSOING and S.10.

OPERATIONS.
3. The 231st and 229th Inf.Bdes will capture the above line but will not pass on beyond it.
   Strong picquets will be established on the high ground and an Outpost Line of Resistance will be selected between the above line and the River MARCQ by the B.G.s.O, 231st and 229th Inf.bdes in consultation.
   If touch has been lost with the enemy, stabding patrols of K.E.H. will be pushed out East of the outpost line of picquets.

4. If the 59th Division has not come up level with the 74th Division, the 229th Inf.Bde will form a defensive flank through ASCQ and HELLEMMES.

MAIN LINE OF RESISTANCE.
5. The B.G.C., 230th Inf.Bde will select the best Main Line of Resistance on the general line FORT SAINGHIN - SAINGHIN - BATTERIE DU CAMP-FRAINCAIS or through ASCQ if the 59th Div. has advanced to that point.
   The 230th Inf.Bde, 179 Army R.A. Bde & Support Coy, M.G.Bn will then be moved by order of B.G.C., 230th Inf.Bde to suitable billets covering this line.
   All necessary reconnaissances will be carried out for occupying the main line of resistance at short notice.

DIVISIONAL RESERVE.
6. The Reserve Coy, M.G.Bn will march at 0900 tomorrow to LESQUIN under orders of OC, M.G.Bn and will remain in Divisional Reserve.

ROYAL ENGINEERS.
7. All crossings over the River LA MARCQ and road craters will be repaired under orders of C.R.E. For this purpose all Field Companies, R.E. (less sections with Adv.Guards) and the Pioneer Bn will come under his orders.
   Special attention will be paid to the bridge at PONT a TRESSIN (M.20) and the road ENNEQUIN - RONCHIN - MERCHIN - ASCQ - CHERENG.

8./

8. ACKNOWLEDGE.

C.Brood

Lieut.Colonel,
General Staff,
74th (Yeomanry) Division,

Issued at *1845*

Copies to:-
No, 1. G.O.C.
    2. 'G'
  3-5. 'Q'
    6. C.R.A.
    7. C.R.E.
    8. Signal Coy,
    9. M.G.Bn.
  10. 229th Inf.Bde
  11. 230th   "   "
  12. 231st   "   "

13. A.D.M.S.
14. Div. Train.
15. III Corps.
16. 55th Division.
17. 57th Division.
18. 59th Division.
19. 52nd Bde. R.G.A.
20. 21st Sqdn R.A.F.
21-22. War Diary.
23. File.
24. *N°.4. Balloon Sect.*

SECRET.   Copy No. 21

74th DIVISION ORDER No.103.

19th October 1918.

Ref.Maps. Sheets 36 & 37, 1:40,000.

INFORMATION.

1. Our troops hold BOURGHELLES (S.18) - CAMPHIN - BAISIEUX - TEMPLEUVE (H.33) and 74th Division is pushing on tonight to the line T.4 - N.16.
Headquarters of Inf.Bdes are as follows:-
    229th Inf.Bde   ...   ...   M.20.b.7.9.
    230th   "   "   ...   ...   M.20.b.7.9.
    231st   "   "   ...   ...   X.5.a.0.6.
55th Division is directed on the line BACHY - Custom House (T.8).
The enemy is still opposing us with weak rearguards only.

INTENTION.

2. The G.O.C. intends to capture the line ORCQ (O.26) - O.14.c. tomorrow.
The 55th Division will advance to the line U.3 - U.2 - O.32.

BOUNDARIES.

3. The Southern Divisional Boundary is amended to the line S.2.c.0.0. - M.34.c.0.0. - N.34.c.0.0. - N.30.c.0.0. and thence grid East.

OPERATIONS.

4. (a) The First Objective for 55th and 74th Divisions will be the line T.6.d. - N.36.Central - N.29.b. - N.17.d.
231st and 229th Inf.Bdes will advance at 0800 and capture the above line.
As soon as 55th Division troops have arrived at the point N.35.a.8.5. and have obtained touch with 229th Bde, the 231st Bde Group will be reformed and will go into billets in the villages of BAUDION - LAMAIN - HERTAIN. Bde H.Q. on main CHERENG - TOURNAI road about L'EPINE.
   (b) In conjunction with 55th Division, 229th Bde will then advance to the capture of the Second Objective ORCQ - O.14.c.
   (c) Liaison posts will be established with flank Divisions as follows:-
    55th Division - QUATRE CHINS T.3.b.7.7. by 231st Bde.
                    Farm, N.35.a.8.5. by both 231st & 229th Bdes
                    Houses, O.25.d.1.2. by 229th Bde.

    57th Division - Railway crossing N.14.c.4.7.
                        "   "   N.15.c.8.9.
                    Wood.   O.13.b.8.0.

   (d) The 230th Bde Group will march to BAISIEUX tomorrow starting at 0800 and will billot at BAISIEUX and CAMPHIN, Bde H.Q. BAISIEUX.
   (e) The Reserve Coy, M.G.BN, will march to SIN starting at 0800 and will remain in Divisional Reserve.

MAIN LINE OF RESISTANCE.

5. The B.G.C., 231st Bde will select the best main line of Resistance on the general line N.29.d. - N.17.d.
The 231st Bde Group will make all necessary reconnaissances for the occupation of this line by both 231st and 230th Bde Groups in the event of an attack by the enemy.

6. /

- 2 -

6. **REPAIR OF ROADS.**

   The C.R.E. will supervise the filling in of all craters, special attention being paid to the main CHERENG - TOURNAI Road.

   It is the duty of every unit, which is stationary, even temporarily, in the neighbourhood of a road crater, to set to work to repair it immediately, and to report the presence of the crater, and the progress of the work to Div. H.Q. Even men temporarily halted by the road side can assist materially by throwing in stones and earth, (timber from houses must not br used for this purpose) until they have to move forward again. Advanced Guards, if unable to get on with this work should immediately call upon the local inhabitants to assist.

7. **REPORTS.**

   Reports to WATTIGNIES Chateau (W.1.c.7.3.) up to 1200 tomorrow. At which hour Div.H.Q. will open at PONT a TRESSIN (M.21.a.3.3).

8. ACKNOWLEDGE.

                                                C.Br...th
                                                Lieut.Colonel,
                                                General Staff,
                                                74th (Yeomanry) Division.

Issued at 2030.

Copies to:-

No.1.	G.O.C.	13.	A.D.M.S.
2.	'G'	14.	Div Train.
3-5.	'Q'	15.	III Corps.
6.	C.R.A.	16.	55th Division.
7.	C.R.E.	17.	57th Division.
8.	Signal Company.	18.	52nd Bde R.G.A.
9.	M.G.Bn.	19.	31st Sqdn, R.A.F.
10.	229th Bde.	20.	No.4. Balloon Sec.
11.	230th "	21-22.	War Diary.
12.	231st "	23.	File.

"A" Form.
MESSAGES AND SIGNALS.

Army Form C.2121.
(In pads of 100)

Prefix	Code	m	Words.	Charge.	This message is on a/c of:	Recd. at .... m.
Office of Origin and Service Instructions.			Sent At ....m. To .... By		War Service. (Signature of "Franking Officer.")	Date .... From .... By ....

TO:
- GOC 231 Bde M.G. Bn ADMS 3 CORPS
- 229 Bde C.R.A. Q Div Train 21 SQDN RAF
- 230 Bde CRE Signals 55 DIV 52 Bde R.F.A.
- 57 DIV No 4 Balloon

Sender's Number: G.314
Day of Month: 20
In reply to Number:
AAA Sectr

& line ORCQ – 0.14 captured without serious opposition 229 Bde will at once secure bridges at 0.23.a, 0.17 and 24.8 and railway bridges 0.16.d forming bridgehead about FAUBOURG DU CHATEAU aaa 231 Bde Group will advance to ORCQ billeting in ORCQ and MARQUAIN aaa Bde HQ in MARQUAIN aaa Main line of resistance 0.26 – 0.19 aaa 230 Bde Group will advance to cross-roads N.21.d.8.4 billeting LAMAIN – HAUBION – HERTAIN aaa Bde H.Q. about L'EPINE aaa Reserve M.G. Coy will advance to BAISIEUX aaa Above moves will take place on initiative of 229 Bde close touch being kept by all units with unit in front aaa 55 DIV will be crossing at bridge 0.30.c.8.3 aaa CRE will supervise construction of pontoon bridge if required aaa

From ....
Place ....
Time ....

The above may be forwarded as now corrected. (Z)

Censor. Signature of Addressor or person authorised to telegraph in his name.
* This line should be erased if not required.

"A" Form.
MESSAGES AND SIGNALS.

| Sender's Number. | Day of Month. | In reply to Number. | A A A |

and will move up all necessary bridging material forthwith to position of assembly on MARQUAIN - TOURNAI road aaa NO troops will enter TOURNAI aaa NO civilians will be allowed to enter or leave the town aaa 229 Bde will picquet all exits from town on East bank of river to south Div boundary where mixed posts will be formed with 5J-Div aaa 231 Bde will picquet all entrances on West bank as far south as bridge O.30.C.8.3 exclusive aaa 229 and 231 Bdes will form mixed picquet at bridge O.23.a.0.7. aaa Damage to TOURNAI will be avoided as far as possible tactical operations being carried out North & South of town

From 74 DW
Place
Time 1000

SECRET.   Copy No. 21

74th DIVISION ORDER No.104.

20th October 1918.

Ref.Maps.   Sheets 36 & 37, 1:40,000.

INFORMATION.

1. Our troops hold the line N.30.d.5.5. - N.30.b.9.0. - N.24.b.8.4. - N.18.Central.
   The 55th Division continues the line on the right through O.31.a. and probably the high ground in O.32.c. thence to PIC-AU-VENT.
   The 57th Division holds a line East of BLANDAIN.N.12.d-O.1.c.
   The enemy holds the wood in O.13.d. and the high ground in O.19.b. and d.

INTENTION.

2. The G.O.C. intends to push on tomorrow to form a bridge-head East of TOURNAI as indicated in No.G.314.

OPERATIONS.

3. (a) The 229th Inf.Bde will advance in conjunction with the 55th Division at o800 and cross the River ESCAUT North of TOURNAI and form a bridgehead from WARCHIN (exclusive) to O.17.Central.
   The 55th Division will continue the line from WARCHIN (inclusive) to GUERONDE.
   (b) Liaison posts will be established as the advance progresses by the 229th Bde with flank Divisions as follows:-

   55th Division - Houses O.25.d.1.2.
                     Cutting O.27.c.6.0.
                     Railway P.19.b.9.1.

   57th Division - Wood O.13.b.8.0.
                     Road O.16.a.2.0.

   (c) All entrances to TOURNAI will be picquetted as ordered in No.G.314.
   Each Brigade will detail an officer not under the rank of Major who will be responsible that the above orders are strictly enforced and only experienced N.C.O's are put in charge of picquets.
   (d) The move of 230th and 231st Bde Groups as ordered in G.314 is cancelled. Further orders will be issued as the situation developes.

OUTPOST and MAIN LINES OF RESISTANCE.

4. The line selected by B.G.C., 231st Bde on the general line N.29.d. - N.17.d. will be the main line of resistance.
   The outpost line of resistance will be the picquet line.

5. Reports to Div.H.Q. PONT A TRESSIN (M.21.a.3.3).

6. ACKNOWLEDGE.

C Brook

Lieut.Colonel.
General Staff,
74th (Yeomanry) Division.

Issued at 21/30

Distribution as usual.

SECRET.

Appendix XVII

Copy No......

74th DIVISION ORDER NO 105.

21st October 1918.

1. Brig. Gen. C.E.HEATHCOTE, C.M.G., D.S.O. will act as Military Governor of TOURNAI.

2. 231st Infantry Brigade is placed at the disposal of the Military Governor for closing the entrances to TOURNAI, maintaining order etc.

3. All the picquets established by 229th Infantry Brigade as ordered in G.314 dated 20th October will be taken over by 231st Brigade as soon as possible. The closest possible touch being maintained between 229th and 231st Infantry Brigades.

4. All troops of 231st Brigade will be billetted outside the line of picquets.

5. The remaining troops of 231st Brigade Group (less Tunnellers) will revert to Divnl Control as soon as the above orders come into force.

6. No Officers or Men will be allowed to enter TOURNAI without a pass signed by the Div. H.Qrs.

7. Further instructions are contained in Appendix 'A'.

8. ACKNOWLEDGE.

C Brook

Lieut Colonel.
General Staff.
74th (Yeomanry) Division.

Issued at... 2230

Copies to :-

No 1. G.O.C.
    2. 'G'
3 -5. 'Q'
    6. C.R.A.
    7. C.R.E.
    8. Signal Coy.
    9. M.G.Bn.
   10. 229th Inf. Bde.
   11. 230th Inf. Bde.
   12. 231st Inf. Bde.
   13. A.D.M.S.
   14. Div. Train.
   15. III Corps.
   16. 55th Division.
   17. 57th Division.
   18. 52nd Bde R.G.A.
   19. 21st Sqdn R.A.F.
   20. No 4 Balloon Section.
   21.- 22. War Diary.
   23. File.

Divisional Order No 104.

APPENDIX 'A'

ORDERS FOR THE MILITARY OCCUPATION OF TOURNAI.

1. The H.Qrs of the Military Governor will be established on the MARQUAIN - TOURNAI road as close to TOURNAI as possible.
    The H.Qrs will be clearly marked and an Officer's Guard mounted.

2. Picquets will be placed on all roads leading into the town.
    Additional picquets will be detailed to deal with emergencies. These picquets need not be mounted but will be ready to act at short notice.

3. No troops will be allowed to enter the town without passes and no civilians will be permitted to leave it on any account.

4. Passes to enter the town may be issued by the Military Governor to troops under his Command as required by the military situation.
    All other passes must be countersigned by Divnl H.Qrs.

5. The French Mission, accompanied by certain Staff Officers specified on the pass will be allowed to enter the town by the gate at 0.28.b.6.7. as soon as its capture has been effected.

6. *See Amendment No. 2* Any British Officer or man found coming out of the town without a pass will be arrested and sent under escort to Divisional H.Qrs.

7. Lewis Guns will be sited so as to bear on all entrances to the town.

8. *See Addendum No. 1* The Military Governor will use his own discretion as to the advisability of sending troops into the town in the event of any disturbances occurring.
    The inside of the town will not be regularly patrolled without further instructions.

9. Guards and sentries will be kept well clear of the entrances they are guarding until they have been examined by the R.E. and reported clear of mines and booby traps.

S E C R E T.
****

Copy No. 21

ADDENDUM NO 1 to 74TH DIVISION ORDER NO. 105.

Appendix 'A'. para 4.
  add
    "Cars carrying authorised flags may enter without passes.

  para 8.

  Delete. last sentence and add.
    "Guards will be placed as soon as possible on
      (a)   All municipal buildings.
      (b)   Main Post and Telegraph Offices, and Telephone Exchanges.
      (c)   All main Bridges.
      (d)   Railway Station.
      (e)   Such other places as may be asked for by the Civil Administration".

C Broad

Lieut-Colonel,
General Staff,
74th (Yeomanry) Division.

22nd October 1918.

Copies to all recipients of 74th Division Order No. 105.

S E C R E T.
* * * * *

AMENDMENT NO. 2 to 74TH DIVISION ORDER NO. 105.

Para 6 is cancelled and the following is substituted.
~~No officers~~ or men will be allowed to enter TOURNAI ~~without~~ a pass signed by the Military Governor.

C Broad

Lieut-Colonel,
General Staff,
74th (Yeomanry) Division.

25th October, 1918.

Copies to all recipients of 74th Division Order No. 105.

SECRET.
******

Appendix XVIII   Copy No. 21

74TH DIVISION ORDER NO 103.

22nd October 1918.

1. The 230th Infantry Brigade will relieve the 229th Infantry Brigade in the line on the night October 23rd/24th.

2. On relief, 229th Infantry Brigade be disposed in the billets occupied by 230th Infantry Brigade.

3. Sections R.E. and M.G. Coys will remain attached to their present Brigades.

4. The troop K.E.H. at present attached to 229th Infantry Brigade will be transferred to 230th Infantry Brigade.

5. Instructions regarding Artillery reliefs will be issued separately by the C.R.A.

6. The Tunnellers at present attached to 229th Infantry Brigade will on relief be transferred to 230th Infantry Brigade and vice versa.

7. Details of relief to be arranged direct between B.G's. C..

8. Completion of relief to be wired to Divisional H.Q.

9. ACKNOWLEDGE.

C Bwod

Lieut Colonel,
General Staff,
74th (Yeomanry) Division.

Issued at 2000

Copies to :-

No			
1.	G.O.C.	13.	A.D.M.S.
2.	'G'	14.	Div. Train.
3 -5.	'Q'	15.	III Corps.
6.	C.R.A.	16.	55th Division.
7.	C.R.E.	17.	57th Division.
8.	Signal Coy.	18.	52nd Bde R.G.A.
9.	M.G.Battn.	19.	21st Sqd R.A.F.
10.	229th Inf. Bde.	20.	No 4 Balloon Sec
11.	230th Inf. Bde.	21 - 22.	War Diary.
12.	231st Inf. Bde.	23.	File.

SECRET.   S.G. 143.

To all recipients of D.O. 106.

Reference 74th Division Order No 106.

Headquarters of 229th Infantry Brigade on relief will be at CHATEAU LUCHIN. M.36.a.

Headquarters of 230th Infantry Brigade will remain at CHATEAU D'ESCANIN.

[signature]

Lieut Colonel.
General Staff.
74th (Yeomanry) Division.

23rd October 1918.

"A" Form
MESSAGES AND SIGNALS.

Army Form C. 2121
(in pads of 100.)

TO	To all recipients of D.O. 106.

Sender's Number.	Day of Month.	In reply to Number.	AAA
G.396	23		

DW. Order 106 is Cancelled AAA Acknowledge.

From: 74 DW
Time: 1200

Sd. W.R. Beckwith
Major

"A" Form — MESSAGES AND SIGNALS.
Army Form C. 2121 (in pads of 100.)

TO	229 Bde	CRA		Signals	52 Bde MGA	JOC
	230 Bde	CRE	ADVS	3 Corps	55 Div	4 Balloon Sec
	231 Bde	ADMS	Train	57 Div	21 Sqn RAF	

Sender's Number.	Day of Month.	In reply to Number.	AAA
G.397	23		

Ref. G.396 relief of 229 Bde by 230 Bde will take place night 24/25 AAA Details of relief as given in Div. Order 106 AAA

Asked 229 + 230 Bdes to Ack.
Rep'd all concerned.

From: 74 Div
Time: 1500

(Z) H. J. Sharp
Capt.

Appendix XIX

SECRET.   Copy No....21

74th DIVISION ORDER No.107.

24th October 1918.

Ref.Maps. Sheets 36 & 37.

1. (a) THE OUTPOST LINE OF RESISTANCE will run approximately
as follows;-
O.26.c.0.0 - O.25.d.4.5 - O.25.b.3.3 - O.19.b.0.5 -
                                           - to junction with
57th Division in   O.13.a.5.0.
   (b) The defence of this line will be arranged by B.G.C.,
230th Inf.Bde, and the necessary posts, etc dug forthwith.
   (c) The M.G.Company attached to the Brigade will be
disposed in depth so as to defend not only the Outpost
Line of Resistance but also the ground between it and the
Main Line of Resistance.
   (d) The Artillery attached to the Brigade will be disposed
in depth to cover the above line with forward sections for
wire cutting, harassing fire, etc.
   (e) The points of junction with flank Divisions are
approximately as follows;-
          55th Division - O.26.c.0.0.
          57th Division -   O.13.a.5.0.
   The exact points will be fixed by B.G.C., 230th Bde
in consultation with flank Brigades of the above Divisions.

2. (a) THE MAIN LINE OF RESISTANCE will run approximately
as follows;-
N.29.d.6.0 - N.29.Central - N.23.c.9.1 - N.23.b.4.9 -
N.17.d.8.0 - N.17.b.9.0. with a refused flank in N.17.b.
   (b) The 231st Inf.Bde is detailed for the defence of this
line. B.G.C., 231st Bde will arrange for the necessary
posts to be dug forthwith.
   (c) The M.G.Companies attached 229th and 231st Inf.Bdes
will be disposed so as to cover this line under arrangements to be made by O.C., M.G.Battn. in consultation with
B.G.C., 231st Bde. The above companies will both come
under the command of 231st Bde.
   (d) The Artillery Brigades attached 229th and 231st Inf.
Bdes will be disposed in depth to cover the above line
under arrangements to be made by the C.R.A.
   (e) The above troops need not actually be in position
provided that the line can at any time be manned at half
an hours notice.
   (f) The point of junction with 55th Division is
approximately N.35.b.
   The exact point will be fixed by B.G.C., 231st Bde
with flank Bde of 55th Division.

3. ACTION IN CASE OF ATTACK.
   (a) IN THE OUTPOST SYSTEM.
       The 230th Bde will fight on the Outpost Line of
Resistance and will employ the Brigade Reserve to regain
any portion lost.
       In the event of an enemy attack being in such strength
as to render the retention of the Outpost Line of Resistance impossible, all the troops detailed for the defence
of this line will fight a rearguard action back to the
Main Line of Resistance, falling back on previously
selected positions but this action will only take place
when the B.G.C. has expended all the resources at his
disposal.
   (b)/

- 2 -

(b) ON THE MAIN LINE OF RESISTANCE.
This is the line for the retention of which the Division will expend the whole of its resources.

(c) THE DIVISIONAL RESERVE will be prepared to,-
    (i) Counter-attack to regain any portion of the Main Line of Resistance temporarily occupied by the enemy.
    (ii) To reinforce the Division on either flank.

(d) THE ACTION OF THE ARTILLERY will be,-
    (i) When observation is obtainable to engage any parties of the enemy, each battery in its own zone.
    (ii) When observation is impossible,-
        (1) To engage hostile forming up places.
        (2) To fire down roads and tracks and other likely avenues of approach.
        (3) To concentrate on the villages of OROQ and MARQUAIN should they be lost and so prevent him either assembling in these villages or debouching from them.

4.   The 229th Infantry Brigade and the remaining Company, M.G.Battn will remain in Divisional Reserve at two hours' notice.

5.   The 230th Infantry Brigade will place examining posts on all roads crossing the Outpost Line of Resistance.
    No civilians will be allowed to pass Eastwards of this line.
    All suspects from either direction will be sent to Divisional H.Q.
    All roads in front line leading towards the enemy will be barricaded.

6.   The above dispositions will be taken up forthwith, completion will be reported to Divisional H.Q. Exact dispositions will be forwarded as soon as possible.

7.   The disposition of Troop, K.E.H., Pioneer Bn and Field Companies, R.E. will remain unchanged.

8.   ACKNOWLEDGE.

C. Broad

Lieut.Colonel,
General Staff,
74th (Yeomanry) Division.

Issued at 2230.

Copies to:-
No.1.	G.O.C.	13. A.D.M.S.
2.	'G'	14. Div.Train.
3-5.	'Q'	15. III Corps.
6.	C.R.A.	16. 55th Division.
7.	C.R.E.	17. 50th Division.
8.	Signal Coy.	18. 52nd Bde, R.G.A.
9.	M.G.Bn.	19. 21st Sqdn, R.A.F.
10.	229th Inf.Bde.	20. No.4. Balloon Sec.
11.	230th " "	21-22. War Diary.
12.	231st " "	23. File.

Secret

Reference Div. Order No 107.

Cancel para 1 (b) and substitute

"The outpost system will be held by 2 battalions organised in depth to include the Outpost Line of Resistance with one battalion in Brigade Reserve".

[signature]
Lieut Colonel.
General Staff.
74th (Yeomanry) Division.

28th October 1918.

Copies to all recipients of Div. Order No 107.

SECRET.　　　　　　　　　　　　　　　　　　　　　　　Copy No. 21

Appendix IX

24th October 1918.

74TH DIVISION ORDER NO. 108.

1. 230th Infantry Brigade Group will maintain close touch with the enemy by means of constant patrolling.

2. The wire along the front will be cut and hostile strong points, houses, etc occupied by the enemy bombarded and preparations made to undertake any minor operation which would be beneficial in advancing our line towards TOURNAI.

3. When the enemy retires the immediate objectives of 230th Brigade are as follows :-
   (a) To cross the River ESCAUT by the bridges at O.23.a. c.b. and 4.7.
   (b) To form a bridgehead from WAVRIN (exclusive) to O.17.central.
   (c) To capture RUMILLIES (P.15) keeping touch with the 55th Division on the railway P.16.c. and with the 57th Division on the high ground in P.9.c.
   (d) East of River ESCAUT, the tactical boundary between 55th and 74th Divisions will be the railway from P.19.central to P.16.c.

4. 229th Brigade will be prepared to advance in support of 230th Brigade and will, on the advance being resumed, be rejoined by the F.A. Brigade and Machine Gun Company temporarily placed at the disposal of 231st Brigade for the defence of the Main Line of Resistance.

5. 231st Brigade will be prepared to picquet the Town of TOURNAI under instructions already issued.

6. (a) The Artillery is given full liberty of action West of the River ESCAUT as regards engaging all localities occupied by the enemy except in the Town of TOURNAI itself.
   (b) Hostile batteries will be engaged whenever observation is possible or definite information as to their location is obtainable, except in inhabited villages when reference will be made to Divisional Headquarters.
   Area shoots will not be employed.
   (c) Harassing fire may be employed as required but should be limited to shrapnel when engaging roads, bridges etc in the neighbourhood of houses where civilians may still be in occupation.

7. ACKNOWLEDGE.

C Broad

Lieut-Colonel,
General Staff,
74th (Yeomanry) Division.

Issued at 2230

Copies to :-
No. 1.	G.O.C.	13.	A.D.M.S.
2.	'G'.	14.	Div.Train.
3-5	'Q'.	15.	III Corps.
6.	C.R.A.	16.	55th Division.
7.	C.R.E.	17.	57th Division.
8.	Signal Coy.	18.	32nd Bde, R.G.A.
9.	M.G.Battn.	19.	21st Sqdn R.A.F.
10.	229th Inf. Bde.	20.	No. 4 Balloon Secn.
11.	230th Inf. Bde.	21-22	War Diary.
12.	231st Inf. Bde.	23.	File.

SECRET.
******

Copy No............

Appendix XI
19

74TH DIVISION ORDER NO 109.

29th October 1918.

1. Divisional Orders No 105 and No 108 are cancelled and the following substituted.

2. Brigades will be described in this order as the Advanced Guard Brigade, the TOURNAI Brigade, and the Reserve Brigade.

3. So soon as there are signs that the enemy is withdrawing, units of the Advanced Guard Brigade will follow him up without waiting for orders.

4. The immediate objectives of the Advanced Guard Brigade are :-
    (a) To cross the River ESCAUT by the bridges at O.23.a.0.6. and 4.7.
    (b) To form a bridgehead from WARCHIN (exclusive) to O.17. central.
    (c) To capture RUMILLIES (P.15) keeping touch with the 55th Division on the railway in P.16.c. and with the 57th Division on the high ground in P.9.c.

    After the capture of these objectives the Advanced Guard Brigade will be prepared to undertake any further operations if ordered.

    East of the River ESCAUT the Southern Divisional Boundary will be the railway from P.19.central to P.16.c.

5. The Advanced Guard Brigade will picquet the exits of TOURNAI East of the River from O.23.a.0.6., where a liaison picquet will be formed with the TOURNAI Infantry Brigade to O.30.c.8.3. where a liaison picquet will be formed with the 55th Division. The duty of these picquets will be to prevent all civilians leaving the town on any pretext.

    The TOURNAI Infantry Brigade will picquet the western exits from O.30.c.8.3. to O.23.a.0.6. and will arrange to take over the posts on the East side from the Advanced Guard Brigade as soon as practicable.

6. The TOURNAI Infantry Brigade will advance to carry out its duties as soon as the situation permits.

    Troops not required for duty will be billeted immediately West and South of TOURNAI.

7. Groups will be formed as under :-

Advanced Guard.

Infantry Brigade.
1 Coy Machine Gun Battn.
44th Brigade, R.F.A.
439th Field Coy, R.E.
Section R.E,
Det. 251 Tunnelling Company, R.E.
1 Company Pioneer Battn.
Company Divisional Train.
~~Field Ambulance.~~

TOURNAI Brigade Group.

Infantry Brigade.
Section R.E.
Det. 251 Tunnelling Coy, R.E.
Company Divisional Train.
~~Field Ambulance.~~

- 2 -

Divisional Reserve.

Reserve Infantry Brigade.
117th Brigade, R.F.A.
179th (Army) Brigade, R.F.A.
R.A.R.E. (less 1 section).
R.M.R.E. (less 1 section).
Pioneer Battn. (less 1 Coy).
Machine Gun Battn (less 1 Coy).

8. The work of bridging the river will be carried out in accordance with arrangements already made by C.R.E.

9. As soon as the advance commences Headquarters of Advanced Guard and TOURNAI Brigades will be established in ORCQ, where Brigade forward stations have already been established.
The first move of Divisional Headquarters will be to ORCQ.

10. Further orders for the TOURNAI Infantry Brigade are in the attached Appendix, 5 copies of which are issued to each Infantry Brigade.

11. Trench and Loop wireless Sets will be taken by Brigade and Battalion Headquarters. All formations must be prepared to rely largely on visual signalling. Power Buzzers will not be taken.

12. ACKNOWLEDGE.

A.C.Temperley

Lieut-Colonel,
General Staff,
74th (Yeomanry) Division.

Issued at............ 1500

Copies to :-

No.		
1.	G.O.C.	
2.	'Q'.	
3-5.	'Q'.	
6.	C.R.A.	
7.	C.R.E.	
8.	Signal Coy.	
9.	M.G.Battn.	
10.	229th Inf. Bde.	
11.	230th Inf. Bde.	
12.	231st Inf. Bde.	
13.	A.D.M.S.	
14.	Div. Train.	
15.	III Corps.	
16.	55th Division.	
17.	57th Division.	
18-19.	War Diary.	
20.	File.	

S E C R E T.
* * * * *

APPENDIX.

ORDERS FOR THE MILITARY OCCUPATION OF TOURNAI.

1.   is appointed Military Governor.

2. The Headquarters of the Military Governor will be established on the MARQUAIN - TOURNAI road as close to TOURNAI as possible.
    The Headquarters will be clearly marked and an Officer's Guard mounted.

3. Picquets will be placed on all roads leading into the town.
    Additional picquets will be detailed to deal with emergencies. These picquets need not be mounted but will be ready to act at short notice.

4. No civilians will be permitted to leave the town on any account.

5. No officers or men will be allowed to enter TOURNAI without a pass signed by the Military Governor, except Officers in cars carrying authorised flags, who may enter without passes.

6. The French and Belgian Missions, accompanied by certain Staff Officers specified on the pass will be allowed to enter the town by the gate at O.28.b.6.7. as soon as its capture has been effected.

7. Lewis Guns will be sited so as to bear on all entrances to the town.

8. The Military Governor will use his own discretion as to the advisability of sending troops into the town in the event of any disturbances occuring.
    Guards will be placed as soon as possible on,-
  (a) All Municipal buildings.
  (b) Main Post and Telegraph Offices, and Telephone Exchanges.
  (c) All main Bridges.
  (d) Railway Station.
  (e) Such other places as may be asked for by the Civil Administration.

9. Guards and sentries will be kept well clear of the entrances they are guarding until they have been examined by the R.E., and reported clear of mines and booby traps.

Issued with 74th Division Order No. 109.

S E C R E T.

AMENDMENT TO DIVISIONAL ORDER 109.

Erase "Field Ambulance" wherever it occurs in para. 7.

A.C.(signature)

Lieut-Colonel,
General Staff,
74th (Yeomanry) Division.

29th October 1918.

To all recipients of 74th Div. Order No 109.

S E C R E T.
* * * * * *

Copy No..........

74TH DIVISION ORDER NO 109.

29th October 1918.

1. Divisional Orders No 105 and No 108 are cancelled and the following substituted.

2. Brigades will be described in this order as the Advanced Guard Brigade, the TOURNAI Brigade, and the Reserve Brigade.

3. So soon as there are signs that the enemy is withdrawing, units of the Advanced Guard Brigade will follow him up without waiting for orders.

4. The immediate objectives of the Advanced Guard Brigade are :-
   (a) To cross the River ESCAUT by the bridges at O.23.a.0.8. and 4.7.

The objectives of the Division and of the flank Divisions also the inter-Divisional boundaries are shewn on the attached map.
The second objective of the Division on the left is MELLES.

After the capture of these objectives the Advanced Guard Brigade will be prepared to undertake any further operations if ordered.

East of the River ESCAUT the Southern Divisional Boundary will be the railway from P.19.central to P.18.c.

5. The Advanced Guard Brigade will picquet the exits of TOURNAI East of the River from O.23.a.0.6., where a liaison picquet will be formed with the TOURNAI Infantry Brigade to O.30.c.8.3. where a liaison picquet will be formed with the 55th Division. The duty of these picquets will be to prevent all civilians leaving the town on any pretext.
The TOURNAI Infantry Brigade will picquet the western exits from O.30.c.8.3. to O.23.a.0.6. and will arrange to take over the posts on the East side from the Advanced Guard Brigade as soon as practicable.

6. The TOURNAI Infantry Brigade will advance to carry out its duties as soon as the situation permits.
Troops not required for duty will be billeted immediately West and South of TOURNAI.

7. Groups will be formed as under :-

Advanced Guard.

Infantry Brigade.
1 Coy Machine Gun Battn.
44th Brigade, R.F.A.
439th Field Coy, R.E.
Section R.E.
Det. 251 Tunnelling Company, R.E.
1 Company Pioneer Battn.
Company Divisional Train.
Field Ambulance.

TOURNAI Brigade Group.

Infantry Brigade.
Section R.E.
Det. 251 Tunnelling Coy, R.E.
Company Divisional Train.
Field Ambulance.

SECRET.
******

Copy No.........

74TH DIVISION ORDER NO 109.
****

29th October 1918.

1. Divisional Orders No 105 and No 108 are cancelled and the following substituted.

2. Brigades will be described in this order as the Advanced Guard Brigade, the TOURNAI Brigade, and the Reserve Brigade.

3. So soon as there are signs that the enemy is withdrawing, units of the Advanced Guard Brigade will follow him up without waiting for orders.

4. The immediate objectives of the Advanced Guard Brigade are :-
   (a) To cross the River ESCAUT by the bridges at O.23.a.0.8. and 4.7.
   (b) To form a bridgehead from WARCHIN (exclusive) to O.17. central.
   (c) To capture RUMILLIES (P.15) keeping touch with the 55th Division on the railway in P.16.c. and with the 57th Division on the high ground in P.9.c.

   After the capture of these objectives the Advanced Guard Brigade will be prepared to undertake any further operations if ordered.
   East of the River ESCAUT the Southern Divisional Boundary will be the railway from P.19.central to P.16.c.

5. The Advanced Guard Brigade will picquet the exits of TOURNAI East of the River from O.23.a.0.6., where a liaison picquet will be formed with the TOURNAI Infantry Brigade to O.30.c.8.3. where a liaison picquet will be formed with the 55th Division. The duty of these picquets will be to prevent all civilians leaving the town on any pretext.
   The TOURNAI Infantry Brigade will picquet the western exits from O.30.c.8.3. to O.23.a.0.6. and will arrange to take over the posts on the East side from the Advanced Guard Brigade as soon as practicable.

6. The TOURNAI Infantry Brigade will advance to carry out its duties as soon as the situation permits.
   Troops not required for duty will be billeted immediately West and South of TOURNAI.

7. Groups will be formed as under :-

Advanced Guard.

Infantry Brigade.
1 Coy Machine Gun Battn.
44th Brigade, R.F.A.
439th Field Coy, R.E.
Section R.E.
Det. 251 Tunnelling Company, R.E.
1 Company Pioneer Battn.
Company Divisional Train.
~~Field Ambulance.~~

TOURNAI Brigade Group.

Infantry Brigade.
Section R.E.
Det. 251 Tunnelling Coy, R.E.
Company Divisional Train.
~~Field Ambulance.~~

- 2 -

Divisional Reserve.

Reserve Infantry Brigade.
117th Brigade. R.F.A.

8. Bridges are being built by XI Corps at O.23.d.3.3. and O.23.c.8.7. III Corps is building bridges at O.29.b.6.8. and to the South.
As far as possible, III Corps bridges (when built) will be used by this Division for the movement of troops and supplies. The Northern portion of the town will be left clear for XI Corps.

9. As soon as the advance commences headquarters of Advanced Guard and TOURNAI Brigades will be established in ORCQ, where Brigade forward stations have already been established.
The first move of Divisional Headquarters will be to ORCQ.

10. Further orders for the TOURNAI Infantry Brigade are in the attached Appendix, 5 copies of which are issued to each Infantry Brigade.

11. Trench and Loop wireless Sets will be taken by Brigade and Battalion Headquarters. All formations must be prepared to rely largely on visual signalling. Power Buzzers will not be taken.

12. ACKNOWLEDGE.

13. The Divisional road will be RUMILLIES - HAVINNES - BECLERS Stn - BECLERS - THIMOUGIES Road. The Divisional cable will be laid along this route and all Brigade Headquarters will be located in its vicinity.

Issued at............ 1500

General Staff,
74th (Yeomanry) Division.

Copies to :-

No.				
1.	G.O.C.		13.	A.D.M.S.
2.	'G'.		14.	Div. Train.
3-5.	'Q'.		15.	III Corps.
6.	C.R.A.		16.	55th Division.
7.	C.R.E.		17.	57th Division.
8.	Signal Coy.			
9.	M.G.Battn.		18-19.	War Diary.
10.	229th Inf. Bde.		20.	File.
11.	230th Inf. Bde.			
12.	231st Inf. Bde.			

- 2 -

Divisional Reserve.

Reserve Infantry Brigade.
117th Brigade, R.F.A.
179th (Army) Brigade, R.F.A.
R.A.R.E. (less 1 section).
R.M.R.E. (less 1 section).
Pioneer Battn. (less 1 Coy).
Machine Gun Battn (less 1 Coy).

The work of bridging the river will be carried out in accordance with arrangements already made by C.R.E.

9. As soon as the advance commences Headquarters of Advanced Guard and TOURNAI Brigades will be established in ORCQ, where Brigade forward stations have already been established.
The first move of Divisional Headquarters will be to ORCQ.

10. Further orders for the TOURNAI Infantry Brigade are in the attached Appendix, 5 copies of which are issued to each Infantry Brigade.

11. Trench and Loop wireless Sets will be taken by Brigade and Battalion Headquarters. All formations must be prepared to rely largely on visual signalling. Power Buzzers will not be taken.

12. ACKNOWLEDGE.

A.C.Semperley

Lieut-Colonel,
General Staff,
74th (Yeomanry) Division.

Issued at............. 1.500

Copies to :-
No. 1. G.O.C.
2. 'Q'.
3-5. 'Q'.
6. C.R.A.
7. C.R.E.
8. Signal Coy.
9. M.G.Battn.
10. 229th Inf. Bde.
11. 230th Inf. Bde.
12. 231st Inf. Bde.
13. A.D.M.S.
14. Div. Train.
15. III Corps.
16. 55th Division.
17. 57th Division.
18-19. War Diary.
20. File.

SECRET.
* * * * * *

APPENDIX.

ORDERS FOR THE MILITARY OCCUPATION OF TOURNAI.

1. .... is appointed Military Governor.

2. The Headquarters of the Military Governor will be established on the MARQUAIN - TOURNAI road as close to TOURNAI as possible.
   The Headquarters will be clearly marked and an Officer's Guard mounted.

3. Picquets will be placed on all roads leading into the town.
   Additional picquets will be detailed to deal with emergencies. These picquets need not be mounted but will be ready to act at short notice.

4. No civilians will be permitted to leave the town on any account.

5. No officers or men will be allowed to enter TOURNAI without a pass signed by the Military Governor, except Officers in cars carrying authorised flags, who may enter without passes.

6. The French and Belgian Missions, accompanied by certain Staff Officers specified on the pass will be allowed to enter the town by the gate at O.28.b.6.7. as soon as its capture has been effected.

7. Lewis Guns will be sited so as to bear on all entrances to the town.

8. The Military Governor will use his own discretion as to the advisability of sending troops into the town in the event of any disturbances occuring.
   Guards will be placed as soon as possible on,-
   (a) All Municipal buildings.
   (b) Main Post and Telegraph Offices, and Telephone Exchanges.
   (c) All main Bridges.
   (d) Railway Station.
   (e) Such other places as may be asked for by the Civil Administration.

9. Guards and sentries will be kept well clear of the entrances they are guarding until they have been examined by the R.E., and reported clear of mines and booby traps.

Issued with 74th Division Order No. 109.

Appendix XXII

SECRET.   Copy No. 18

74th DIVISION ORDER No.110.

31st October 1918.

1. The bombardment will be continued tomorrow and hostile machine gun positions will be gassed if the wind is favourable.

2. These demonstrations, coupled with operations further to the North and to the South may induce the enemy to expedite his withdrawal.
To ascertain this 230th [231st] Brigade will conduct an operation on the morning of Nov.2nd in conjunction with an attack by the 55th Division on our right.

3. At 0515 - Divisional Artillery will open an intense bombardment along the road in O.27.a. & c, O.21.a. & c, O.15.c.
At 0520 - patrols will be sent forward simultaneously along the Divisional front to test the enemy line.
At 0523 - the standing barrage will lift from the road to the enemy front line system.
At 0526 - the barrage will lift from the front line to the second system.
At 0541 - it will lift off the second system.

4. Should the patrols draw fire they will return to our lines. Should the enemy have retired or show signs of weakening, the patrols will continue their advance under the barrage and will be supported.
The advance will continue and ultimately the whole Advanced Guard Brigade will be set in motion in accordance with Divisional Order No.109.
There will be no advance beyond the enemy wire South of the LILLE - TOURNAI Road owing to mines.

5. A machine gun barrage will be placed on the first and second objectives and will lift 200 yards ahead of the artillery barrage.

6. 230th Brigade Group will be ready to move at one hour's notice after 0630.   All 1st Line Transport will be in readiness to join units at short notice.

7. The C.R.E. will arrange for all bridging material to be ready for loading and for transport and teams to be standing by from 0800, if the Advanced Guard is moving forward.

8. Watches will be synchronized by the General Staff at 1400 on November 1st.

9. ACKNOWLEDGE.

ACTempertey
Lieut.Colonel.
General Staff,
74th (Yeomanry) Division.

Issued at 2000.

Distribution overleaf.

Copies to:-
- No. 1. G.O.C.
- 2. 'G'.
- 3-5. 'Q'.
- 6. C.R.A.
- 7. C.R.E.
- 8. O.C., Signal Coy.
- 9. "   M.G.Battn.
- 10. 229th Infantry Brigade.
- 11. 230th   "   "
- 12. 231st   "   "
- 13. A.D.M.S.
- 14. Div Train.
- 15. III Corps
- 16. 55th Division.
- 17. 47th Division.
- 18-19. War Diary.
- 20. File.

SECRET.

Proposed bridging arrangements for L'ESCAUT RIVER.

2 PONTOON BRIDGES.- to be erected by 439 Field Coy R.E. and 1 Company, 1/12 Loyal North Lancs Pioneers at most suitable sites between O.16.d.5.3. and O.23.a.3.4.
    6 pontoons and 439 Field Company Trestle wagon will be held in readiness to move up to site of bridge as soon as possible
    Teams and wagons will then return for Pontoon Park equipment to erect the second bridge. - (5 pontoons have been asked for)
    On completion of trestle bridge by R.A.R.E., pontoon bridge of Companies' equipment will be dismantled and wagons returned to units.

1 TRESTLE BRIDGE, to take 3 ton lorries, will be erected by R.A.R.E. at the most suitable site between the same limits.
    5 lorries have been applied for to report to O.C. R.A.R.E. at M.18.c.3.9. at short notice to carry up prepared material. Two trips will probably be required.

INFANTRY BRIDGES. - 1 section R.A.R.E. with advanced Brigade will make the following arrangements:-
    4 scaling ladders and 6 light 15 feet bridges will be placed at disposal of leading Battalion to assist patrols in crossing over debris of demolished bridges.
    4 rafts with line and pickets will be prepared and placed in convenient sites for leading Companies to carry forward and use for crossing the river. Two Sappers from the section will be detailed to accompany each raft.
    Division have arranged for 10 G.S. wagons to report to the advanced Brigade at short notice; on them will be loaded the remaining cork floats and duck boards at L'EPINE, with which the remainder of the Section and 20 Pioneers detailed by O.C. 1/12 Loyal North Lancs will erect two Infantry Bridges at most convenient sites between O.16.d.5.3. and O.23.a.3.4.

    2 Companies 1/12 Loyal North Lancs will be available for clearing roads and R.M.R.E. in reserve will stand by ready to move at short notice.

29/10/1918.
                              Lieut-Colonel R.E.
                        C.R.E. 74th (Yeomanry)Division.

            Copies to:- O.C.R.M.R.E.
                        O.C.R.A.R.E.
                        O.C. 439 Field Coy R.E.
                        O.C. 1/12 Loyal North Lancs.
                        229th Brigade.
                        230th Brigade.
                        231st Brigade.
                          C.R.A. 74th Div.
                        'G.S.' 74th Divn.
                        'Q'. 74th Division.
                        C. E. 3rd Corps.

"B" Form.
MESSAGES AND SIGNALS.

Army Form C. 2122.

Prefix OHM Code 1015 m.

Office of Origin and Service Instructions: YED
Words: 46
Received At 10.40 m. From CCO By AA
Sent

TO: 55 Div

Sender's Number: G31
Day of Month: 12

Amend SG 24/Y dated Oct 11th as follows para 2 last line but one for intense read normal para 3 last line for 40 minutes read 60 minutes aaa Addressed 3 Corps reptd other recipients of SG 24/Y

Amend 252

From: 74 Div 0950

SECRET.

S.G.24/7.

Headquarters,

III Corps.

1. The line on which the Infantry will form up for the attack on the railway line, and the actual objective is shown on the attached tracing.

2. The attack will be made by two companies, 230th Infantry Brigade on the Right and one battalion, 229th Infantry Brigade on the Left.

The advance will be under a creeping barrage at 100 yards in 4 minutes, starting 200 yards East of the forming up line. The barrage will remain stationary for 4 minutes before beginning to advance.

The protective barrage will be placed 300 yards beyond the final objective and will remain ~~intense~~ normal for 15 minutes after which it will die away.

3. It is requested that a standing barrage may be placed by batteries of the 55th Division on the railway in U.6.a. and b. and O.36.d. from Zero to Zero + 60 minutes.

4. The co-operation required from the Heavy Artillery is as follows.

   (a) Counter-battery work from Zero onwards. Special attention being paid to hostile batteries firing from the S.E.

   (b) Co-operation in the creeping barrage by howitzer fire on LACHERIE (O.36.d.) - O.36.a. - the railway line from O.35.b.4.7. to O.23.a.4.4. - wire and houses O.30.c. and a. - O.24.c. and a. and finally the SANTES line viz. P.31.c. - OPTIC Trench - PAYS PERDU - BRICKFIELDS (O.24.b.7.3) - FORT DU MIN D'HAUBOURDIN (P.19.a).

5. 5 a.m. is proposed for Zero Hour.

6. Will you kindly inform me if the above arrangements agree with those of the XI Corps. If the Zero hour suggested is not suitable to them, can it be made as near 5 a.m. as possible as it is necessary for the Left Brigade to get over the forward slope before broad daylight.

C Brough
Lieut Colls
for
Major-General,
11th October 1918. Commanding 74th (Yeomanry) Division.

Copies to:- 229th Infantry Brigade.
             230th   "   "
             231st   "   "
             C.R.A.
             C.R.E.
             O.C., M.G.Bn.
             O.C., 52nd Bde. R.G.A.
             47th Division.
             55th Division.

D. D. & L., London, E.C.
(P6975) Wt.W11200/H2695 500,000 12/16 W21 H16/580

COVER
FOR
BRANCH MEMORANDA.

Unregistered.

(76)

Referred to	Date	Referred to	Date
23rd ~~Yf B~~			
~~74th (Yeo) Division~~			

Vol. 8

General Staff.
74th Division.
November 1918.

Army Form C. 2118.

WAR DIARY
INTELLIGENCE SUMMARY
(Erase heading not required.)

General Staff,
74th (Yeomanry) Division.

Instructions regarding War Diaries and Intelligence Summaries are contained in F.S. Regs. Part II and the Staff Manual respectively. Title pages will be prepared in manuscript.

Sheet 37. 1:40,000.

Place	Date	Hour	Summary of Events and Information	Remarks and references to Appendices
Field.	1st Nov.	0520	Situation unchanged.	
		1200	One L.F.E.A. flew over our lines (O.19) dropping propaganda.	
		1650	Situation unchanged.	
	2nd	0509	Situation unchanged.	
		0515	A bombardment of Divisional artillery of all calibres on selected targets coupled with operations of Flank Divisions. Patrols along Divisional front sent forward to test enemy lines.	
		0715	Patrols unable to reach objectives owing to heavy M.G. fire. Enemy put down heavy M.G. and artillery barrage immediately our barrage opened. Orders to patrols were to return to our lines should they draw fire.	
		0800	Line remains unchanged.	
		1720	Situation unchanged.	
	3rd	0515	Situation unchanged.	
		1700	Situation unchanged.	
	4th	0500	Situation unchanged. Quiet night.	
		1200	231st Infantry Brigade notified of intense 5 minute bombardment by Artillery of all calibres at 1800 to-day on selected targets. Posts in O.21.a. and O.15.c. withdrawn.	
		1220	One Company of Pioneers attached to 231st Brigade to be employed on erecting shelters.	
		1310	Wire from III Corps cancelling bombardment of TOURNAI Barracks.	
		1600	Increased enemy artillery activity in vicinity LAMAIN. MARQUAIN and ORCQ heavily shelled.	
		2115	Between 2025 and 2105 enemy attempted raid on post at O.20.d.9.7. after heavily shelling it with 5.9s and 4.2s. Strength of raiding party estimated at 20. Raid was repulsed by L.G. fire. The post had no casualties.	
	5th	0515	Situation unchanged.	
		1500	Amendments to Divisional Order No 109 issued.	Appendix 1
		1600	Numerous coloured Very lights sent up by enemy from TOURNAI Church.	

Army Form C. 2118.

WAR DIARY
or
INTELLIGENCE SUMMARY.
(Erase heading not required.)

Instructions regarding War Diaries and Intelligence Summaries are contained in F.S. Regs., Part II and the Staff Manual respectively. Title pages will be prepared in manuscript.

Place	Date	Hour	Summary of Events and Information	Remarks and references to Appendices
	Nov 6th	0500	Situation unchanged.	
		1700	Situation unchanged.	
		1835	Enemy heavily shelled area HERTAIN - LAMAIN and cross roads in N.21.d.	
	7th	0510	Situation unchanged. Gas shelling on MARQUAIN during night.	
		1030	Wire from III Corps. German plenipotentiaries expected. Careful watch to be kept along whole Divisional front.	APP. 2
		1520	Orders issued for relief of left Brigade 55th Division by 229th Brigade on night of Nov 8th/9th.	
		1730	Situation unchanged. Artillery quiet on the whole except for a sharp concentration against one of our Battery positions at 1215 - 1245 and slight gas shelling MARQUAIN same hour.	
	8th	0530	231st Brigade report situation unchanged. Gas shelling nil.	
		0700	231st Brigade reported that civilian lady came in from TOURNAI and stated enemy left TOURNAI about 0300 this morning.	
		0730	Forward Brigade 55th Division report enemy has evacuated front posts opposite 55th Division front.	
		0745	231st Brigade report patrols reached 100X east of cross roads at O.27.a.50.35 without encountering any opposition. No enemy seen.	
		0855	231st Brigade report patrols reached FAUBOURG de LILLE at O.28.a.2.3. at 0605 and were pushing on. 1 German M.G. captured.	
		0920	Pilot 21st Squadron reports all bridges in TOURNAI blown up except at O.23.a.3.4. Civilians seen in town west of river. Heavy M.G. fire experienced over right bank of river, causing forced landing at L'EPINE.	
		0930	Relief of Left Brigade 55th Division by 229th Brigade cancelled.	
		1000	21st Squadron report our troops in O.29.c.9.3.	
		1020	231st Brigade report FAUBOURG de LILLE clear of the enemy. Patrols entered TOURNAI at 0930. Patrols West of L'ESCAUT were fired at by M.G's from East of L'ESCAUT river bank. All bridges reported destroyed. Road in FAUBOURG de LILLE mined, but not gone up. 231st Brigade H.Q. established in ORCq.	
		1120	Identification of P/W captured FAUBOURG de LILLE belongs 2 Coy, 15 R.I.R. 2 Gd.R. Div.	

Army Form C. 2118.

WAR DIARY
or
INTELLIGENCE SUMMARY.
(Erase heading not required.)

Instructions regarding War Diaries and Intelligence Summaries are contained in F. S. Regs., Part II. and the Staff Manual respectively. Title pages will be prepared in manuscript.

Place	Date	Hour	Summary of Events and Information	Remarks and references to Appendices
			Div Order No 111 issued	App 9
	Nov 8th	1115	Situation. 24th Welsh, one Company along West bank of L'ESCAUT. Enemy snipers and M.G. on East bank. One Company on line 0.21.d. and.b. 2 Companies along left sector old front line. 25th R.W.F. along old front line. 10th K.S.L.I. moving to MARQUAIN. Patrols working West bank of river N. and S. of Bridge 0.23.a.0.6. P/W 15 R.I.R. captured FAUBOURG de LILLE states. Retirement began 0200 this morning to line about 3 kilometres W. of LEUZE where resistance will be offered for 8 days. P/W battalion dug trenches and erected wire on this front a week ago.	
		1215	Situation. Patrols 231st Brigade still held up at river. Support Companies 24th Welsh in line 0.15.d.9.4. to 0.21.b.5.0. 2 Companies in old line 0.15.c. and 0.21.a.	
		1400	Situation unchanged. L.G. and rifle posts covering bridges 0.23.a.0.6., 0.23.a.2.4. and 0.23.c.8.7. In touch with 47th Division on left at 0.22.a.9.9.	
		1430	21st Squadron report considerable M.T. in small batches along roads E. of TOURNAI going E. during morning at points Q.32.central, P.6.d., K.33.a., also few cyclists in K.31. Explosion seen on railway between TOURNAI and Q.35. also numerous fires in back areas. A.A. fire experienced vicinity LEUZE. M.G. fire active E. outskirts TOURNAI and back area.	
		1600	Situation unchanged. Enemy harassing western outskirts of TOURNAI, and FAUBOURG de LILLE with H.V., 4.2" and 77 mm.	
		1803	dispositions 230th Brigade for night. 10th Buffs picquetting western exits of TOURNAI. Enemy still hold right bank of river with M.Gs. Sussex remains at LAMAIN. Suffolks at HERTAIN for present until right bank of river is gained. FAUBOURG de LILLE heavily shelled since 1400.	
	9th	0500	Situation. Enemy still holding right bank of river opposite 231st Brigade front. Hostile artillery very quiet and no gas shelling reported.	
		0800	55th Division report infantry footbridge established V.2.central at 0330. 1 Company over river. Pontoon bridge erected at 0.36.b.8.7. and bridgeheads established at CHERCQ and 0.36.b.	
		0840	Phone message from 231st Brigade to say that infantry footbridge erected at 0.22.b. 70.95.	
		0850	Air report. Our troops passing through GALONNE. Civilians waving flags in villages between TOURNAI and LEUZE.	

Army Form C. 2118.

WAR DIARY
or
INTELLIGENCE SUMMARY.
(Erase heading not required.)

Instructions regarding War Diaries and Intelligence Summaries are contained in F.S. Regs., Part II. and the Staff Manual respectively. Title pages will be prepared in manuscript.

Place	Date	Hour	Summary of Events and Information	Remarks and references to Appendices
	Nov 9th	0940	Infantry foot-bridge erected O.22.b.6.9. 10th K.S.L.I. all across.	
		0950	229th Brigade ordered to move in accordance with G. 723 of today.	
		1010	Orders issued for Advanced Guard Brigade to make good line East of BECLERS - THIMOUGIES	App 4
			55th Division Mobile column will move forward East of this line to seize high ground East of LEUZE. 9th Cavalry Brigade will assist in pursuit tomorrow.	
			47th Division report. Right Brigade not yet across canal. Left Brigade across and advancing Eastwards.	
		1103	10th K.S.L.I. established bridgehead. 25th R.W.F. now passing through 10th K.S.L.I.	
		1110	55th Division report. Advance troops East of road V.5, V.11. Pontoon Bridge at V.3.c.0.2.	
		1130	47th Division occupied MONT St AUBERT without opposition.	
		1210	Aeroplane report. Enemy cavalry in farm P.14.a.5.8. Our troops just West of this farm.	
		1230	Air report. Road and railway destruction TOURNAI - LEUZE completed. Destruction of railway and roads being carried out this morning between LEUZE and ATH.	
		1255	10th K.S.L.I. holding line O.17.b.5.3., O.18.d.4.9., P.13.c.6.2., P.19.b.7.2., with patrols pushed out in front. Liaison established with 55th Division at P.19.b.8.2.	
		1400	Pontoon bridge over river O.22.b.95.70.	
		1450	Air report. Our men seen resting along road in Q.32. Enemy cavalry seen Q.15.b.2.4. R.22.a. and b. Enemy fires and explosions seen vicinity of LEUZE - ATH and on railway N. from LEUZE.	
		1610	Warning Order issued to Brigades. Advanced Brigade will resume advance tomorrow.	App. 5
			1st Objective high ground R.14.a. - R.2.	
			2nd Objective Railway in R.18. - R.6.	
			229th Brigade group to move eastwards in support.	
			(M.G.Batta less 1 Company.	
			(117th Brigade R.F.A.	
		1930	Second pontoon bridge over river at O.23.a.1.6.	
		1700	Sheet 38. Situation. Leading Battalion 231st Brigade were beyond FAINTEAU and advancing on second objective. No opposition. 1 Battalion in Support on N. and S. line through FAINTEAU. Third Battalion HAVINNES. In touch with 55th Division. Not in touch with 47th Division on left.	

Army Form C. 2118.

WAR DIARY
or
INTELLIGENCE SUMMARY.
(Erase heading not required.)

Instructions regarding War Diaries and Intelligence Summaries are contained in F. S. Regs., Part II. and the Staff Manual respectively. Title pages will be prepared in manuscript. Sheet 38.

Place	Date	Hour	Summary of Events and Information	Remarks and references to Appendices
	Nov. 9th	1830	47th Division reports. Advanced troops have reached line J.27.central - J.33.central - P.3.central. Advance will resume tomorrow at 0700.	
		1845	Situation. 231st Brigade established on Second Objective. No contact with enemy. Civilians say enemy left THIMOUGIES 1600.	
		1900	Order issued confirming Warning Order sent out during afternoon and ordering further advance eastwards. Divisional Headquarters closing PONT à TRESSIN and opening O.18.c.2.7. same hour.	
		2300	Div Order No 113 issued	App 6
	10th	0530	Situation quiet. No enemy in vicinity and no hostile artillery whatever.	
		0950	Situation sent to Corps. At 0850 advanced troops had reached wood in Q.5.d. and Q.11.b. Single rifle shots heard coming from wood in Q.6. but otherwise no opposition encountered.	
		1200	Situation 231st Brigade. Final objective established along railway R.5. and 6. Patrols in BOIS ST MARTIN, R.6.a. and b. No contact with enemy. Liaison with cavalry at HACQUEGIES L.27. Not in touch with 55th Division, but patrols out. Roads all mined but not gone up. 231st H.Q. HERQUEGIES.	
		1210	Air report. Our advanced troops in N.10.d.70.95., N.5.c.80.75., N.16.b.7.8. and moving towards ATH. Bridges intact exception of rly bridges at N.12.c.3.7. and N.12.c.3.m. Crater along railways E. and W. of ATH. Roads East of river undamaged. M.G. fire experienced East of ATH also A.A.	
		1235	Identification ALSATIAN deserter in TOURNAI - 2nd Coy, 64 Labour Battalion.	
		1420	G.S.O. 2 spoke to 231st Brigade and received dispositions - also to G.O.C., 74th Division who stated he had given B.G.C., 231st Brigade orders "Not to advance further today".	
		1440	Situation to Corps. At 1200 final objective gained along railway R.5. and 6. Patrols in BOIS ST MARTIN. R.6.a. and b. No contact with enemy. Liaison with cavalry HACQUEGNIES. (as above at 1200.)	
		1540	Brigade H.Q., 229th LA ROSIER FARM Q.9.c., 230th TOURNAI, 231st Brigade HERQUEGIES.	
		1615	Warning order issued. G.772. "B' teams ordered to join Battalions.	App. 7
		1730	231st Brigade have patrols on line M.3. - M.9. Air report states Situation unchanged. cavalry seen in rifle Range N.5.d., N.10.b. & d., N.16.b. A.A. and M.G. fire encountered East of DENDRE. Road and Railway west of GHISLENGHEM - CAMBRON - CASTEAU cratered.	

Army Form C. 2118.

WAR DIARY
or
INTELLIGENCE SUMMARY.
(Erase heading not required.)

Instructions regarding War Diaries and Intelligence Summaries are contained in F. S. Regs., Part II. and the Staff Manual respectively. Title pages will be prepared in manuscript.

Place	Date	Hour	Summary of Events and Information	Remarks and references to Appendices
	Nov. 10th	1905	Main Cable route RUMILLIES – MELLES – QUARTES – FRASNES – LAHAMARDE road.	
		1915	Order No G.773 issued.	
		1925	231st Brigade report. Outpost line established with 55th Division at M.7.b. and M.8.d.4.8. and with 47th Division. No contact with enemy during day.	
		2340	Locations 231st Brigade. H.Q. R.8.a.0.8.; 10th K.S.L.I. R.2.c.3.3., 25th R.W.F. R.5.c.5.9.; 24th Welsh L.33.d.8.5., L.T.M.B. R.2.c.3.2.	
	11th	0520	Situation unchanged.	
		0845	Air report. Civilians waving flags in all towns and villages from river to main road running N. & S. through squares L, R, and X. Our advanced troops in ATH at O.26.central and on road to CHEVRES. Craters at road junction O.34.d.3.3. *over canal.*	APP. 8
		0845	Order issued G. 796.	
			Hostilities cease 1100 today afterwards no further movement eastwards. Outposts will be put out and all military precautions taken, contact with enemy will be avoided. Troops at present in movement will halt at 1100 and occupy best available billets.	
		0940	Infantry not to be in advance of cavalry screen at 1100.	
		1300	Divisional Headquarters opened FRASNES-Les-BUISSENAL L.23.a.4.6.	
		1800	Order sent to 231st Brigade to issue instructions to 19th Hussars (attached) to rejoin 9th Cavalry Brigade at MAFFLE, O.20.b.	
		1930	Situation to Corps. 231st Brigade have posts on canal at I.31.b.3.9., I.20.c.1.1., I.15.c.3.9., I.10.b.2.8., G.29.d.2.3., G.29.b.7.7. Right post 29th Division C.23.c.2.7. No touch with 55th Division. 231st Brigade H.Q. and 24th Welsh OEUDEGHIEN, K.S.L.I. OSTICHES. 25th R.W.F. PERUWELZ. 229th Brigade H.Q., LAHAMADIE. 230th Brigade billetted HACQUEGNIES.	
		2030	Order No G.809 issued.	APP. 9
		2315	Order No G.815 issued.	APP. 10
	12th	0500	Situation unchanged.	
		0955	III Corps handed over administration of TOURNAI to XI Corps at 1000 today.	

Army Form C. 2118.

WAR DIARY
or
INTELLIGENCE SUMMARY.
(Erase heading not required.)

Instructions regarding War Diaries and Intelligence Summaries are contained in F. S. Regs., Part II. and the Staff Manual respectively. Title pages will be prepared in manuscript.

Place	Date	Hour	Summary of Events and Information	Remarks and references to Appendices
	Nov. 12th	1535	3 Officer O.Rs P/W captured by 29th Division brought to Corps. Prisoners stated they had been taken after Armistice, but this was definitely proved incorrect.	
			All available troops employed on roads tomorrow. 229th Brigade from road junction I.8. across river in area occupied today – 230th Brigade from CONTREPRE G.8 to road junction in B.28 inclusive.– 231st Brigade from road junction in B.28 exclusive and area OSTICHES – REBAIX – RAPIGNIES.	
		1810	Area of 231st Brigade amended as follows – 231st Brigade LAHAMADIE – LESSINES road from road junction in B.28 exclusive to road junction B.30.b.9.7. inclusive thence RAPAGNIES – REBAIX – OSTICHES to road junction B.28.	
		2245	Posts on outpost line located as follows :– J.20.c.1.3., J.20.c.1.9., J.13.b.4.0., J.7.c.8.5., J.1.c.5.0., J.1.b.0.3., B.25.d.1.0., B.25.b.4.0., B.19.d.4.0., B.19.d.4.3.	
	13th	0715	Civilians allowed to pass through outpost line from EAST to WEST only.	
		0920	Instructions issued to 229th Brigade regarding P.M. taking over posts – (G.848.)	App.11
		1006	Orders issued to Brigades. No enemy aircraft to be allowed to cross the line.	App.12
			Army Commander at Headquarters. He stated the Division would form part of the Army of occupation, and would be under the Second Army.	App.13
		1750	Reference G.848 posts established by P.M., Fifth Army are responsible only for examination and control of civil population. 229th Brigade will still maintain complete system of outposts.	
	14th	1430	Conference. Corps Headquarters.	
		2330	Divisional Order No 114 issued.	
	15th	1500	Divisional Order No 115 issued.	
		2000	Divisional Order No 116 issued.	
	16th	—	Move of 230th and 231st Brigades in accordance with Divisional Order 116 completed.	
	17th	—	Move of 229th and 231st Brigades completed.	

Army Form C. 2118.

WAR DIARY
or
INTELLIGENCE SUMMARY.
(Erase heading not required.)

Instructions regarding War Diaries and Intelligence Summaries are contained in F. S. Regs., Part II. and the Staff Manual respectively. Title pages will be prepared in manuscript.

Place	Date	Hour	Summary of Events and Information	Remarks and references to Appendices
	Nov. 18th	—	Two battalions from each Brigade Group moved to vicinity of TOURNAI – LEUZE railway in accordance with G.830 to work on railway. 242nd Army Brigade, R.F.A. joined Division and went into billets in L.33.b.	App/14
	19th	1100	229th Infantry Brigade H.Q. moved to LEUZE.	App. 15
	20th		Work on TOURNAI – LEUZE railway continued.	" 16
	21st		Organization of Recreation and Education in Division.	" 17
	22nd			
	23rd			
	24th			
	25th		"	
	26th			
	27th			
	28th			
	29th			
	30th			

A. Sanderson
Major,
General Staff,
74th (Yeomanry) Division

SECRET.
******

AMENDMENTS TO
74th (YEOMANRY) DIVISION ORDER NO 109.

1.   Para 4. - Cancel last two sub-paras and substitute :-

   " The objectives of the Division and of the flank Divisions, also the inter-Divisional boundaries are shown on the attached map.

   The second objective of the Division on the left is MELLES. "

2.   Cancel para 8 and substitute :-

   " Bridges are being built by XI Corps at O.23.d.3.3. and O.23.c.8.7. III Corps is building bridges at O.29.b.6.8. and to the South.

   As far as possible, III Corps bridges (when built) will be used by this Division for the movement of troops and supplies. The Northern portion of the town will be left clear for XI Corps."

3.   Add fresh para -

   " 13. The Divisional Road will be RUMILLIES - HAVINNES - BECLERS Stn - BECLERS - THIMOUGIES Road. The Divisional cable will be laid along this route and all Brigade Headquarters will be located in its vicinity."

4.   ACKNOWLEDGE.

ACTemperley
Lieut Colonel.
General Staff.
74th (Yeomanry) Division.

5th November 1918.

Addressed all recipients of Divisional Order No 109.

"A" Form
MESSAGES AND SIGNALS.

Army Form C. 2123
(In pads of 100.)

TO	229 Bde	47 Div	C.R.A.	A.D.M.S.	G.O.C.
	230 Bde	55 Div	C.R.E.	Signals	Div Train
	231 Bde	3 Corps.	M.G.Bn.	'Q'.	

Sender's Number.	Day of Month.	In reply to Number.	AAA
* G. 675	7		

229 Bde will relieve left Bde of 55 Div in line on night Nov 8/9th aaa C.R.A. will arrange for relief of F.A. Bde covering this Sector aaa M.G.Bn will arrange to relieve Machine Gun Coy of 55 Div aaa All reliefs to be arranged direct between those concerned aaa Completion to be reported by wire

Added all concerned.

From 74 Div
Place
Time 1520

(Sd.) A. GALLOWAY, Capt GS

"A" Form
MESSAGES AND SIGNALS.

Army Form C.2121 (In pads of 100)

TO	229 Bde	47 Div	C.R.A.	A.D.M.S.	G.O.C.
	230 "	55 Div	C.R.E.	Signals.	Div. Train
	231 Bde	3 Corps	M.G.Bn.	'Q'.	

Sender's Number.	Day of Month.	In reply to Number.	AAA
* G. 695	8		

G. 675   is   cancelled   A.A.A.

Added all concerned.

From: 74 Div
Time: 0930

(Sd.) A. GALLOWAY, Capt
G.S.

SECRET.

Copy No. 19

Appendix III

74TH DIVISION ORDER NO 111.

8th November 1918.

1. Under instructions received from III Corps, 2 Battalions of the 1st Portuguese Brigade, 1st Division and 1 section of the 6th Field Ambulance will be attached to the 74th Division.

2. These Battalions which have been reorganised and are reported to be complete with equipment and transport will be attached as follows :-

    22nd Battn to 230th Brigade.
    34th Battn to 229th Brigade.

    B.Gs.C. these Brigades will make arrangements to receive these Battalions on November 11th.

3. These Battalions will be under the disciplinary control and supervision of the Brigadier Generals Commanding the Brigades to which they are attached.

4. The section of the 6th Field Ambulance will come under the orders of the A.D.M.S., 74th Division.

5. Separate instructions are being issued regarding the method of training and employment of these Battalions.

6. Each Battalion will be accompanied by complete echelons of 1st Line and Mechanical Transport (namely 2 G.S. Wagons for supplies and 2 Lorries per Battalion). Of these the Train vehicles will be attached to the Train of the 74th Division, and the M.T. vehicles to the M.T. Company of the 74th Division.

7. A Liaison Officer and Medical Officer will accompany each Battalion. It is also hoped to arrange for a Liaison Officer to be attached to Divisional Headquarters.

8. III Corps "Q" will issue special instructions on the following points :-
    (a) Feeding arrangements.
    (b) Clothing, Arms and equipment.
    (c) Discipline.
    (d) Pay.

9. ACKNOWLEDGE.

A C Temperley.

Lieut-Colonel,
General Staff,
74th (Yeomanry) Division.

Issued at... 1230

Copies to:-

1.	G.O.C.	13.	A.D.M.S.
2.	'G'.	14.	Div. Train.
3-5.	'Q'.	15.	III Corps.
6.	C.R.A.	16.	55 Div.
7.	C.R.E.	17.	47 Div.
8.	Signals.	18.	British Mission, 1st Portuguese Division.
9.	M.G. Battn.	19-20.	War Diary.
10.	229th Inf. Bde.	21.	File.
11.	230th " "	22.	74 M.T. Coy.
12.	231st " "		

"A" Form
Army Form C. 2121
(In pads of 100.)

MESSAGES AND SIGNALS. No. of Message............

Prefix........Code..........m.	Words	Charge	This message is on a/c of:	Recd. at......m.
Office of Origin Service Instructions	Sent			Date............
Urgent Cher: Pte 229+231	At.......m.		.............Service.	From ....
Priority to remainder	To........			
	By........		(Signature of "Franking Officer")	By ....

TO:
229 Bde	O.C.	Train	3 Corps
230 Bde	Signals	to	
231 Bde	R.A.M.C.	55 Div	G.O.C.

Sender's Number.	Day of Month.	In reply to Number.	AAA
G. 732	8		

Ref TOURNAI Sheet 1/100,000 aaa Advanced Gd Bde will make good line East of BECLERS - THIMOUGIES today aaa 74th Div will stand fast on that objective aaa 55 Div Mobile column will move forward East of this objective to seize high ground East of LEUZE aaa 9th Cav Bde will assist in pursuit tomorrow aaa Next objective of XI Corps is high ground N. of FRASNES - lez - BUISSENAL aaa Corps Boundaries aaa North - MONTREUIL au BOIS - BAS DOUX - DAMERIE - HOUTAING (all inclusive) - 400 yds South of BOUVIGNIES aaa South PIPAIX - ERVEAU (both excl) - BLICQUY (incl) - TONGRES and CHIEVRES (both excl) aaa ACK Added all concerned.

From 74 Div
Place
Time 1010

"A" Form
MESSAGES AND SIGNALS.

Army Form C. 2121 (In pads of 100.)

Urgent Operation Priority to 229 and 251 Bdes ...

Appendix 5

TO:
- 229 Bde — C.R.A. — "Q" — Train — 47 Div
- 230 Bde — C.R.E. — M.G.Bn. — 21 Sqd RAF
- 251 Bde — Signals — A.D.M.S. — X Corps — 55 Div

Sender's Number: G 755 Day of Month: 9

AAA

Div Order No 112 AAA Advanced Guard Bde will continue advance to-morrow at 0800 AAA First objective high ground R.14.a. - R.2. Second objective Railway in R.12 - R.6. AAA Dividing line between 55 and 74 Div BECLERS - ALTIERE - LAMOURETTE (both incl to 55 Div) - L.8.a.0.0. AAA 47 Div objective MOUSTIER (L.29.) AAA 55 Div objective MONTROR (M.32.) - LE CHAPITRE (M.8.) AAA One regt 9th Cav Bde moving via MERQUEGIES to MOUSTIER to join XI Corps aaa 229 Bde group as detailed in warning order will cross R. ESCAUT by bridge at O.29.b.9.7. and will concentrate in area THIMOUGIES - BECLERS - HAVINNES area AAA Head of column to pass eastern edge of MARQUAIN at 0900 AAA Brigade Staff Officer to be at bridge to regulate traffic AAA

"A" Form
MESSAGES AND SIGNALS.

Army Form C. 2121
(In pads of 100.)

No. of Message............

Prefix.........Code.........m.	Words	Charge.	This message is on a/c of :	Recd. at......m.
Office of Origin and Service Instructions	Sent		..............................Service.	Date............
....	At ....m.			From ....
....	To			
....	By		(Signature of "Franking Officer")	By...............

TO {

- 2 -

| Sender's Number. | Day of Month. | In reply to Number. | AAA |

D.A.C. less one section to CRCQ AAA
One section D.A.C. and 6" how battery
to RUMILLIES AAA D.A.C. and 6" battery
not to enter MARQUAIN before 1100 aaa
Div H.Q. closes in present position
and opens at O.18.c.2.7. at 1200 AAA
ACKNOWLEDGE AAA Added all concerned

From: 74 Div
Place:
Time:

The above may be forwarded as now corrected. (Z)

..................................(Sd) A.C. TEMPERLEY, Lt Col
Censor. Signature of Addressor or person authorised to telegraph in his name
GS*
* This line should be erased if not required.

Order No. 1625. Wt. W3253/ P 511. 27/2. H. & K., Ltd. (E. 2634).

Appendix 6/20

S.D.1.A.

Copy No......

74th. DIVISION ORDER NO.113.

Ref. Sheet 37.1:40,000.

9th. November 1918.

1. Reference 74th Div. Order No.111.

The 1st and 3rd Battalions and Section No.6 Field Ambulance 1st Portuguese Division will move from LESQUIN to the area LAMAIN - HAUDION - HERTAIN on November 11th and will billet in the villages as follows:-

1st Battalion in LAMAIN.
3rd Battalion in HERTAIN.
Section No.6 Fld.Amb. in HAUDION.

2. Advance Parties accompanied by two British liaison Officers will meet billeting party detailed by 74th Division at the cross Roads in N.21.d. at 10.00 on 11th Nov.

3. No restrictions as to route but the head of the Column is to reach Cross Roads in N.21.d. by 12.00 on 11th Novr.

4. On arrival in billets 1st Battalion will come under the orders of B.G.C. 230th Infantry Brigade and Section No.6 Field Ambulance will come under the orders of A.D.M.S. 74th Division.

5. On 12th November 3rd Battalion will march at 6 a.m. to join 229th Infantry Brigade. Route and destination to be notified later.

6. Four lorries accompanying Portuguese troops will report empty to the O.C., 74th Div.M.T.Coy. on the morning of the 11th November and four G.S. wagons will report empty to O.C., 74th Div.Train on the morning of the 12th November. Locations of these Units will be communicated later. 15 O.R. will be detailed from each Battalion to report respectively to O.C. Train and O.C.,M.T.Coy as loading parties.

6. ACKNOWLEDGE.

Wm Beckwith Major
for Lieut.Colonel,
General Staff,
74th (Yeomanry) Division.

Issued At..2300......

Copies to:-
    No. 1. G.O.C.
        2. Senior Bn.Cmdr.
            1st & 3rd Port.Bns.
    3 - 6. Lieut.Milne Liaison Officer.
        7. Belgian Mission.
        8. 229th Inf.Brigade.
        9. 230th Inf.Brigade.
      10. A.D.M.S.
      11. 'Q'.
      12. D.A.P.M.
      13. O.C., 74th M.T.Coy.
      14. O.C., 74th Div.Train.
      15. British Mission 1st Portuguese Divn.
      16. IIIrd Corps.
      17. Signals.
      18. File.
  19 - 20. War Diary.

"A" Form
MESSAGES AND SIGNALS.

Army Form C. 2121
(In pads of 100.)

Urgent Op Priority

(Sgd) A.C.

TO:
- 229 Bde
- 230 Bde.
- 231 Bde.

Sender's Number: G. 772
Day of Month: 10

AAA

Warning Order aaa 231 and 229 Bdes will move eastwards tomorrow at 0800 aaa 230 Bde will move eastwards immediately it is relieved in TOURNAI units marching eastwards as relieved aaa 11th Corps ordered to complete relief by 1000.

From: 74 Div.
Time: 1615

(Sd.) A.C. CRAIG Lt.

"A" Form
MESSAGES AND SIGNALS.

Army Form C. 2121
(In pads of 100.)

Prefix........Code........m, Words. Charge.

Office of Origin and Service Instructions

Operation
Priority.
(Sd.) G.B.

This message is on a/c of:
Appendix 8

TO	229 Bde	C.R.A.	Train	M.G.Bn.
	230 Bde	C.R.E.	Signals	
	231 Bde	A.D.M.S.	Q.	

Sender's Number: G. 796
Day of Month: 11
AAA

Hostilities cease 1100 today after which hour no further easterly movement will take place aaa outposts will be put out and all military precautions taken aaa Contact with enemy will be avoided aaa Troops at present in movement will halt at 1100 and occupy best available billets or return to last nights billets if no facilities exist. AAA 230 Bde will stand fast AAA

From 74 Div.
Place
Time 0845

(Sd.) C. BROAD Lt. Col. G.S.

"A" Form
MESSAGES AND SIGNALS.

Army Form C.2121
(In pads of 100.)

Prefix........Code...........m, | Words. | Charge.
Office of Origin and Service Instructions

Urgent Oper Pri.
to 229 & 231 Bdes.

(Sd.) W.M.BECKWITH Major,
By......G.S.

This message is on a/c of:
Appendix 9
..............Service.

Recd. at............m.
Date............
From............
By............

TO:
229 Bde	C.R.A.	Train	55 Div
230 "	C.R.E.	Q	29 Div
231 "	A.D.M.S.	M.G.Bn.	III Corps.

| Sender's Number | Day of Month | In reply to Number | AAA |
| G.809 | 11 | | |

Ref. Sheet 38 - 1:40,000 AAA Probable moves
for 12th inst AAA 229 Bde Group will pass
through 231 Bde and occupy most advantageous
line from junction with 55 Div about J.25.b.
to D.19.central AAA Posts under officers
will be placed on all roads crossing outpost
line to prevent civilians passing E. or W.
AAA 229 Bde Group will billet E. of R. DENDRE
AAA Boundary between 55 and 74 Div. railway
line from GHISLENGHIEN to LACQUESAINT AAA
Special parties to be detailed to keep touch
with flank divs AAA 231 Bde Group will
remain in present billets and withdraw outposts
when 229 Bde has passed through AAA 230 Bde
Group to which 60 pr battery will be attached
will move into billets vacated by 229 Bde
Group on main road between LA MAMAIDE and

From
Place
Time

The above may be forwarded as now corrected. (Z)

"A" Form
MESSAGES AND SIGNALS.

Army Form C. 2121
(In pads of 100.)

		2.	
Sender's Number.	Day of Month.	In reply to Number.	AAA

G.7.d. orders to move and times later AAA
AUK.
~~Addressed all concerned.~~

From: 74 Div.
Place:
Time: 2030

(Sd) W.M. BECKWITH, Major,

"A" Form
MESSAGES AND SIGNALS.

Army Form C. 2121
(In pads of 100.)

URGENT OP·PTY·
229 Bde
230 "   (Sd)
231 "   C.B.

This message is on a/c of: *Appendix X*

TO				
	229 Bde	C.R.A.	Train	55 Div
	230 Bde	C.R.E.	Q	29 Div
	231 Bde	A.D.M.S.	M.G.Bn.	III Corps.

Sender's Number.	Day of Month.	In reply to Number.	
* G. 815	11		AAA

Movements detailed in G. 809 will be carried out tomorrow aaa 229 and 230 Bdes to start at 0900 aaa If any opposition is encountered 229 Bde will halt on the line where opposition is met with and establish outposts aaa Acknowledge aaa Addsd all concerned.

From 74 Div
Place
Time 2315

(Sd) C. BROAD, Lt. Col. GS

SECRET.   Copy No. 16

74th DIVISION ORDER No.114.   Appendix XI

14th November 1918.

1.   The following forecast of probable moves is issued for information.

   November 16th.
   (a) 230th Brigade Group (less 230th Field Ambulance and
       M.G's) to HEFQUELGIES - PIRE - THIMOUGIES - MAVIPRES -
       Grande MASURE Area.

   (b) 231st Brigade Group (less Artillery & M.G.s) to
       REBAIX - BIGAUDE - BUISSENAL - MOUSTIER -
       COCQUEREAUMONT - Gd MARAIS - MAINVAULT Area.

   (c) 44th Brigade R.F.A. and No.2 Sec. D.A.C. to ANVAING
       - FOREST - POPUELLES - QUARTES Area.

   (d) M.G.Coys of above Brigades to ELLIGNIES LEZ FRASNES -
       ELMOTE - DIME Area.

   November 17th.
   (a) 231st Brigade Group (less Artillery & M.G's) to CORDES
       - HAUT REJET - MOURCOURT - MELLES Area.

   (b) 229th Brigade Group (less Artillery & M.G.'s) to
       REBAIX - BIGAUDE - BUISSENAL - MOUSTIER -
       COCQUEREAUMONT - Gd.MARAIS - MAINVAULT Area.

   (c) 117th Brigade R.F.A. and No.1 Sec.D.A.C. to ANVAING
       - FOREST - POPUELLES - QUARTES Area.

   (d) H.Q., M.G.Bn & M.G.Coys, 229th Brigade Group to
       ELLIGNIES LEZ FRASNES - ELMOTE - DIME Area.

   NOTES:- 1.   Divn.H.Q., Pioneer Battalion, 230th Field Amb,
           H.Q. Div.Train, No.3 Sec.D.A.C. will probably remain
           in present locations.

        2.   H.Q.,D.A.C. and Mobile Vet.Section will move to
           ANVAING - FOREST - POPUELLES - QUARTES Area.

        3.   Maps showing exact boundaries of areas will be
           issued tomorrow with the order to move.

        4.   The 229th Brigade will be relieved in the line
           by a Brigade from the II Corps.
             230th & 231st Brigade Area will be taken over on
           Nov.16th by troops from the II Corps.

                                           C Broad

                                       Lieut.Colonel.
                                       General Staff,
                                   74th (Yeomanry) Division.

Issued at ... 2330

Copies to:- No.1. G.O.C.   No.13. A.D.M.S.
            2.   14. Div.Train.
            3-5.
            6. C.R.A.
            7. C.
            8. Signal Coy.
            9. M.G.Bn.   15. War Diary.
           10. 229th Inf.Bde.   File.
           11. 230th   "   "
           12. 231st   "   "

SECRET.

COPY NO......19

Appendix XII

74th DIVISION ORDER NO.115.

15th November 1918.

Ref. sheet TOURNAI 1:100,000 2nd Ed.

1.   The new Divisional Boundaries and the allotment of billeting areas are shown on the attached map.

2.   230 Brigade Group less 230 Field Ambulance will march to Area E on 16th instant via CONTREPRE - FRASNES - HACQUEGNIES, hour of start to be fixed by B.G.C. 230 Brigade but the rear of the column will be clear of the V of BOIS LEFEBVRE by 1045.

On arrival at HACQUEGNIES the M.G.Coy attached 230 Brigade Group will come under orders of O.C. M.G.Battalion and will be billeted in Area B.

3. (a) 231 Brigade Group (less 44 Brigade R.F.A., No.2 Sec. D.A.C. and M.G.Coy) will march to Area A on 16th inst via any route other than LESSINES - TOURNAI road. Hour of start to be fixed by B.G.C. 231st Inf.Brigade.

(b) 44th Brigade R.F.A., No.2 Sec.D.A.C. and M.G.Coy. attached 231 Brigade Group will march under orders of B.G.C. 231 Brigade Group on Nov.16th to Cross Roads 500 yards N.E. of HACQUEGNIES following immediately in rear of 230 Brigade Group.

On arrival at the above point, these Units will revert to control of C.R.A. and O.C.,M.G.Battalion respectively and billet in Areas C and B respectively.

4.   Divisional Headquarters, Pioneer Battalion, 230th Field Ambulance, H.Q. and No. 1 Coy Div.Train, No.3 Sec.D.A.C. will remain in present locations.

5.   H.Q. D.A.C. and Mobile Veterinary Section will move on November 16th to Area C under orders of C.R.A.

6.   Orders regarding move of 231st Brigade Group to Area D and relief of 229th Brigade Group will be issued later.

7.   ACKNOWLEDGE.

C Bwd

Lieut.Colonel,
General Staff,
74th (Yeomanry) Division.

Issued at...1500...

Copies to:-
```
       No. 1. G.O.C.                No. 13. A.D.M.S.
           2. 'G'.                      14. Div. Train.
         3-5. 'Q'.                      15. III Corps.
           6. C.R.A.                    16. 55th Division.
           7. C.R.E.                    17. 29th Division.
           8. Signal Coy.            18-19. War Diary.
           9. L.S.Bn.                   20. File.
          10. 229th Inf.Bde.
          11. 230th   "    "
          12. 231st   "    "
```

Appendix XIII

SECRET.

Copy No. 19

74th DIVISION ORDER No.116.

15th November 1918.

Ref.Map. TOURNAI 1;100,000 2nd Edition.

1. The 229th Brigade Group will be relieved in the line on 17th instant by an Infantry Brigade, 29th Division. B.G.C. of this Brigade has been instructed to report at H.Q., 229th Infantry Brigade tomorrow.
   All details will be arranged direct between B.G's.C. concerned.
   Completion of relief will be wired to Divisional H.Q. by 229th Infantry Brigade.

2. (a) 229th Brigade Group, less 117th Bde.R.F.A. & No.1 Section, D.A.C., will, on completion of relief, march to billetting area 'A'.
   No restriction as to roads.
   (b) 117th Brigade.R.F.A. & No.1 Section, D.A.C. will on completion of relief, march under orders of B.G.C., 229th Infantry Brigade to cross roads 500 yds N.E. of HACQUEGNIES.
   No restriction as to route.
   On arrival at above point, these units will revert to control of C.R.A. and billet in area 'C'.

3. The 231st Brigade Group will march on 17th instant to billetting area 'D'.
   No restrictions as to route.
   Hour of start to be fixed by B.G.C., 231st Infantry Brigade.

4. The H.Q., M.G.Bn. and two companies attached 229th Infantry Brigade will on 18th inst. march to billetting area 'B' under orders of B.G.C., 229th Infantry Brigade.
   No restrictions as to route. Hour of start to be fixed by B.G.C., 229th Infantry Brigade.
   On arrival in area 'B', the H.Q., M.G.Bn and above two companies will revert to Divisional control.

5. ACKNOWLEDGE.

C Broad

Lieut.Colonel,
General Staff,
74th (Yeomanry) Division.

Issued at 2000.

Copies to:-
No. 1. G.O.C.
2. 'G'
3-5. 'Q'
6. C.R.A.
7. C.R.E.
8. Signal Coy.
9. M.G.Bn.
10. 229th Infantry Bde.
11. 230th " "
12. 231st " "
No.13. A.D.M.S.
14. Div.Train.
15. III Corps.
16. 55th Division.
17. 29th Division.
18-19. War Diary.
20. File.

"A" Form
MESSAGES AND SIGNALS.

Army Form C. 2121
(In pads of 100.)

Prefix......Code......m. | Words. | Charge.

Office of Origin and Service Instructions

Operation Priority to 229, 230 and 231 Bdes.

(Sd) A.C. CRAIG Lt.

This message is on a/c of: *Appendix XIV* Service.

TO:	229 Bde	3 Corps	C.R.A.	Train.
	230 Bde	74 Div Sigs	C.R.E.	D.A.D.V.S.
	231 Bde	Q.	A.D.MS.	

Sender's Number: G. 830
Day of Month: 17
AAA

Each Inf Bde will detail two Bns for work on LEUZE - TOURNAI railway aaa Bns will rendezvous for work 0830 19th inst aaa 231 Bde P.23.a.1.7. and Q.14.c.7.8. 230 Bde Q.28.a.6.0. and Q.35.d.9.3. 229 Bde X.2.a.1.7. and R.34.b.3.1. aaa One Bn each location aaa All available tools will be taken aaa Hours of work 0830 to 1600 aaa Work under supervision 5th Bn Canadian Rlwy Troops aaa Billets allotted will be notified later aaa Troops will move to billets on 18th inst under orders of B.Gs.C. Bdes aaa Fld Coys R.E. not required aaa Bdes will report by wire which Bns are detailed aaa ACKNOWLEDGE Added 229 230 231 Bdes reptd all concerned.

From: 74 Div.
Place:
Time: 1510

(Z) (Sd) A.C. CRAIG. Lt.

Appendix XV

G. 8/2.

MINUTES OF CONFERENCE AT DIVISIONAL SPORTS MEETING 18th inst.

1. A preliminary Meeting of representatives from all Units in the Division was held at Divisional Headquarters on 18th inst., when it was decided to form a Divisional Sports Committee.
The following were elected to act on the Committee :-

   President.

   Brig. Gen. F.S. THACKERAY. D.S.O., M.C.

   Secretary.

   Major J.P. HEYWOOD LONSDALE.

   Members.

   Captain H.L. JEAKES. M.C.

   also 1 representative from each Infantry Brigade Group, (including Field Coy, R.E., Field Ambulance and Company Divisional Train.)

   1 representative from R.A.
   1   "   from Divisional Troops.

2. DUTIES OF COMMITTEE.
   1. Central Financial Control.
   2. Organization of Competitions on a Divisional basis.
   3. Hire of lands, and settlement of claims made for lands used for recreations and competitions.
   4. Purchase and retail of equipment.
   5. Representation of Division at Corps and Army Sports Meetings.

3. The Committee was authorised to organize Brigade Committees and decide as to their duties.

4. The question as to the starting of Brigade Concert Parties was left for the Committee to consider - also the question of starting a pack of Hounds or beagles.

5. It was decided that units should begin as soon as possible to work up the interest of both Officers and men in the following recreations :-

   Football, Boxing, Cross-country running, Wrestling on horseback, Tugs of War, Riding and jumping, Tent-pegging, Hockey, Baseball, Basket Ball, Wrestling, also (indoor games), Whist Drives, Chess, Halma, Draughts, Dominoes, Ping Pong.

6. Units were to be asked by their representatives attending the meeting to send in as soon as possible, through their Brigade representatives, all requirements as to outfit and equipment for games suggested.

7. The names of the representatives of each Brigade Group are to be sent in to Divisional H.Q. by Noon on 20th inst.

8. /

8. All competitions will be carried out under rules as laid down in S.S. 137.

****

Distribution :-

        229th Infantry Brigade. (5)
        230th   "   "   (5)
        231st   "   "   (5)
        C.R.A.   (5)
        C.R.E.   (5)
        74th Battn, L.G.C.
        74th Div. Signal Coy.
        A.D.M.S.
        74th Divisional Train.
        74th M.T. Coy.
        Pioneer Battalion.

Appendix XVI

G. 8/3.

MINUTES OF CONFERENCE HELD BY DIVISIONAL

RECREATION COMMITTEE ON 23RD INST.

A Meeting of the Divisional Recreation Committee was held at Divisional Headquarters on Saturday, November 23rd when the following points were discussed and decided on:-

1. That Brigade Committees should be formed and should consist of a President and one Member from each unit in the Brigade Group. The Divisional representative of the Group being an ex officio member of the Committee.

2. The duties of Brigade Committees were to consist of
    1. Organisation of competitions within the Group.
    2. Hiring of lands, or any places wanted for the holding of recreations of any kind.
    3. Supervising the arrangements made by Battalion Committees.
    4. General supervision of all Sports, Games and Competitions etc. in the Brigade.
    5. Appointment of representative on the Divisional Committee.

3. It was decided that all equipment should be bought by the Divisional Committee and retailed by them to units. The Brigade Committee advising the Divisional Committee as to the proportion to be given to each unit when the total requirements of units cannot be met.

4. In case of the required amount of equipment not being procurable at the E.F.C., it was decided to try and buy it in England at the wholesale prices.

5. With regard to hiring of lands it was decided that units were to make as good an arrangement as possible, and in case of no satisfactory agreement being arrived at, then it should be put before the Divisional Committee and settled by the Claims Officer.

6. The question of a pack of beagles or hounds was left over for the present until more information on the subject was available.

7. As much equipment as possible was to be bought at once. The Divisional Funds would advance the money required as a loan, the debt being finally met by units or by any funds which could be obtained from Government for these purposes.

8. Brigade Committees were to report whether they could raise Concert Parties. The Divisional Committee was prepared to assist Brigade Concert Parties with a loan for starting their troupes.

9. Units were to be instructed by Brigade Committees to apply to the Stationery Services for S.S. 137, i.e., the Rules under which all Competitions were to be held.

Distribution :-
   Sports Representative,
      229th, 230th, 231st Brigade Group.
   D.A.
   Divisional H.Q. Group.
      (at M.G. Battn).
   Major LONSDALE.

Appendix XVII

G. 38/35.

74TH (YEOMANRY) DIVISION.

ORGANISATION OF EDUCATION.

1. The Education of the Division will be organised as nearly as possible on the same lines as a University.

2. The following is the method which will be carried out throughout the Division, —
Div HQ will be the organizing and directing Staff & will be responsible for :-
   (a) General Organization.
   (b) Arrangement of Classes for technical instruction in subjects which require practical demonstration such as Workshop training, electricity, Motor Mechanics etc.
   (c) Providing extra lectures and instruction in special subjects and arranging for the interchange of instructors between Groups.
   (d) The Provision of the necessary books and materials required.
   (e) Arrangements for examinations.
   (f) Arrangement for the attendance of students at special Courses outside the Division.

3. GROUPS. The Division will be sub-divided into five groups constituted as follows :-

   No 1 Group. **Divisional Headquarters Group.**

   Divisional H.Q.
   H.Q. and No 1 Section Divisional Signal Coy.
   H.Q. and No 1 Company, Divisional Train.
   H.Q. Divisional Engineers.
   M.T. Company.
   1/12th North Lancs (Pioneers).
   74th Battn, M.G.C.
   74th Div. Employment Company.

   No 2 Group. Divisional Artillery, 242nd Army Brigade R.F.A. and Mobile Veterinary Section.

   No 3 Group. 229th Infantry Brigade with attached Field Company, Field Ambulance and Company Train.

   No 4 Group. 230th Infantry Brigade with attached units as above.

   No 5 Group. 231st Infantry Brigade with attached units as above.

   The Headquarters of each Group will be responsible for

   (a) Supervision of the Education throughout the Units comprising the Group.
   (b) Organisation of Central Group Schools for instruction in those special subjects which can be taught by means of lectures and book work, and which are beyond the scope of units.
   (c) Organisation and General supervision of schools of such technical and commercial instruction as can be arranged with units such as R.E. and R.A.M.C. within the Group.
   (d) The Compilation and keeping up to date of a list of Instructors with the subjects in which they are qualified to instruct.

In /

- 2 -

In this list should be included those officers and O.R. who have a good knowledge of certain subjects and who, with a short training should make efficient instructors.

A further list will be kept of lecturers on General subjects stating the subjects on which they are prepared to lecture.

A copy of these lists to be forwarded to Divisional H.Q. and Amendments notified from time to time.

(e) Responsibility that a Nominal Roll is kept at the Headquarters of each Unit showing the following information for each man in the Groups on proforma below,-

Rank and Name.	Occupation before War.	Occupation desired after War.	Courses attended with Dates.	Remarks.

A duplicate copy of this proforma for each Unit in the Groups will be kept at Group Headquarters.

(f) Application by the Group Education Officer to Divisional Education Officer for all Books and material required for instruction.
(g) Responsibility for provision as far as possible and application when necessary to Divisional H.Q. of proper facilities for education such as Halls, lighting etc.
(h) The keeping of such Records and Returns as are required by Divisional H.Q.
(j) Responsibility for keeping Registers of attendance of Students by Educational Officers in order that certificates may be granted.

4. Each Unit (Battalion, Brigade R.A., Field Company, Field Ambulance and Company Train) will carry out the General Elementary Training of all ranks under the supervision of the Group H.Q.

It is also suggested that Unit classes could be organised in such subjects as Shoemaking and Tailoring in which trades most units are in possession of an expert.

5. In order to make the chain of responsibility complete and to assist in the organisation of the education of the Group it will be necessary for a Group Education officer to be selected in each Group. This officer must be in addition to the Education Officer of each unit in that Group.

All Education Officers will give their whole time to the education in their Groups and Units and will be struck off all other duties.

6. When necessary a certain proportion of technical troops will be attached to those Groups who have no R.E. Company or Field Ambulance attached to them.

7.

7. If there is sufficient demand and the necessary instructors are forthcoming, Classes for officers will be organised.

A. Sanderson Major

Lieut-Colonel,
General Staff,
74th (Yeomanry) Division.

20th November, 1918.

Copies to :-

329th Infantry Brigade. (10)
330th   "   "   (10)
231st   "   "   (10)
C.R.A.   (12)
C.R.E.   (4)
A.D.M.S.   (4)
1/12th North Lancs (Pioneers) through
                 C.R.E. (2)
O.C., 74th Div. Train.   (5)
O.C., 74th Bn. M.G.C.   (5)
O.C., 74th Div. Sig. Coy. (4)
O.C., 74th Div. Emp. Coy. (2)
74th Div. Education Officer. (2)

SECRET.   Copy No. 16

74th DIVISION ORDER No.110.

31st October 1918.

1. The bombardment will be continued tomorrow and hostile machine gun positions will be gassed if the wind is favourable.

2. These demonstrations, coupled with operations further to the North and to the South may induce the enemy to expedite his withdrawal.
To ascertain this 230th Brigade will conduct an operation on the morning of Nov.2nd in conjunction with an attack by the 55th Division on our right.

3. At 0515 - Divisional Artillery will open an intense bombardment along the road in O.27.a. & c, O.21.a. & c, O.15.c.
At 0520 - patrols will be sent forward simultaneously along the Divisional front to test the enemy line.
At 0523 - the standing barrage will lift from the road to the enemy front line system.
At 0526 - the barrage will lift from the front line to the second system.
At 0541 - it will lift off the second system.

4. Should the patrols draw fire they will return to our lines. Should the enemy have retired or show signs of weakening, the patrols will continue their advance under the barrage and will be supported.
The advance will continue and ultimately the whole Advanced Guard Brigade will be set in motion in accordance with Divisional Order No.109.
There will be no advance beyond the enemy wire South of the LILLE - TOURNAI Road owing to mines.

5. A machine gun barrage will be placed on the first and second objectives and will lift 200 yards ahead of the artillery barrage.

6. 230th Brigade Group will be ready to move at one hour's notice after 0830. All 1st Line Transport will be in readiness to join units at short notice.

7. The C.R.E. will arrange for all bridging material to be ready for loading and for transport and teams to be standing by from 0800, if the Advanced Guard is moving forward.

8. Watches will be synchronized by the General Staff at 1400 on November 1st.

9. ACKNOWLEDGE.

                                                 ACTemperley
                                                              Lieut.Colonel.
                                                              General Staff,
                                                         74th (Yeomanry) Division.

Issued at 2000.

                Distribution overleaf.

Copies to:-
No. 1. G.O.C.
2. 'G'.
3-5. 'Q'.
6. C.R.A.
7. C.R.E.
8. O.C., Signal Coy.
9. "   M.G.Battn.
10. 229th Infantry Brigade.
11. 230th   "   "
12. 231st   "   "
13. A.D.M.S.
14. Div Train.
15. III Corps.
16. 55th Division.
17. 47th Division.
18-19. War Diary.
20. File.

SECRET.

Headquarters,
  III Corps.
    55th Division.
    47th Division.

    Herewith table of bombardments of hostile positions opposite this Divisional Front during next 3 days with a view to destruction of enemy personnel.

4th November, 1918.

Major-General,
Commanding 74th (Yeo) Division

S E C R E T.   Copy No. 9

Royal Artillery Order No.66.
-by-
Brigadier General L.J. HEXT, C.M.G.
Commanding Royal Artillery 74th (Yeo) Division.

4th November, 1918.

1. Concentration of all Guns and howitzers of the 44th Brigade, R.F.A. that can reach the target will take place according to the attached bombardment table.
Heavy Artillery are co-operating under orders being issued direct by III Corps H.A.

2. All concentrations will last for 5 minutes with the exception of concentrations 7 & 8 which will last for 10 minutes.

3. Rate of Fire.

    18-pdrs.   INTENSE, except in concentrations 7 & 8.

    4.5" Hows. RAPID.

4. Ammunition for 18-pdrs.

    50% A and 50% AX except in concentrations 7 & 8 when shrapnel only will be used.

5. Watches will be synchronised from this office at 1530 and 2100 today and at 0830 and 1400 on November 5th.

ACKNOWLEDGE.

                                                   Major R.A.
                                              Brigade Major R.A.
Issued at 1430   74th (Yeomanry) Division.

Copy.No. 1 - 5. 44th Bde. R.F.A.   6. 74th D.A.C.
         7 -11. H.Q., 74th (Yeo) Divn. 12. H.Q. 231st Inf. Bde.
         13.   R.A. IIIrd Corps.   14. IIIrd Corps H.A.
         15.   52nd Bde. R.G.A.   16. 164th (S) Bty. R.G.A.
      17 & 18.   War Diary.   19. File.

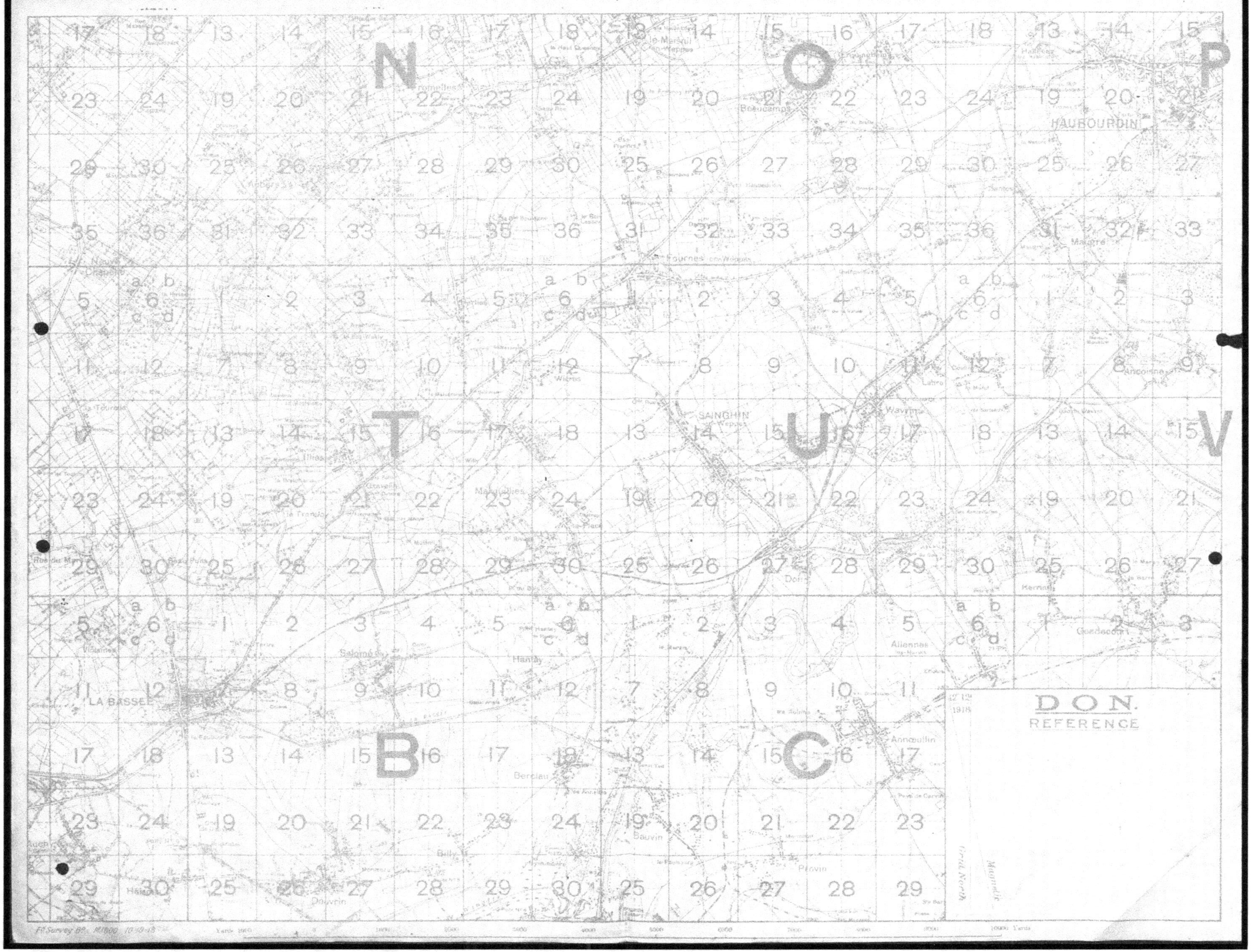
DON.
REFERENCE
N
O
P
T
U
V
B
C
HAUBOURDIN
Beaucamps
Fromelles
Fournes en Weppes
SAINGHIN en Weppes
Wavrin
Maugre
Ancoisne
Illies
Marquillies
Don
Allennes
Hantay
Salomé
LA BASSEE
Violaines
Berclau
Annoeullin
Bauvin
Provin
Billy
Douvrin
Herrin
Gondecourt
Magnetic
Grid North
1918
Yards

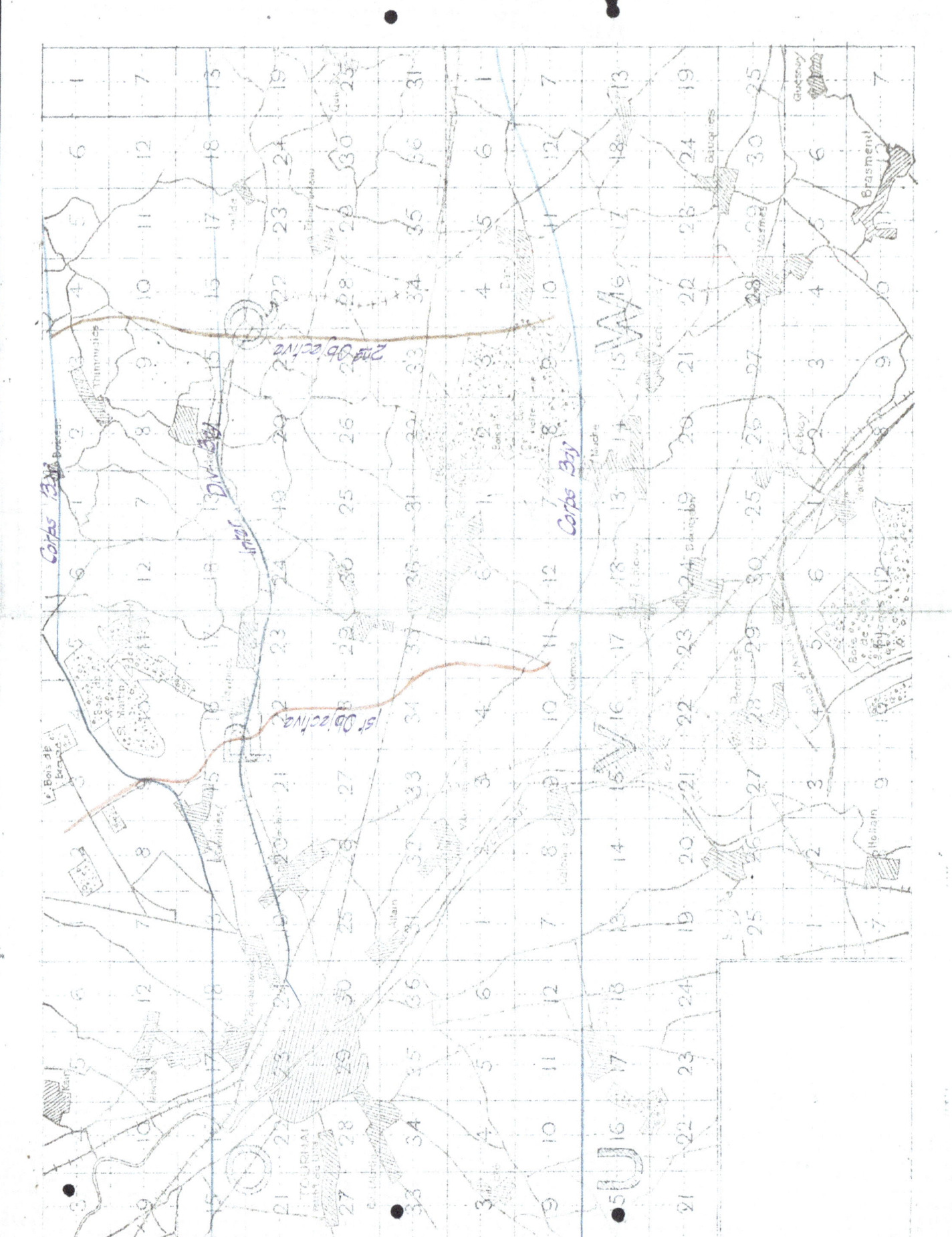

BOMBARDMENT TABLE.

No.	Target.	Description.	Date.	Time.	Remarks.
1	O.21.a.9.8. to O.21.a.85.15.	Occupied road and M.G. positions.	Nov. 4th.	1800 to 1805	Infy. posts in O.21.a & O.15.d. to withdraw.
2	O.27.c.60.65. to O.27.c.65.20.	Sunken road and occupied M.G. positions.	4th.	1925 to 1930.	
3.	As in 2		5th	0510 to 0515.	
4	As in 1		5th	0535 to 0540.	As in 1.
5.	O.21.d.75.90.	M.G. positions in or near house.	5th	1005. to 1010.	
6.	O.21.b.35.05.	M.G. & T.M. positions.	5th	1040 to 1045.	
7.	From O.27.b.65.25. to O.2C.a.05.30.	FAUB^G de LILLE.	5th	1200 to 1210.	4.5" Hows and H.A. Gas shell if wind suitable 18-prs.Shrapnel only. Rate of fire-1st 2 mins INTENSE. Last 8 mins. RAPID.
8	As in 7.		5th	1640 to 1650.	As above.
9.	O.27.a.8.4.	M.G. in house.	5th	1810 to 1815.	Post in O.27.a. to withdraw.
10.	O.27.a.5.5.	Enemy post.	6th	0520 to 0525	Posts in O.27.a., O.26.b., O.21.c. to withdraw.
11	O.15.d.75.05.	M.G. position in trench in front of houses.	6th	0840 to 0845.	
12	O.27.a.90.	Earthworks.	6th	0930 to 0935.	
13.	O.22.a.05.80.	M.G. position.	6th	1055 to 1100.	
14	O.22.c.55.60.	Emplacements.	6th	1235 to 1240.	
15.	O.27.a.5.8.	Enemy post.	6th	1820 to 1825.	Posts in O.27.a., O.26.b. & O.21.c. to withdraw.

BELGIUM 1:100,000   TOURNAI

TOURNAI 2ND EDITION

BOMBARDMENT TABLE.

No.	Target.	Description.	Date	Time	Remarks.
16	O.21.b.6.4.	Earthwork.	Nov. 6th.	1855 to 1900.	

4th November, 1918.

[signature]
Major. R.A.
Brigade Major. R.A.
74th (Yeomanry) Division.

www.ingramcontent.com/pod-product-compliance
Lightning Source LLC
Chambersburg PA
CBHW080851010526
44117CB00014B/2231